Business Result

Advanced | Teacher's Book

Rachel Appleby & Heidi Grant

Class DVD worksheets by
John Hughes & Shaun Wilden

OXFORD
UNIVERSITY PRESS

OXFORD
UNIVERSITY PRESS

Great Clarendon Street, Oxford OX2 6DP

Oxford University Press is a department of the University of Oxford.
It furthers the University's objective of excellence in research, scholarship,
and education by publishing worldwide in

Oxford New York

Auckland Cape Town Dar es Salaam Hong Kong Karachi
Kuala Lumpur Madrid Melbourne Mexico City Nairobi
New Delhi Shanghai Taipei Toronto

With offices in

Argentina Austria Brazil Chile Czech Republic France Greece
Guatemala Hungary Italy Japan Poland Portugal Singapore
South Korea Switzerland Thailand Turkey Ukraine Vietnam

OXFORD and OXFORD ENGLISH are registered trade marks of
Oxford University Press in the UK and in certain other countries

ISBN: 978 0 19 476823 8   (Book)
ISBN: 978 0 19 473946 7   (Pack)

Printed in China

This book is printed on paper from certified and well-managed sources.

ACKNOWLEDGEMENTS

Accompanying Teacher's DVD produced by: MTJ Media, Oxford, UK

*The author and publisher would like to thank the following for their kind assistance with
the accompanying Teacher's DVD:* Rebecca Turner, Jennie Cadd, Conal Keith, Eiko
Kunitomo, Yoshihiko Nakao, Paowitoo Werawath, Seung Shik Shin (Luke),
Irina Keist, Piraporn Thaijaidee, Piyaphol Vudhivorn, Saengwongkij, Sabiha
Iqbal, Satoko Ueyama, Mariusz Kawa, Saad Alnesafi, Raul Cadalso, Sylwia
Kawa, Deborah Lisburne (Saïd Business School, University of Oxford, UK),
Helen Hawari (Oxford Brookes University, UK), Catriona Davidson (The
Eckersley School of English, Oxford, UK), Elaine Allender (British Study
Centres, Oxford, UK), David Newton (OISE, Oxford, UK), Stephanie Davis
(OISE, Oxford, UK), Meriel Steele (Oxford English Centre, Oxford, UK), Rosa
Lucia (Oxford School of English, Oxford, UK), Richard Walton (St. Clare's,
Oxford, UK), Alice Berkeley

Cover photo by: Chris King

Contents

The course

Who is *Business Result* for?

Business Result is a comprehensive multi-level course in business English suitable for a wide range of learners. The main emphasis is on *enabling* your students; helping them to communicate more effectively in their working lives.

In-work students

Unlike many business English courses, *Business Result* addresses the language and communication needs of employees at all levels of an organization who need to use English at work. It recognizes that the business world is truly international, and that many people working in a modern, global environment spend much of their time doing everyday tasks in English – communicating with colleagues and work contacts by phone, via email, and in a range of face-to-face situations such as formal and informal meetings / discussions, and various planned and unplanned social encounters. It contains topics relevant to executive-level learners, but doesn't assume that the majority of students will be international managers who 'do business' in English – the activities allow the students to participate in a way that is relevant to them, whatever their level in their company or organization.

Pre-work students

Business Result can also be used with pre-work students at college level. The course covers a variety of engaging topics over the twelve units, so students without much work experience will receive a wide-ranging overview of the business world, as well as acquiring the key communication skills they will need in their future working lives. Each unit in this *Teacher's Book* contains suggestions for adapting the material to the needs of pre-work students.

One-to-one teaching

Many of the activities in the book are designed for use with groups of students, but they can also be easily adapted to suit a one-to-one teaching situation. Notes in the individual *Teacher's Book* units offer suggestions and help with this.

What approach does *Business Result* take?

Business Result helps students communicate in English in real-life work situations. The priority at all times is on enabling them to do so more effectively and with confidence. The target language in each unit has been carefully selected to ensure that students will be equipped with genuinely useful, transferable language that they can take out of the classroom and use immediately in the workplace.

The course recognizes that, with so many businesses now being staffed by people of different nationalities, there is an increasing trend towards using English as the language of internal communication in many organizations. As well as learning appropriate language for communicating externally – with clients or suppliers, for example – students are also given the opportunity to practise in situations that take place within an organization, such as informal meetings or social chat.

The main emphasis of the course is on the students speaking and trying out the target language in meaningful and authentic ways; it is expected that a large proportion of the lesson time will be spent on activating students' interest and encouraging them to talk. The material intentionally takes a communicative, heads-up approach, maximizing the amount of classroom time available to focus on and practise the target language. However, you will also find that there is plenty of support in terms of reference notes, written practice, and review material.

The syllabus is essentially communication-driven. The focus on *Business communication skills* as the core of each unit ensures that students are provided with a range of phrases they can use immediately, both in the classroom and in their day-to-day work. The topics in each of the twelve units have been chosen because of their relevance to modern business and the world of work. Vocabulary is presented in realistic contexts with reference to authentic companies or organizations. Grammar is also a key element of each unit, ensuring that students also pay attention to accuracy and become more proficient at expressing themselves clearly and precisely.

Student's Book

The Student's Book pack

The *Student's Book* pack offers a blend of classroom teaching and self-study, with an emphasis on flexibility and time-efficiency. Each of the twelve *Student's Book* units provides around four hours of classroom material with the potential for two to three hours of additional study using other components in the package.

The reading texts are a suitable length for this level, and with an emphasis on listening and speaking, written exercises are kept to a minimum. Instead, students are directed to the *Practice file* at the back of the book; here they will find exercises which can be used as supplementary material in class or for homework.

Encourage your students to look at and use the *Interactive Workbook* on DVD-ROM – there are cross-references at appropriate points in each unit. Here they will find a range of self-study material to help them review, consolidate, and extend their learning.

Writing is a feature of the course, but is not part of the main *Student's Book* units. The *Interactive Workbook* has an email writing section with exercises and model emails related to the content of every unit. There is also a writing file on the *Business Result* website.

Key features of a unit

Each unit has five sections – *Working with words, Business communication skills, Language at work, Practically speaking,* and the *Case study* – the first four deal with core vocabulary associated with the unit theme, key functional expressions, and related grammar. Each ends with a fluency task to enable students to personalize the target language. Every unit ends with a *Case study*.

Unit menu

This lists the key learning objectives of the unit.

Starting point

Each unit opens with some lead-in questions to raise awareness of and interest in the unit theme. Use these questions to help you to establish what students already know about the topic and how it relates to their own working lives. They can usually be discussed as a class or in small groups.

Working with words

This section introduces key vocabulary in a variety of ways, such as authentic reading texts, listenings, and visuals. Students are also asked to find common collocates that will help them to expand their personal lexicon more rapidly. This section also offers opportunities to work on reading and listening skills. There is a glossary of all target lexis, plus other reference vocabulary, on the *Interactive Workbook* in both PDF and interactive formats.

Business communication skills

This section focuses on one of four broad communication themes – meetings, presenting, telephoning, and negotiating. These are treated differently throughout the book so that, for example, students practise giving a briefing at a formal meeting as well as brainstorming ideas at a less formal meeting. They compare the different language needed for giving formal and impromptu presentations. Typically, the section begins with students listening to an example situation (a meeting, a presentation, a teleconference). They focus on *Key expressions* used by the speakers which are listed on the page. They are given the opportunity to practise these in various controlled and open work-related tasks.

Language at work

This section focuses on the key grammar underpinning the communication skills section that precedes it. The grammar is reviewed from a communicative point of view; this will meet your students' expectations with regard to learning form and meaning, but also reminds them how the grammar they need to learn commonly occurs in business and work situations. At this level, there is an emphasis on revision and a focus on the more lexical areas of grammar.

Practically speaking

This section looks at various useful aspects of everyday communication from a 'how to' perspective. It covers some of the more informal, but very practical aspects of social interaction in the workplace – for example, showing understanding, expressing personal views, or raising a difficult point.

Case studies

All units end with a *Case study*. This gives students an opportunity to recycle the language from the unit, demonstrate progress, and use their knowledge and ideas to resolve an authentic problem or issue. The *Case studies* have been compiled using authentic content and the contexts connect with the unit theme. The content is accessible, and preparation time is minimized by including only as much information as can be assimilated relatively quickly in class. Even so, you may wish to optimize classroom time even further by asking students to read the background material before the lesson.

The *Case studies* follow a three-part structure:

Background – a short text (or texts) about a real company, product, or related situation.

Discussion – discussion questions on key issues arising from the background information and associated issues, providing a natural bridge to the task.

Task – a discussion, meeting simulation, or series of tasks, aimed at resolving a core issue related to the case and providing extended practice of the target language of the unit.

Culture question

Awareness is raised of how national and company cultures can influence business interaction via a series of discussion questions.

Key word

Commonly occurring words with multiple meanings are explored through short exercises.

Additional material

At the back of the *Student's Book*, you will find the following sections.

Practice files

This provides unit-by-unit support for your classroom work. Each file provides additional practice of target language from the three main unit sections: *Working with words, Business communication skills,* and *Language at work*. This can be used in two ways:

For extra practice in class – refer students to this section for more controlled practice of new vocabulary, key expressions, or grammar before moving to the next stage. The optimum point at which to do this is indicated by cross-references in the *Student's Book* unit and the teaching notes in this book.

For self-study – students can complete and self-check the exercises for review and revision outside class.

Answers for the *Practice file* appear on pages 123–127 of this book, and on the student's website.

Language reference

Grammar explanations relating to the *Language at work* sections.

Useful phrases

Lists of phrases relating to the *Practically speaking* sections.

Information files

Additional information for pair / group activities and case studies.

Audio scripts

Interactive Workbook

This is a self-study component on DVD-ROM and online. It contains

- interactive Exercises and Tests for each unit, with answers
- interactive Email exercises, plus a model email for each unit
- interactive Phrasebank – students can create their own personalized 'Phrasebook' (DVD-ROM only)
- interactive Glossary for students to test their vocabulary
- *Student's Book* audio in MP3 format
- a video clip for each unit with interactive exercises.
- reading and discussion activities (online only).

To access the online content, students will find an access card on the inside cover of the *Student's Book*. This contains an access code to unlock the online content. Students need to go to **www.oxfordlearn.com** to activate their code, and then follow the instructions online to access the content.

Teacher's Book

What's in each unit?

Unit content

This provides an overview of the main aims and objectives of the unit.

Context

This section not only provides information on the teaching points covered in the unit, but also offers some background information on the main business theme of the unit. This will include reference to its importance in the current business world as well as a brief discussion of related issues, such as cross-cultural awareness or technology. If you are less familiar with the world of business, you will find this section especially helpful to read before starting a unit.

Teaching notes and answers

Notes on managing the *Student's Book* exercises and various activities are given throughout, with suggested variations that you might like to try. You will find comprehensive answers to all *Student's Book* exercises, as well as notes on possible responses to discussion questions.

Extension

With some students it may be appropriate to extend an exercise in some way or relate the language point more specifically to a particular group of students. Suggestions on how to do this are given where appropriate.

Extra activity

If you have time or would like to develop further areas of language competence, extra activities are suggested where they naturally follow the order of activities in the *Student's Book*. For example, the *Teacher's Book* may suggest tasks to exploit a particular listening activity more fully. Alternatively, if your students need to write emails, extra follow-up ideas are provided.

Alternative

With some students it may be preferable to approach an activity in a different way depending on their level or their interests. These options are provided where appropriate.

Pronunciation

Tips on teaching pronunciation and helping students improve their intelligibility are provided where there is a logical need for them. These often appear where new vocabulary is taught or for making key expressions sound more natural and fluent.

Dictionary skills

It's helpful to encourage students to use a good dictionary in class and the relevant notes suggest moments in the lesson when it may be helpful to develop your students' skills in using dictionaries. They also offer ideas on how new language can be recorded by students appropriately in their notebooks.

Pre-work learners

Although most users of *Business Result* will be students who are already in work, you may also be teaching classes of students who have little or no experience of the business world. Where necessary, you may want to adapt certain questions or tasks in the book to their needs, and extra notes are given for these types of learners.

One-to-one

In general, you will find that *Business Result* can be used with any size of class. However, with one-to-one students you will find that activities which have been designed with groups of students in mind will need some adaptation. In this case, you may wish to follow the suggested alternatives given in this book.

Feedback focus

Throughout the course, students are involved in speaking activities using the new language. You will want to monitor, correct, and suggest areas for improvement as well as acknowledging successes. During and after many of the freer practice activities it will be helpful to follow the guidelines in the teaching notes on what to monitor for and ways of giving feedback.

Watch out

This is a note to highlight any potentially problematic language points, with suggestions on how to pre-teach certain vocabulary or clear up misunderstandings.

Photocopiable tests (pages 96–119)

There are two types of test to accompany each unit. These can be administered at the end of each unit in order to assess your students' learning and allow you, the student, or the head of training to keep track of their overall progress.

Progress test

Each of these twelve tests check key vocabulary, key expressions, and grammar for the unit. They provide a final score out of 30. Students will need between fifteen and twenty minutes to complete the test, although you can choose to set a time limit that would be appropriate for your students.

Speaking test

To help you assess communicative performance, students are given a speaking task that closely resembles one of the speaking activities in the unit. Students get a score out of a possible ten marks.

How to manage the speaking test

In most cases, the speaking test is set up as pair work. The pairs carry out two role-plays. The marking criteria require students to perform five functions in the conversation and it is advised that you make students familiar with these criteria beforehand. You can grade each of the five stages using a straightforward scoring system of 0, 1, or 2, giving a final score out of ten. This kind of test can be carried out during the class, perhaps while other students are taking the written progress test, or you can set aside a specific time for testing.

Note that if testing is not a priority, the role-plays can also be used as extra classroom practice without necessarily making use of the marking criteria.

Teacher-Training DVD

The *Teacher's Book* at each level of *Business Result* is accompanied by a teacher-training *DVD* which demonstrates how sections from the *Student's Book* and the *Business Result* website can used. It addresses key issues relevant to the level and looks at various classroom approaches. The DVD also includes commentary from teachers and one of the *Student's Book* authors, and addresses many of the questions that teachers have to ask themselves when teaching business English. The *Advanced DVD* uses sections from *Student's Book Unit 11*, and the *Writing bank*, found on the *Business Result* website.

Orientation through the course

Watching the DVD is a fast way to familiarize yourself with the course – how the course is organized, its approach to business English, and ways of using the material in the classroom.

Supporting new teachers

If this is your first time teaching business English, you will find watching the DVD especially helpful. It provides guidance, advice, and tips on working with business English students.

Teacher development

You may be a more experienced teacher, in which case the DVD will address many issues you are already familiar with, but perhaps never have the opportunity to discuss with fellow professionals.

Teacher training

Directors of Studies or teacher trainers will be particularly interested in using the DVD as part of a complete teacher-training package. Each section of the DVD forms the basis of a training session lasting approximately 45 minutes. You can use the DVD in different segments with ready-to-use worksheets (with *Answer key*) on pages 128–135 of this *Teacher's Book* and training notes that are available from the *Business Result* website (see below). Simply photocopy the worksheets and download the training notes to use in conjunction with the DVD in your staff training and development sessions. Note that DVDs at other levels of *Business Result* address different business English themes; together, the DVDs from the different levels form an entire training package in teaching business English. See the website for more information.

Class DVD

The *Teacher's Book* pack also includes a DVD for use in the classroom. It includes one clip for every unit of the *Student's Book*. The clip can also be found on the *Interactive Workbook* on DVD-ROM packaged with the *Student's Book*.

You can use the DVD in class to complement your lessons. Each clip has a worksheet offering a complete lesson to accompany it. The worksheet can be downloaded from the Class DVD, along with an answer key and transcript.

The *Student's Book* flags up the appropriate moment to show the DVD in class with this icon: **VIDEO**

Teacher's website

The Teacher's website can be found at **www.businessresult.co.uk/ teachers**. It contains a range of additional materials, including

- needs analysis form – for use at the start of the course
- progress test record
- course management and assessment tools
- DVD training notes
- wordlists
- writing bank and reading bank.

Using the course

How to use *Business Result*

From start to finish

You can, of course, use *Business Result* in a linear fashion, starting at *Unit 1* and working your way through each unit in turn. If you do so, you will find it works well. Each section of the unit is related thematically to the others; there is a degree of recycling and a steady progression towards overall competence, culminating in the *Case study*. Timing will inevitably vary, but allow approximately four classroom hours for each unit. You will need more time if you intend to do the *Practice file* activities in class.

The 'fast-track' option

If you have less time, and wish to focus more on developing your students' communication skills, create a 'fast-track' course using the central section of each unit: *Business communication skills*, and the *Case study*. This will still provide a coherent balance of input and output, and students will spend more of their time actively engaged in using the language. You should find with this option that each unit provides at least two hours of classroom material.

Include *Practically speaking* if you wish – allow approximately 30 minutes extra. If your students need grammatical support or revision, use as much of the *Language at work* section as you feel is appropriate, or refer students to notes in the *Language reference* section.

Mix and match

If your students have less specific needs and you would like to 'cherry pick' what you feel are the most interesting and relevant sections of the book, this approach should work well. You will find that all the sections are essentially free-standing, despite being thematically linked, and can be used independently of the rest of the unit.

The Expert View from Cranfield School of Management

Cranfield University School of Management is one of the world's leading business schools, and one of only a small number of schools worldwide designated as 'triple-accredited'. It offers a widely respected international MBA programme, as well as a range of MSc and Executive Development courses.

The partnership between OUP and Cranfield provides authentication for key aspects of the course material, particularly the *Case studies*. Each *Case study* is accompanied by a brief commentary on the topic or issue covered. These short texts are written by members of the School of Management academic staff, leading practitioners in their field, and in some cases by former course participants who work in international business. They offer insights and advice on the *Case study* theme, and an extended version of many of them can be found on the *Business Result* website. There is also an introductory section in the *Student's Book* which includes information about Cranfield and some biodata on the contributors.

Further information about Cranfield programmes can be found at: **www.cranfield.ac.uk/som**

1 | Connections

Unit content

By the end of this unit, students will be able to
- describe cross-cultural experiences
- report back on research
- use tenses appropriately
- introduce themselves to a group.

Context

Building connections with other people and companies is integral to the success of any business, and in today's global business climate this often means building relationships with people and companies from different cultures. This is not always easy, since people from different cultures tend to interpret and evaluate situations in different ways. In order to develop successful business relationships across cultures, there needs to be appreciation of and respect for these cultural differences.

One of the key issues arising when cultures meet in a business context is the difference in value systems and how this has an impact on styles of decision-making. For example, people from individualistic ('I') cultures (e.g. the USA) tend to value personal goals and concerns over group goals and concerns, and personal rights over collective responsibilities. In contrast, people from collectivistic ('we') cultures (e.g. many countries in Africa and Asia) tend to value group goals and concerns over personal ones, and collective needs over personal needs. In a decision-making meeting, those from an individualistic culture might be more likely to behave competitively rather than cooperatively, and favour a decision that would maximize rewards or individual profit, whilst those from a collectivist culture are more likely to try to maintain group harmony and protect the interests of the whole group. If there is a lack of cultural awareness, these different approaches could cause misunderstandings or conflict.

In this unit, students have the opportunity to discuss different cross-cultural experiences. They then practise the language of participating in an informal meeting. They also review past, present, and future tenses. In the *Case study* they investigate possible international locations for a successful business based in Spain.

Starting point

1, 2 As a lead-in, write the words *cultural awareness* and *company culture* on the board. Ask students what they think these words mean and write their ideas on the board (e.g. *cultural awareness* = understanding and respecting the fact that people from different cultures have different values, customs, languages, and traditions; *company culture* = accepted behaviour within a company, reflected in the organizational structure, work environment, dress code, values, working hours, and overtime, etc.). Students then work in pairs and discuss the questions.

Watch out! This can be a very sensitive topic. Throughout the unit, try to avoid generalizations and stereotyping.

> **Possible answers**
> 1 Cultural awareness is needed if you are doing business with someone from another culture. Simple rules of etiquette are important so that you don't appear impolite. For example:
> - In Japan, people greet each other by bowing.
> - In France, you shouldn't use the familiar 'tu' form, or use first names unless invited to do so.
> - In America, you might have lunch out of a box during a meeting, and drink a coffee out of a plastic cup while walking to work. In Italy you would be more likely to take a visitor for a longer lunch in a nice restaurant, and talk business over a coffee in a café. Americans are clock-watchers whereas Italians place more importance on social rapport.
> 2 Company culture is influenced by styles of decision-making and by accepted styles of relationships between management and staff. The culture of the country where a company is based will determine what these accepted styles are.

Pre-work learners

Write the following questions on the board and ask students to discuss them in pairs.
- *What cultural differences have you experienced when holidaying in other countries?*
- *What aspects of the culture in your country might be difficult for a foreign visitor to understand?*

Extra activity

Write the following numbers on the board and ask students if they have any significance in their culture.
- *13*
- *888*
- *4*

Now write the following questions on the board and ask students to discuss their ideas in pairs.
1 *Which of these numbers is considered lucky in China? Why?*
2 *Which is considered unlucky in the UK? Why?*
3 *Which is considered unlucky in Japan? Why?*

Answers: 1 = 888 – eight represents prosperity and joy in China; 2 = 13 – the reason is not known for sure, but it could be linked to Christian tradition (the disciple who betrayed Jesus was the thirteenth to sit at the table at the Last Supper); 3 = 4 – in Japan the word for four is similar to the word for death.

Working with words

1 Students read the statements and decide if they agree with them. They can then discuss their answers in pairs.

> **Possible answers**
> 1 No. Every company has its own way of doing things.
> 2 Not necessarily more weight, but body language / gestures communicate meaning and people also judge others according to how they are dressed, etc.
> 3 No. Some cultures are very time-conscious – being on time is very important; in other cultures it's less important.
> 4 No. Within every culture individuals vary enormously.
> 5 Yes. It's important to be open and accept that there are situations you won't necessarily understand.
> 6 Yes. It helps you to understand different styles and approaches to business and enables you to avoid offending business contacts from other cultures.

2 Students read the text and compare their answers in **1**. They then decide which piece of advice they find most useful.

> **Answers**
> 1 Each organization has its own culture, personality, and way of doing things.
> 2 Noticing how people act, dress, and treat each other can be helpful.
> 3 Cultures may have totally different concepts of time.
> 4 Values and behaviour are also influenced by background, experience, and personality.
> 5 It's important, but this can be difficult. Business is about managing unknowns.
> 6 It gives you a better insight into working across cultures.

Extension

If your students lack knowledge about different cultures, ask them to do some research online for homework. Ask them to choose one country that interests them and to prepare a short talk for the next lesson giving advice about working with people from that country and / or visiting that country.

3 Students complete the phrases with verb + noun collocations from the text.

Alternative

Before students attempt **3**, ask them to see how many phrases they can complete without referring back to the text. Then give them just 30 seconds to find the answers in the text.

> **Answers**
>
> | | | | |
> |---|---|---|---|
> | 1 | build | 7 | form |
> | 2 | keep | 8 | manage |
> | 3 | process | 9 | work |
> | 4 | read | 10 | build |
> | 5 | take | 11 | weigh up |
> | 6 | keep | 12 | give |

4 Students now match the collocations from **3** to the definitions.

> **Answers**
>
> | | | | |
> |---|---|---|---|
> | a | 5 | g | 11 |
> | b | 2 | h | 7 |
> | c | 6 | i | 10 |
> | d | 1 | j | 3 |
> | e | 4 | k | 12 |
> | f | 9 | l | 8 |

5 Students work in small groups. If possible, put students from the same nationality or company together. Alternatively, ask students to compare the advice they would give about their culture / company. Encourage them to use the collocations from **3** during their discussion.

6 01 ▷ Students listen and answer the question.

> **Answers**
> **Speaker 1:** negative
> **Speaker 2:** positive
> **Speaker 3:** positive

7 01 ▷ Students decide what each adjective is used to describe. They then listen again and compare their answers.

> **Answers**
>
> | | | | |
> |---|---|---|---|
> | 1 | *P* | 7 | *P* |
> | 2 | *PL* | 8 | *E* |
> | 3 | *E* | 9 | *P* |
> | 4 | *E* | 10 | *P* |
> | 5 | *PL** | 11 | *PL* |
> | 6 | *P* | 12 | *E* |
>
> * *up-and-coming* can also be used to describe a person who is likely to become famous in the future

8 Students work in pairs. They match the definitions and then write their own.

> **Answers**
> a 4   d 9
> b 7   e 11
> c 8   f 10
>
> *open-minded* = open to new ideas
> *out-of-the-way* = isolated, not central
> *time-consuming* = something that takes a lot of time
> *up-and-coming* = popular, likely to be successful in the future
> *self-assured* = confident about yourself
> *unexpected* = something you hadn't imagined, a surprise

9 Students work in pairs and describe their experiences using the adjectives from **7**.

Pre-work learners

Write the following questions on the board and ask students to answer them in pairs, using adjectives from **7**.
- *How are you viewed at your place of study?*
- *What is your place of study like?*
- *Have you ever had a part-time job, or had a work placement? If so, what was the experience like?*

Extra activity

Ask students to work in pairs and brainstorm the opposites to the adjectives in **7**.

Possible answers: 1 narrow-minded; 2 central; 3 quick / rapid; 4 interesting; 5 past-it; 6 timid / shy; 7 reserved; 8 exciting; 9 head-in-the-clouds; 10 difficult / demanding; 11 high-profile; 12 expected.

>> If students need more practice, go to **Practice file 1** on page 102 of the **Student's Book**.

10 Allow time for students to think about one of the situations. They should then talk about their experiences with a partner, answering questions 1–4. Encourage them to use vocabulary from **3** and **7**.

Feedback focus

Monitor for use of the new vocabulary. At the end of the activity, ask students to summarize their partner's situation. Give feedback on the use of vocabulary and correct mistakes if necessary.

(i) Refer students to the **Interactive Workbook Glossary** for further study.

Business communication skills

1 Ask students to read the *Context*. They can then discuss the question in pairs.

> **Possible answers**
> Johanna will probably be expecting to hear details about the location, the facilities available, any competition in the area, property prices, etc.

Extra activity

Write the following questions on the board. Ask students to work in pairs and discuss the answers (see answers in brackets).
- *What is the capital city of Poland?* (Warsaw)
- *What is the population of Poland?* (38.5 million)
- *What is the name of the sea to the north of Poland?* (the Baltic sea)
- *In which part of the country is the mountain location of Zakopane?* (the south)

Students might also be interested to know that the main industries in Poland are electronics, vehicles, and construction.

2 02▷ Students listen and complete Johanna's notes. They should also note down whether each piece of information comes from a personal observation or a third party / another source.

> **Answers**
> **Probable location** = the Krakow area (third party / another source)
> up-and-coming (third party / another source)
> **+ points** = beautiful, lively, a lot going on (personal observation)
> the area is being pushed for development (third party / another source)
> **- points** = a number of hotels already catering for the business market (personal observation)
> **Conclusions / action points** = several interesting sites worth considering outside Krakow (third party / another source)
> **Action** = go exploring, visit other sites (third party / another source)

3 02▷ Students listen again and note down the phrases. They can then work with a partner and discuss why these phrases are used.

Watch out! You may have to pause the audio at various points to allow students enough time to note down the phrases.

Answers

The client has told us that the site is likely to be around the Krakow area. (Johanna may want to emphasize this is not her decision.)

Apparently, it seems that Krakow is quite an up-and-coming place. (Johanna hasn't been there herself and is judging based on what she has heard.)

(The city centre) is really beautiful and lively. **I get the impression that** there's a lot going on there. (It was his subjective opinion which others may or may not share.)

According to the local tourist office, they're really pushing the area for development. (This is what Peter was told, but it may not be 100% accurate.)

From what I could see, there are already a number of hotels catering for the business market. (In his short time of looking around the city, Peter felt there was already competition.)

I gathered from the locals that there were several interesting sites worth considering nearby. (The locals told Peter there were other sites of interest around the city.)

As it was made clear that I should go exploring, I cut this short so that I could visit other sites. (Peter had been told to look at other alternatives and find out more.)

4 Students work in pairs and read their information. Allow them five minutes to prepare to report their findings. Encourage them not to just read their information. When they are ready, they should report back to each other. They can then discuss the differences in their information.

Alternative

Students could select a town or area that they know well to talk about.

5 03, 04▷ Students listen and complete the notes.

Answers

1 Mountain site
Zakopane – more of a ski resort than a business centre
activities: skiing, walking, saunas
location: at least a couple of hours' drive from the airport
local workforce: level of English a problem – it's not their *first* second language

2 City outskirts site
the edge of Krakow
infrastructure: already in place
facilities: local facilities are first class
possible site for purchase: old brewery to acquire and refit

6 03, 04▷ Students listen again and answer the questions.

Answers

1	Extract 2	4	Extract 2
2	Extract 2	5	Extract 3
3	Extract 3	6	Extract 3

7 05▷ Students listen and match the pairs of sentences to 1–6 in **6**.

Answers

a	6	d	5
b	3	e	1
c	2	f	4

8 Students work in pairs and have the conversations. Encourage them to use the phrases from the *Key expressions*.

Possible answers

1 **A** The major advantage is that by arranging the desks on the outside of the room, we'd have more space.
  B I'm a bit reluctant to do that – what would we do with the empty space in the middle?
2 **A** I'm just not 100% convinced that now is the right time to buy.
  B That's not a reason to avoid discussing it with them.
3 **A** I've got to say that you'd be exactly the right person for this project.
  B I can't promise anything. I'm not sure that I can commit to such a long-term project.
4 **B** It's not that I'm not willing to work Saturdays, it's just that I'd like to avoid it, if possible.
  A I'm sure you'll agree that if we work on the next two Saturday mornings, we'll meet the deadline.

» If students need more practice, go to **Practice file 1** on page 102 of the **Student's Book**.

9 Students work in pairs. Allow time for them to prepare what they will say. They can then take turns to report back to each other. If the students can't think of a time when they had to report back, they can turn to the *File* for ideas.

10 Students discuss whether the language they used when reporting back in **9** gave the intended impression (e.g. positive or negative) to their partner.

Feedback focus

Give positive feedback to students who used the *Key expressions* correctly.

ⓘ Refer students to the **Interactive Workbook Email** and **Phrasebank** sections for further study.

Language at work

1 Students read the extracts and match the sentences to the meanings.

> **Answers**
>
> | | | | |
> |---|---|---|---|
> | 1 | e* | 5 | a |
> | 2 | c | 6 | g |
> | 3 | d | 7 | f |
> | 4 | b | | |
>
> * In this example, what was decided in the past didn't happen, but this structure can also be used to describe a past plan that *did* actually happen at a later time.

Extra activity

Ask students to work in pairs and identify the tenses / structures that are used in the *italic* sections of the sentences in **1**.
   Answers: 1 past perfect; 2 modal *should*; 3 *be going to*; 4 present perfect; 5 present continuous; 6 past perfect continuous; 7 future continuous.

2 Students work in pairs and compare the sentences with those in the audio scripts.

> **Answers**
>
> **a** This sentence suggests that this is a repeated action, i.e. the client has told us this several times. The sentence used in the audio suggests that they only told them once.
>
> **b** There is only a slight difference in meaning. This sentence suggests that the action started in the past and is still continuing. In the script, the emphasis is on the fact that it is happening now and there is no mention of the past.
>
> **c** This sentence emphasizes that the action was in progress over a period of time in the past. The sentence in the script implies that more information will follow, i.e. it sounds more like the beginning of a story.
>
> **d** There is very little difference in meaning here. Both sentences refer to a plan that was made in the past. The sentence in the script could also imply that the plan didn't happen, depending on intonation and what follows.
>
> **e** This sentence refers to something in the past that you didn't do, but that would have been advisable to do and you regret not doing it. The sentence in the script is a simple recommendation.
>
> **f** This sentence implies that there is a possibility it will be a bit more complicated. The sentence in the script suggests that it definitely will be more complicated, as *going to* is usually used to make a prediction based on evidence.
>
> **g** This sentence implies that the action will be completed by a given time in the future. The sentence in the script suggests that the action will be in progress at a given time in the future.

Alternative

Ask students to identify the tenses / structures in sentences a–g before they turn to the audios scripts.
   Answers: a present perfect continuous; b present perfect continuous; c past continuous; d past simple; e modal + *have* + past participle; f modal + verb; g future perfect.

>> Refer students to the **Language reference** section on page 126 of the **Student's Book** for more information.

3 Students read the email and correct any mistakes. They should then look for verbs where a different tense could be used. They can then check their answers in pairs.

> **Answers**
> **Mistakes:**
> ~~had been skimming~~ have been skimming
> ~~was gathering~~ have gathered
> ~~should have pointed out~~ should point out
> ~~are being expected~~ are expected
> ~~had heard~~ have heard
> ~~we try~~ we have been trying / we tried
> ~~have been insisting~~ have insisted
> ~~I'll have got back to you~~ I'll get back to you
> ~~I know what will be happening~~ I'll know what is happening
> **Alternative verb forms:**
> It won't be (isn't going to be) as straightforward as we had hoped. – tone doesn't change
> If we haven't heard (don't hear) by then. – tone doesn't change
> We need (will need) to take legal action. – tone doesn't change
> We need to take (we will be taking) legal action. – tone changes: the alternative sounds like a definite plan, so is more formal / decisive

>> If students need more practice, go to **Practice file 1** on page 103 of the **Student's Book**.

4 Students work in pairs and find out as much information as they can abut each other. Encourage them to use a variety of tenses in their conversations.

Feedback focus

Note down any incorrect uses of tenses during the activity. Afterwards, write the errors on the board for the whole class to correct.

Pre-work learners

Tell students that it's the first day at their new place of study and they're trying to get to know each other during a break. Write the following topics on the board and ask students to talk about them with a partner.

- *a major change (perhaps you've moved town to study at the place you are now)*
- *how you ended up choosing the course you're on*
- *any present projects (perhaps you've joined a club / sports team)*
- *your regrets and hopes*
- *your predictions*

Practically speaking

1 As a lead-in, write the following statement on the board and ask students if they agree with it. Then ask them to work in pairs and discuss the questions.
   - *First impressions are always right.*

2 06▷ Students listen and answer the questions.

Possible answers
Answers will vary, but students might make some of the following observations.
Speaker 1: hasn't structured her presentation very well, although her warning that she can talk too fast might be appreciated.
Speaker 2: she's much more formal, but could be seen as arrogant because she gives herself lots of credit (although she does want to share her knowledge, which is positive).
Speaker 3: this is very informal (some might see this as good, others will see it as bad) and he is also quite boastful.

3 Students order the information and compare their answers in pairs.

Answers
1 who they are
2 role
3 reason for being there
4 achievements / activities
5 aspirations

4 06▷ Students listen again and complete the phrases. They can then work with a partner and match the phrases to the topics in **3**.

Answers
1 my name's, I'm from
2 I'm accountable for
3 I've now managed to
4 Lately I've been concentrating on
5 I'm ready to
6 those of you who don't know me already, I am
7 My responsibilities include
8 I'm empowered to, have the task of
9 I'd like to point out that, I have been continually improving
10 I hope to
11 As most of you will know
12 Basically my role is to
13 This entails a lot of
   who they are: 1, 6, 11
   role: 2, 7, 8, 12, 13
   reasons for being there: 5, 10
   achievements / activities: 3, 4, 9
   aspirations: 10

» Refer students to the **Useful phrases** section on page 134 of the **Student's Book** for extension and revision.

5 Allow time for students to prepare their introductions. Encourage them to choose phrases from **4** to use in their introduction. Then ask each student to introduce himself / herself to the class.

Feedback focus

Give feedback on the use of language in the introductions and the impression each student made on the rest of the class.

Alternative

If you have access to the necessary equipment, you could film the introductions. Ask students to prepare their introductions for the next lesson. You can then film and play back the footage to the class. Ask students to watch themselves and their classmates and comment on the following.
Language
- expressions used (particularly new ones from the unit)
- accuracy of tense use
- range of vocabulary
Delivery
- pace
- pronunciation of key words
- body language (gestures, eye contact)

Key word

Students match the phrases to the definitions.
Answers: 1 b, 2 e, 3 a, 4 d, 5 c

Culture question

Students can discuss the questions in pairs, before feeding back to the rest of the class.

ⓘ Refer students to the **Interactive Workbook Exercises and Tests** for revision.

Case study

Background

This *Case study* presents an innovative start-up company based in Spain that provides corporate management services to visitors to Madrid. They would like to expand and use a location outside Spain. The topic allows students to consider the issues that a company needs to address when planning this kind of expansion. The *Task* then enables students to practise the language of the unit while discussing the strengths and weaknesses of three possible new locations.

Allow a few minutes for students to read the *Company profile* and the texts. Be prepared to answer any questions about vocabulary.

Discussion

1–4 Students can discuss these questions in pairs, before feeding back to the rest of the class.

> **Possible answers**
> 1 They provide a personalized and friendly service. They help visitors to enjoy the *real* culture of Madrid – they aren't just restricted to the typical tourist areas.
> 2 Answers will vary.
> 3 He needs to think about the competition, the costs of setting up in a new location, potential language problems, how to recruit local staff, customer profile, etc.
> 4 Answers will vary.

Task

1 07▷ Students listen to James' briefing and note the key points to look out for.

> **Answers**
> He wants an overall impression of the place from an outsider's perspective. Restaurants and local delicacies are of particular interest.
> He needs useful information about tourist numbers and origins (where they come from).
> It's important to get specific information on the type of business visitor the city gets. Do they come alone, or with colleagues? What are their activities?
> He wants first-hand knowledge about the local economy – types of businesses or industries, international connections, etc.
> It's also important to find out if there is any competition.
> He also wants to know if there are any language or cultural issues to consider.

2 Divide the class into three groups. Students then turn to their *Files*. Allow time for them to read the information. They should then work with their groups and prepare a list of the strengths and weaknesses of their location.

3 Students now form a new group, with representatives for each location. Each student should introduce himself / herself. They then take turns to report back on their location and discuss their findings. If necessary, refer students to the *Key expressions* list in the *Business communication skills* section.

4 Each group should now agree on the best location for the expansion of Adventurous Appetites and suggest what the next steps should be. They can then summarize their plans for the rest of the class.

Feedback focus

Give feedback on the language students used to introduce themselves and to report back.

Extra activity

Ask students to write a report or an email detailing their group's decision. Ask them to include the following information.
- The main advantages and disadvantages of each location.
- The final decision and reasons for this choice of location.
- The next steps.

One-to-one

Your student can read the *Background* and you can then go through the questions in the *Discussion* together. In the *Task*, your student should read about one location and you should read about another. You can look at the third location together. You can then have the meeting.

≫ Unit 1 **Progress test** and **Speaking test**, pages 96–97.

2 | Careers

Unit content

By the end of this unit, students will be able to
- compare career paths and choices
- manage the discussion and share ideas in meetings
- express different attitudes to the past
- get a point across.

Context

Today most of us need to adopt a more flexible and proactive attitude towards our careers. The notion of a 'job for life' in the same company is no longer valid, even in countries like Japan, where companies have traditionally been more paternalistic towards their staff. Competition for jobs is no longer confined to individual companies or countries: globalization of the economy means that employees are competing for jobs with people in low-cost countries like India and China. Employees at all levels, from the senior manager to the most unqualified production worker, have to be aware of how they can move up in their companies and what additional skills they will need to acquire if they still want to be employable in five or ten years' time.

Companies too realize that a key element in the recruitment and retention of employees is the opportunities they offer them for career development. They can no longer promise them the job security of twenty years ago. However, they can at least provide them with the knowledge and experience they need either to continue to be of value to the company, or to pursue their careers elsewhere, if necessary.

In this unit, students talk about the best ways of moving up in a company and the different career development possibilities on offer. They practise the language of managing discussions and sharing and clarifying ideas. They also review past modals and third conditional sentences for expressing attitudes to the past. In the *Case study* they discuss how to improve staff retention in a pharmaceutical company.

Starting point

1, 2 Students can discuss these questions in pairs before feeding back to the rest of the class. You could circulate and make a note of any incorrect (or correct) past modal forms or conditionals to use when you get to the *Language at Work* section.

Watch out! The second question might be sensitive if students aren't happy with their present job. Don't force them to answer this.

Pre-work learners

Ask students to talk about their study choices instead of career choices. If they have experience of work placements or internships, they could talk about these.

Working with words

1 Check students understand how the game of 'Snakes and Ladders' works (if you land on a snake you slide several steps backwards, if you land on a ladder you climb several steps forwards). Elicit what we mean by 'career ladder' (your movement up the hierarchy of jobs) – the snakes represent the things that hinder our movement up that ladder. Then brainstorm possible snakes and ladders as a class.

Alternative

You could divide the snakes and ladders into two categories (one relating to someone's behaviour and the other relating to external factors). Draw the following table below on the board. Ask students for ideas.

	My behaviour / attitude	Other people / external factors
Career snakes		
Career ladders		

Possible answers: **Snakes:** My behaviour = being quiet and not making yourself known, not willing to do unpaid overtime, having children / taking time off to look after them, poor time management.
External factors = bosses who take all the credit, poor internal communication, back-stabbing, being governed by school holidays, lack of career structure.
Ladders: My behaviour = making sure that you are popular with your boss and colleagues, being seen as a 'winner', being loud and getting noticed by those who matter, being persistent in striving towards your goals, good results in your work.
External factors = bosses who retire or move on, growth of company, possibilities for training.

2 Students read the lists. Allow only a couple of minutes so that they don't read the text in **3**. Ask for a show of hands to see which section they think refers to which category. There may be differences of opinion as different cultures have different views on what could be considered a snake or a ladder. Accept their different opinions without passing judgement.

Watch out! Before they read, you might want to check that students understand the following.
ruthless = hard and cruel, determined to get what you want and not caring if you hurt other people
to do something blindly = to do something without thinking about what you are doing / without reservation

3 Students read the text and discuss their reactions as a class.

> **Possible answers**
> List 1 represents the snakes and list 2 represents the ladders.
> These answers may be surprising as the attitudes / strategies in list 1 seem more openly career-driven. However, the implication in the text is that although some people move up the career ladder with the attitudes / strategies from list 1, they don't hold their positions for long, whereas good companies value the strategies in 2.

4 Students form the multiword combinations and check their answers in texts **2** and **3**.

> **Answers**
>
> | | |
> |---|---|
> | stand up for | come up with |
> | stick up for | keep in with |
> | stay ahead of | hold on to |
> | get on with | look out for |
> | stand out from | move on to |
> | cling on to | stand up to |

5 Students work in pairs to decide on definitions for the multiword verbs. Before they start, you might like to elicit one definition from the class as an example.

> **Possible answers**
> stand up for = to defend an idea or a person
> stick up for = to defend a person (slightly more informal than stand up for)
> stay ahead of = to make sure you have an advantage
> get on with = to continue (without being distracted)
> stand out from = to be recognized as different or better
> cling on to = to keep / not to give to another person (stronger than hold on to)
> come up with = to think of (an idea)
> keep in with = to remain popular with
> hold on to = to keep / not give to another person
> look out for* = to pay attention to OR to take care of someone and make sure nothing bad happens to them
> move on to = to progress
> stand up to = to defend yourself against (a person)
> * Note that two different meanings of this multiword verb are used in the texts

Dictionary skills

Ask students to work in pairs and choose four of the multiword verbs in **4**. Give them three minutes to find them in a dictionary and identify which example sentences in the dictionary entry matches the meaning used in the texts. The winners are the first students to find all four.

6 Students work in pairs and choose the six multiword verbs that they find most useful. They should then write questions to ask another pair. If they find it difficult to make questions only about careers, extend the subject to anything work-related.

> **Possible answers**
> 1 Is it easy to stand up for what you believe in at work?
> 2 Do people in your team stick up for colleagues if they are being unfairly treated?
> 3 What do you think today's employees have to do to stay ahead of the competition?
> 4 Are you a workaholic or do you prefer just to get on with your life?
> 5 If your company asked for voluntary redundancies, would you cling on to your job or offer to leave?
> 6 Can you come up with any ideas for making your job more interesting?
> 7 How important is it for staff in your company to keep in with their boss?
> 8 What perks would you want to hold on to if you changed jobs?
> 9 Do you always look out for new job opportunities in your company?
> 10 What sort of job would you like to move on to next?
> 11 Have you ever had to stand up to your boss?

Alternative

Write the possible answers for **6** on the board with the multiword verbs gapped. Ask students to complete the sentences. They can then ask and answer the questions in pairs.

7 08▷ Before students listen, ask them what they think a career coach is (someone who helps you in planning and managing your career). Ask the class who should be more responsible for career development – the employee or their company. Encourage an exchange of views then refer students to the questions. Students can check their answers in pairs before feeding back to the rest of the class. During feedback, ask students if they agree with the views expressed.

> **Answers**
> 1 False
> 2 True
> 3 False

8 08▷ Students match the verbs to the phrases. They can then listen again to check their answers.

> **Answers**
> | | | | |
> |---|---|---|---|
> | 1 | h | 5 | a |
> | 2 | f | 6 | g |
> | 3 | e | 7 | b |
> | 4 | c | 8 | d |

9 Students match the phrases to the definitions. During feedback, ask students for any examples they can give based on their own experience.

> **Answers**
> | | | | |
> |---|---|---|---|
> | a | 1 | e | 4 |
> | b | 2 | f | 3 |
> | c | 8 | g | 6 |
> | d | 5 | h | 7 |

» If students need more practice, go to **Practice file 2** on page 104 of the **Student's Book**.

10 Students work in pairs. They should work together to prepare an outline for their talk. Ask them to think about where they could incorporate vocabulary from **4** and **8** in their talk. Students then take turns to listen to their partner giving the talk. They can then give feedback to their partner on the language he / she used. If you have time you might like to ask some students to give their talk to the whole class.

Pre-work learners

Ask students to work in pairs and prepare a talk for the next lesson. Tell them that the talk is for recent university graduates and the title is as follows.
 • Building a career – what companies can offer you.
For homework, students could research the subject on the Internet, searching under the keyword *career development*.

Feedback focus

Circulate and note any correct / incorrect use of the phrases from **4** and **8**. After the activity, write these sentences on the board and ask students to identify the correct sentences and amend the incorrect sentences.

ⓘ Refer students to the **Interactive Workbook Glossary** for further study.

Business communication skills

1 Ask students to read the *Context* before asking them to think about what issues may be discussed during the meeting. You could also ask them if their companies have similar problems with recruitment.

> **Possible answers**
> What would the training needs of school-leavers be?
> How would suitable school-leavers be selected?
> What would the conditions of employment for school-leavers be?
> Will they have to work the same number of hours with the same salaries as graduate trainees?
> Will taking on school-leavers have an impact on quality of work completed by the company and therefore affect the company's reputation?
> Would graduates be better for the company?

2 09▷ Students listen and make notes on 1–3. You might need to feed back on questions 1 and 2 first and then play the audio again to allow students to focus on the phrases used. Ask if they can think of any other expressions that might be used to invite someone to contribute, e.g. *Could you / Would you like to / Would you mind ... go(ing) over ... tell(ing) us about / filling us in on ...*

> **Answers**
> 1 The first point is covered.
> 2 Just after each of Arun's contributions to the discussion.
> 3 **start meeting:** ... so let's get started, shall we?
> **establish meeting objectives:** The purpose of today's meeting is to ...
> **ask Arun to present his findings:** Perhaps Arun, you'd like to run us through some of your findings.
> **get Arun to talk about this:** Arun, did you want to talk about staff retention issues as well?

3 10▷ Students listen and discuss the answers in pairs, before feeding back to the rest of the class. You could then ask them what they think of the idea and if a similar policy exists or would be useful in their company (or country).

Answers
1 An in-house training programme would be set up for them, whereby they would work and study at the same time. They would be paid modestly for the five-year duration of the plan.
2 A lot of good students are worried about the cost of being at university and being in debt. They would be happy to have secure employment.
3 She thinks school-leavers are too young to make career decisions, and therefore might not be as committed to the profession as a graduate.

4 Students match the phrases to the functions individually before feeding back to the rest of the class.

Answers
1 b
2 a
3 d
4 c

5 09,10▷ Play the audio twice without stopping. Ask students to note down at least one phrase for each function. Then ask students to compare their answers and add any phrases they missed.

Answers
1 The obvious solution to this problem must be to ...
I know you're not keen on it, Rachel, but ...
I'm sure you'll understand the need to ...
I'm not sure what your feelings are about this, but ...
We were wondering if ...
Given that ... wouldn't it ...?
Something else we've been thinking about is ...
2 I'm sorry, but ...
What makes you so sure?
But surely ...?
... it's interesting you should say that, because actually ...
I suppose so.
But do you really think ...?
3 Could I just say something here ...?
If I could just come in here for a moment ...
Would this be the right moment to mention ...?
4 Can I suggest we come back to ...?
Go ahead.
I'll get on to that in a moment.
Coming back to ...

6 Elicit answers from the whole class.

Answers
1 I know you're not keen on it, Rachel, but ...
You probably won't like this idea ...
I'm not sure what your feelings are about this, but ...
2 Something else we've been thinking about is ...
We were wondering if ...
3 I'm sure you'll understand the need to ...
The obvious solution to this problem must be ...

≫ If students need more practice, go to **Practice file 2** on page 104 of the **Student's Book**.

7 Allow time for students to read through the list, then elicit any other ideas they might have.

8 Students work in pairs and have the meeting. Encourage students to use language from the *Key expressions*. Students can then change roles and have the meeting again.

9 Students work in groups of three. Ask each group to choose a chairperson (Student A).

Allow a few minutes for students B and C to read their *Files* and come up with any new ideas. During this time, ask student A to note down any ideas he / she can think of for each point on the agenda. Students then have the meeting. Encourage them to use language from the *Key expressions* where appropriate. Students should reach a decision on each item of the agenda.

Feedback focus

Ask students B and C to evaluate how well student A managed the meeting and involved both speakers. Ask Student A to evaluate how respectful B and C were of others' opinions, i.e. did they interrupt each other too much or did they criticize ideas too directly?

Extension

Ask students to write up the minutes of the meeting for homework. They can use the agenda to help them structure the minutes. Ask them to include
• at least two ideas that were rejected for each agenda item
• reasons why those ideas were rejected
• one or two ideas that were accepted for each agenda item
• reasons why those ideas were accepted.

Culture question

Students can discuss the questions in pairs before feeding back to the rest of the class. The following ideas may arise, but be careful to avoid over-generalizing.

- Generally, in Asian cultures it is considered impolite to disagree with a hierarchical superior.
- In Northern European cultures diplomacy and politeness are often used to disguise real disagreement.
- In Latin cultures passionate disagreement is fairly common.

ⓘ Refer students to the **Interactive Workbook Email** and **Phrasebank** sections for further study.

Language at work

1 11▷ As a lead-in, write on the board one thing about the past you are happy about, and one thing you regret. For example:
1 *I passed my driving test first time.*
2 *I refused a teaching job in Australia.*

Elicit how you could express satisfaction about **1** and regrets about **2**. Make a note of students' suggestions on the board and ask them to correct any mistakes.
Before they listen to the de-briefing, ask students if they can remember what the initial meeting in *Business communication skills* was about. If they haven't worked on *Business communication skills*, establish the context briefly: four people in an accountancy firm have just had a meeting to discuss the HR department's idea to recruit school-leavers and are saying what they thought of the meeting. Students then listen and complete the sentences.

> **Answers**
> **Conversation 1**
> 1 I'm so glad I finally had
> 2 it's just as well I brought you along
> 3 I'd thought about it, I could have brought
> 4 It would have been good if we'd made
> 5 if only I'd known
> 6 we should have anticipated
> **Conversation 2**
> 7 might have been
> 8 could have been awful if
> 9 suppose I hadn't been there to present
> 10 would have happened if I hadn't suggested
> 11 still don't think Arun brought
> 12 it's a good thing he came

Watch out! You might want to check that students understand *it's just as well*. Explain that it's similar to *it's lucky*.

2 Students can compare their answers in pairs before feeding back to the rest of the class.

Watch out! You might want to check that students understand the following.
relieved = feeling happy because something unpleasant has not happened or is over
hindsight = the understanding that you have of a situation only after it has happened and means that you would have done things in a different way

> **Answers**
> **a** 1, 12
> **b** 2, 8, 9, 10
> **c** 11, 5*
> **d** 3, 4, 5*, 6, 7
> * could be c or d

Pronunciation

Ask students to look at the sentences in **1** again. Write the following tasks on the board (answers are in brackets).
- *Underline any contracted forms. (I'm, I'd x2, we'd x2, hadn't x2, don't).*
- *What other contractions could be used in these sentences? (could've x2, would've x2, should've, might've).*

Then drill the pronunciation of these new contractions and ask students to practise them in pairs. Ask them when it is more suitable to use contracted forms (in spoken language, in less formal situations) and when it is preferable to use full forms (in written language, in more formal situations).

3 Students match the sentences to the structures.

Watch out! If students are unfamiliar with the grammatical terms, ask them to give you examples from the sentences in **2** of a modal, a conditional sentence, a past simple, and a past perfect form.

> **Answers**
> **a** 3, 4, 10
> **b** 6, 7, 8
> **c** 1, 2, 11, 12
> **d** 5, 9

» Refer students to the **Language reference** section on page 126 of the **Student's Book** for more information.

4 Check that students understand how the 'nearly' CV works by asking them to tell you what actually happened, e.g. *When he (or she) graduated from university, he looked for a job to get some experience and was offered a job abroad.* Then focus on the first situation (1a) and elicit sentences using the target structures, e.g. *Maybe he should have done a postgraduate degree. But if he'd done a postgraduate degree, he might not have got useful work experience abroad.* Students then work in pairs. Circulate and ask students to self-correct if you hear any mistakes in the target structures. Feed back on possible answers with the whole class.

>> If students need more practice, go to **Practice file 2** on page 105 of the **Student's Book**.

5 Ask students to think about choices they made in the past and the options they rejected. Give an example, such as a school you decided to study or teach at and another job you refused. If necessary, they could also think about study or job choices, or even towns they decided (not) to live in or houses / flats they decided (not) to buy. Students then discuss their past choices in pairs.

Feedback focus

Circulate and note down three correct sentences you hear and one incorrect. After the activity, dictate the four sentences to the students at normal native speaker speed, using contracted forms where appropriate. Students write down the sentences and identify which one is incorrect.

Pre-work learners

Instead of their work experience, students can focus on schools, academic subjects, sports or other hobbies they chose or didn't choose, good or bad teachers they had or were lucky / unlucky not to have.

Practically speaking

1 Refer students to the photo and the question.

> **Possible answers**
> You can use language to
> • ask if someone has understood
> • give the listener an opportunity to ask for clarification
> • repeat what you said in a different way – perhaps using more simple vocabulary
> • give an example of what you mean.
>
> You could also use your voice or body to
> • change your intonation
> • make gestures
> • refer to visual aids.

2 12▷ Students listen and complete the sentences. You might need to play the audio twice to allow students to note down all the phrases. Students can then check their answers in pairs before feeding back to the rest of the class.

> **Answers**
> 1 would it help if I gave you an example
> 2 I was actually referring to
> 3 if you look at, you'll see
> 4 sorry, let me rephrase that
> 5 What I'm saying is that
> 6 In other words
> 7 the fact of the matter is
> 8 the point I'm trying to make is
> 9 what I mean by 'well-informed' is
> 10 to put it another way

3 Students match the phrases to the techniques.

> **Answers**
> a 4, 6, 10
> b 2, 5, 8, 9
> c 1, 3
> d 7

4 Students work in pairs. Refer them to the agenda, then ask them to read their *Files*. Students then have the meeting. Circulate and ask students to self-correct where necessary.

>> Refer students to the **Useful phrases** section on page 134 of the **Student's Book** for extension and revision.

5 Students work in pairs and take turns to ask and answer questions. Encourage them to use the phrases from **2**.

Key word

Students match the sentences to the uses. They can then check their answers in pairs before feeding back to the rest of the class.
  Answers: 1 d, 2 a, 3 c, 4 b

ⓘ Refer students to the **Interactive Workbook Exercises and Tests** for revision.

Case study

Background

This *Case study* presents a rapidly expanding company that wants to establish a solid career review process. The *Task* then enables students to act as managers and consultants and to discuss ways a company could keep its staff and ensure successful staff development.

As a lead-in, write *rapid expansion* on the board and ask students to brainstorm what problems a company might have if they expand too rapidly. For example: production capacity becomes too small for demand; cash flow problems due to increased production costs versus payment of invoices; staff overworked; difficulty finding new staff, etc.

Refer students to the *Company profile* and then allow them a few minutes to read the two texts. Be prepared to answer any questions about vocabulary. Ask students if their ideas about rapid expansion came up in the texts.

Alternative

Students work in pairs, and each student reads just one of the texts. He / she then summarizes the content for his / her partner.

13▷ Students listen to a manager at Axtrin talking about their connection with tpmg. Ask them to take notes to help them with the discussion questions.

Discussion

1, 2, 3 Students discuss the questions in pairs before feeding back to the rest of the class.

> **Possible answers**
> 1 In the past, staff were able to develop in their own roles and there were no web tools or established procedures to encourage them to look beyond this. However, the new process allowed them to have a longer-term and wider view – they were then able to find out what possibilities there were in the company outside their existing job.
> 2 Axtrin became better able to keep staff. Moreover, the staff would be more satisfied, as they would be more likely to realize their own potential. Ultimately, this could improve the profitability of the company.
> 3 tpmg made the process extremely efficient because they are experienced professionals: they used sophisticated IT tools to set up systems / procedures to develop career reviews.

Task

1 Students read the information about the company, then divide the class into two groups (A and B). If you have a large class, you might want to sub-divide the groups.

Allow each group time to read their *File*. Group A should discuss what they would like tpmg to do for the company. Group B should discuss what they would propose for the company and be prepared to clarify and expand on their ideas.

2 Students then have the meeting. Encourage them to follow the agenda, and ask them to aim to achieve total clarity in the exchange of ideas and equal involvement of all the participants.

Feedback focus

Ask students to comment on their own performance. Write the following questions on the board to help them.
- *Did you cover all points on the agenda?*
- *Were the ideas / proposals clear to all participants?*
- *Were all participants equally involved in the discussion?*

Extension

As a follow-up activity, ask students to send an email to you, summarizing what was agreed. Give feedback on the language used, and also check that both groups had the same impression of what was agreed in the meeting. Deal with any corrections in the next lesson. You could also encourage students to correct each other's emails if you prefer.

One-to-one

Your student can read the *Background* and listen to the manager. You can then do the *Discussion* questions together. In the *Task*, you can play the part of Group A and the student can play the part of Group B.

➤➤ Unit 2 **Progress test** and **Speaking test**, pages 98–99.

3 | Change

Unit content

By the end of this unit, students will be able to
- discuss working practices
- give a formal presentation
- speculate about future changes using different future tenses
- show understanding.

Context

The topic of change is extremely relevant in today's business world. Individuals now fully expect to change jobs throughout their careers. The days of working nine to five in the same company and climbing the career ladder have ended. Companies have always had to embrace change in order to achieve success, and continue to do so to maintain profits. However, they are now increasingly finding that they have to change working practices in line with technological innovations and the increasing concerns about the environment. Implementing change can be a complex process due to the fact that there is a natural tendency to want to avoid change. Companies have to manage any changes extremely carefully if they want to avoid negative reactions from their staff. Communicating exactly what will happen, why, and when, is part of ensuring that staff still feel in control and are more willing to accept change.

In the first section of this unit, students will talk about where they work and how working practices in their company may have changed over time. In the *Business communication skills* section they practise how to give a formal presentation. They then move on to look at the different future tenses needed to speculate about future change. In the *Case study*, they look at the factors involved in changing working environments and discuss ways of improving the work space for a company.

Starting point

As a lead-in you could bring in some photographs of some famous buildings, e.g. The Gherkin in London, The Sydney Opera House, The Reichstag in Berlin, The Burj al Arab in Dubai. Alternatively you could ask students to name some famous buildings they know. Then write the following questions on the board.
1 *Why are these buildings so famous?*
2 *What do you think of the internal / external design of these buildings?*

Discuss these questions as a class. Students can then work in pairs and discuss questions **1–3** in the book before feeding back to the rest of the class. Write any new vocabulary on the board.

Watch out! Be careful if you have students whose work situations may not be secure. In this case you may like to miss out question **3**.

> **Possible answers**
> 1 Answers will vary.
> 2 Flexible working could include working part-time, flexitime, job sharing, working from home, working on short-term contracts, etc.
> 3 Answers will vary. Students may mention changes to working times and hours or the technology used at work, changes in contract, etc.

Pre-work learners

Ask students to think about the building where they are studying or living for the first question. For the third question, ask them to discuss how they think the style and conditions of work are different now from when their parents started work.

Working with words

1 Students read the text and discuss the question in pairs.

   Watch out! Before they read, you might want to check that students understand the following.
   (have) an aversion to = a strong feeling of not liking something / somebody

2 Students read the statements and decide how far they agree with them in relation to their own company. They can then discuss their opinions in pairs before feeding back to the rest of the class.

Alternative / Pre-work learners

Ask students to work in small groups. Write the following instructions on the board.
- *Read the statements in* **2**.
- *Using ideas in the statements and your own ideas, create a list of criteria for the ideal working organization.*
- *Present your ideas to the rest of the class.*

3 Students look back at the texts in **1** and **2** and find words that are similar in meaning to those in *italics* in 1–10.

Answers

1	effective	6	put in place
2	accessing	7	procedure
3	means	8	purpose
4	option	9	dynamic
5	transformed	10	implement

4 Students now decide if the words they found in the texts could replace the words in *italics* in **3**. They should then decide if the meaning of the sentence would change. Ask them to discuss their answers in pairs. They can refer to dictionaries to help them if necessary.

Answers

1 Both words could be used, but the meaning would be slightly different. *Efficient* means that somebody is able to do something well or successfully without wasting time, whilst *effective* means that something works well and the result is good.

2 Only *enter* could be used here as the sentence refers to a period of time. *Enter* means to go into a place or begin a period of time, whilst *access* means to be able to get into something, e.g. a file or a place.

3 Both words could be used, but the meaning would be slightly different. *Ability* means having the skill to do something, whilst *means* are the resources you need to do something.

4 Both words could be used, but the meaning would be slightly different. *Opportunity* means the chance, whilst *option* means the choice.

5 Both words could be used, but *transformed* sounds more dramatic than *changed*. *Change* means to make some alterations, whilst *transform* means to change completely.

6 Only *carry out* is possible as a collocation of *research*. *Carry out* means *to do something*, whilst *put in place* means *to set up something*.

7 Only *process* is possible here. *Process* refers to a series of actions completed in order to achieve something, whilst *procedure* refers to the way or system of doing something.

8 Both words could be used, but the meaning would be slightly different. *Meaning* means the significance of something, whilst *purpose* means the reason for something.

9 Both words could be used, but there would be a slight difference in meaning. *Energetic* means showing a lot of enthusiasm and determination, whilst *dynamic* means being full of energy and new ideas.

10 Only *install* is possible as a collocation of *software*. *Install* means *to put in*, whilst *implement* means *to put in place*.

Extra activity

Draw the table on the board. Ask students to say which verb / noun collocations are possible (answers are in brackets).

Verbs / Multi-word verbs	Nouns
carry out (+ a study, an exercise, a task)	a machine
put in place (+ infrastructure)	innovations
implement (+ change, innovations)	an exercise
install (+ software, a machine)	infrastructure
	a task
	software
	a study
	change

5 14▷ Before students listen, write the words *consultancy* and *consultant* on the board. Ask students to brainstorm the activities that they associate with them (e.g. give advice, increase efficiency, oversee change, maximize profitability, facilitate projects). Then tell students *BICG* stands for *Business Intelligence Consulting Group*. Students then listen and answer questions 1–3.

Answers

1 infrastructure, i.e. information and communication technologies; the physical environment, i.e. architecture and use of office space; cultural aspects, i.e. working practices.

2 They help companies move with the times; implement cost-saving measures; become more productive; have more efficient and effective processes, teams, and working practices; raise the level of motivation.

3 People at the bottom of the hierarchy tend to be quite happy to get something new; those at the top of companies are the champions or sponsors of these new concepts so will naturally be happy about them. However, middle management tend to be very resistant to change.

6 14▷ Students listen again and note down the nouns.

Answers

1	needs / requirements	5	enthusiasm
2	results	6	information / knowledge / ideas
3	problems	7	progress
4	(cultural) change	8	success

7 Students work in pairs and match the nouns to the verbs.

Answers

a	2	e	8
b	1	f	4
c	5	g	7
d	6	h	3

8 Students work in pairs and ask and answer questions about working conditions in their companies. Encourage them to use collocations from **6** and **7**.

> **Possible answers**
> **A** Does your company **accommodate the needs** of its employees?
> **B** Not always. For example, we can't work flexitime. This isn't good for me because I've got children and I can't organize my day so that it fits in with school hours.
> **B** How do managers **assess performance** in your company?
> **A** We have appraisals every fours months and we have performance objectives that we have to meet within a certain period of time.

Pre-work learners

Write the following topics on the board. Pairs then ask and answer questions about them (possible answers are in brackets) using collocations from **6** and **7**.

- *A teacher you know. (How does your teacher **generate enthusiasm** in the class?)*
- *Your place of study. (How is **progress assessed**?)*
- *Your ideal working situation. (How would the company **facilitate** your **development**?)*

>> If students need more practice, go to **Practice file 3** on page 106 of the **Student's Book**.

9 Students work in pairs and read the email. They then have the meeting following stages 1–3.

> **Possible answers**
> **1** Students outline the main points from the email.
> **2, 3** Ideas could include: ensuring that all staff have received adequate training to use new technology in production, introducing flexitime and ensuring that shift times accommodate the needs of employees, introducing bonuses for employees who exceed their targets, etc.

Feedback focus

Circulate, making notes of any errors you want to discuss with the whole class. Give positive feedback to students who use verb / noun collocations from this section.

Extra activity

Ask students to write a report based on the meeting for homework. Ask them to include the following.

- *an outline of the main problems*
- *possible solutions discussed in the meeting*
- *the agreed action plan*

ⓘ Refer students to the **Interactive Workbook Glossary** for further study.

Business communication skills

1 Students read the *Context*. They then work with a partner and discuss the questions.

2 15–18▷ Students listen and fill in the notes on the slides. You might need to allow them to write notes for each extract before moving on to the next extract.

> **Possible answers**
> **1** Research from Henley Management College: middle managers are under increasing pressure and it's going to get tougher.
> **2** Demuting = working remotely from wherever you are. 20th century = 47.6-hour week for British workers. 21st century = new generation of 'career nomads'.
> **3** Employees will be working harder and longer unless organizations devise formal policies to deal with new working practices.
> Shadow careers = amateur activities are pursued to professional standards.
> Local communities could be revived if more people work from home.
> **4** Employers will have to tempt people away from working for themselves, rather than from working for the competition. Employers need to recognize the choice available to the workforce and start planning for it now.

3 15–18▷ Students listen to the four extracts again and note down the phrases used for each category. They can then check their answers with a partner.

4 Students turn to the audio scripts and check their answers.

> **Answers**
> **1** … just to fill you in on some of the background …
> **2** … I'll return to this point later.
> **3** I've divided my talk up into three sections. First of all, I'll …, After that, I'll …, I'll conclude with …
> **4** I'd like to start by saying a few words about …
> **5** By 'demuting' I mean…, Now, I don't know if you're familiar with this term? Well, … refers to …
> **6** OK, moving on now to look at …
> **7** … this is where …, and perhaps here I should just explain what I mean by … – that's when …, So, for example …
> **8** Turning to the next point, …
> **9** … and as I said earlier, …
> **10** Just to digress for a second …
> **11** And this brings me to the last point.
> **12** So, that brings me to the end of my talk. Thank you very much for listening. And I'll be happy to take any questions now.

» If students need more practice, go to **Practice file 3** on page 106 of the **Student's Book**.

5 Students work in pairs and prepare a presentation summarizing what they found out from the audio. They then decide who will deliver each section and practise giving the presentation to each other.

Feedback focus

Circulate, giving help where necessary. Ask students to give their presentations to the rest of the class. Give feedback on the presentation style and use of language.

6 Students prepare their presentations individually. You might need to help them come up with an idea for change, e.g. no more business trips, introduce flexible working, make all offices open-plan, allow employees input on salary scales, allow employees to evaluate their bosses.

Refer them to the *Key expressions* list during preparation and remind them that the tone should be formal.

Alternative

Ask students to prepare the presentation for homework. They can then research the topic further and prepare slides / visuals.

Pre-work learners

Write the following ideas for change at their place of study on the board. Students then choose their favourite idea and prepare to give a formal presentation outlining the change.
- *no more lectures / classes before 11.00 a.m.*
- *limit class sizes to fifteen*
- *introduce online teleconference-style lectures*
- *allow students to design the curriculum*

7 Students listen to the presentations and take notes. Encourage them to ask questions.

Feedback focus

Make notes on the following during each presentation.
- good use of phrases / language
- level of formality (should be formal)
- errors impeding the presentation
- presentation style (e.g. eye contact, voice projection, etc.)

Give each student detailed feedback on their presentation.

Culture question

Discuss these questions as a class.

ⓘ Refer students to the **Interactive Workbook Email** and **Phrasebank** sections for further study.

Language at work

1 If you feel that your students need to revise future tenses before answering these questions, do the following *Extra activity* first.

Extra activity

Write sentences 1–10 from the following table on the board. Ask students to work in pairs to identify the structure used in each sentence (answers are in the table). Whilst they are working on this, write the functions on the board in a mixed order. Then ask students to match the sentences to the functions.

Sentence	Structure	Function
1 *Look at those black clouds – it's going to rain.*	*be going to*	*prediction with evidence*
2 *There will be more floods in the future.*	*will*	*prediction*
3 *I'm not sure what to order from this menu. I know, I'll have chicken.*	*will*	*decision made at time of speaking*
4 *A My train has been cancelled.* **B** *Don't worry, I'll give you a lift.*	*will*	*offer made at time of speaking*
5 *I'm going to learn Italian next year.*	*be going to*	*intention*
6 *At this time tomorrow I'll be giving my presentation to the board.*	*future continuous*	*action in progress at a certain time in the future*
7 *By next summer I will have finished my MBA.*	*future perfect simple*	*action that will be completed at a certain time in the future*
8 *At the end of this month I will have been working at this company for ten years.*	*future perfect continuous*	*action that started previously and will be continuing at a certain time in the future*

9 *The train leaves at 8.30 a.m. tomorrow morning.*	*present simple*	*timetabled event*
10 *I'm meeting my boss at 10.00 a.m. tomorrow, so I can't stay out late tonight.*	*present continuous*	*fixed plan / future arrangement*

Answers

1
   a future simple (*will*)
   b very
   c *is going to* + infinitive
   d very little, but the use of *be going to* would suggest that the speaker thinks there is more evidence in support of the prediction

2
   a future perfect continuous
   b Fairly, but the use of *estimated* in the sentence reminds us that it's a prediction.
   c The future perfect simple could be used.
   d Using the future perfect continuous emphasizes the action of working and implies that it will have started previously and will still be going on at that time in the future, whereas using the future perfect simple would mean that the action may have finished at this point in the future.

3
   a future continuous
   b fairly
   c *will* or *be going to* + infinitive
   d No significant change in meaning, but the use of the future continuous emphasizes the activity of working and raises the level of formality slightly.

4
   a *be going to* + infinitive
   b very
   c *will*
   d Little difference in meaning, but the use of *be going to* rather than *will* suggests that the speaker has evidence to support their argument.

5
   a modal verb + infinitive
   b not certain, but there is a possibility
   c Could be replaced by *is going to have*, *will have* and other modals could be used, e.g. *might / may / would*.
   d It would alter the degree of certainty. *Could / may* means that the speaker thinks it's slightly more likely to happen than if they used *might*, and using *would / will have / is going to have* would mean that the speaker is more certain that there will be 'other positive side effects'.

6
   a future simple
   b fairly
   c As it is a prediction, *will* and *be going to* are interchangeable.
   d *Be going to* implies that the speaker has evidence to support their views.

7
   a *to be* (present simple) + adverb + infinitive
   b fairly
   c several, e.g. *will probably, are going to, are bound to*
   d Some structures change the meaning, i.e. *are bound to* means it is extremely certain.

8
   a future perfect simple
   b fairly
   c Could be replaced by future continuous, e.g. *will be taking place*, or with another modal verb, e.g. *may / might*.
   d Using the future continuous would mean that the change will be in progress in the middle of the 21st century, but using the future perfect simple means that the change will have already occurred by this point. Using different modals would affect the levels of certainty.

9
   a present simple passive + *be* + *-ing* form
   b very
   c No, but word order could change, e.g. *It is expected that people will be working …*
   d It wouldn't.

10
   a modal + adverb + infinitive
   b very
   c *will / be going to*
   d It wouldn't.

Watch out! Remind students that the choice of future structure depends on the context and on the feelings / opinions of the speaker and that often several options are possible grammatically, but they would convey slightly different messages.

Pronunciation

Write the following phrases on the board. Focus on the weak verb forms of *have* and *been*. Ask students to practise saying the weak forms.
   • *will have been working* /wɪl əv bɪn wɜːkɪŋ/
   • *will have taken place* /wɪl əv teɪkən pleɪs/

» If students need more practice, go to **Practice file** 3 on page 107 of the **Student's Book**.

2 19▷ Before they listen, ask students if they think there will be a major change in the way we work in the future. Write the phrases they use to make their predictions on the board. Then students listen to the audio and note down the phrases used. They can then compare the answers with the phrases on the board.

Answers

1 ... **it's bound to** happen sooner or later.
2 **It may happen**, but **it's not very likely**.
3 I think **it's possible that we'll** see new innovations in this area, yes.
4 **It may well be that** things change in the next few years.
5 **Definitely**, yes – **there's certain to be** a major change at some point in the future.
6 I think **it's very unlikely** that will happen, to be honest.
7 Oh most certainly, yes, and **it's highly likely to** impact on all our lives.
8 **It's quite probable that we'll** see some big changes in the near future.
9 **It's certain that** there will be significant changes, yes.
10 Oh **definitely**, and **there's a good chance most of us will** benefit from these changes.

3 Students categorize the phrases. They can then check their answers in pairs before feeding back to the rest of the class.

Answers

1 **certain**: it's bound to, definitely, there's certain to be, it's certain that
2 **probable**: it's highly likely to, it's quite probable that we'll, there's a good chance most of us will
3 **possible**: it may happen, it's possible that we'll, it may well be that
4 **unlikely**: it's not very likely, it's very unlikely

Extension

Elicit phrases for the future that could be used if you think something is impossible (e.g. *we definitely won't …, we've got no hope of -ing …, there's no chance we will …, there's no way we will …*).

4 19▷ Students listen again and note the phrases referring to a point / period of time in the future.

Answers

sooner or later
in the next few years
at some point in the future
in the near future

>> If students need more practice, go to **Practice file 3** on page 107 of the **Student's Book**.

5 Allow students time to note down some ideas before telling their partner about their predictions.

Pre-work learners

Write the following topics on the board. Ask students to choose a topic and make predictions about it.
- *the economy in your country*
- *standards of living in your country*
- *the environment*
- *your future career*
- *your future living arrangements*

(*i*) Refer students to the **Interactive Workbook Exercises and Tests** for revision.

Practically speaking

1 20▷ As a lead-in, write the following work-related problems on the board.
- *My office is too noisy.*
- *I don't like giving presentations.*
- *I have too much work to do.*
- *I'm so disorganized.*

Ask students how they would show understanding if a colleague spoke to them about these problems. Write any suggested language and / or techniques on the board. Then ask them to listen to the audio and identify the problems and the listeners' responses.

Answers

1 The first speaker has a lot of work, and the other speaker responds by empathizing and explaining that they are in a similar situation.
2 The second speaker's presentation didn't go according to plan. The other speaker agrees and says the organization at the conference hasn't been great, and makes a suggestion.
3 The first speaker feels that they are spending most of the time passing on messages now that the team has split up, and cannot get on with work. The other speaker empathizes.
4 The first speaker is annoyed because nobody has responded to a message. The other speaker makes a suggestion.

Watch out! Pre-teaching vocabulary will give the answers to **1**, so just tell students you will deal with unknown words after the listening. You might then want to check that students understand the following.
to be snowed under = to be very busy
treading water = not moving forward
to badger someone = to repeatedly ask someone for something

2 20▷ Students listen again and complete the phrases. They can then compare their answers with a partner before feeding back to the rest of the class.

Answers
1 what you mean
2 hectic over here too
3 hasn't, has it
4 might be worth
5 what you're saying
6 know this is a tricky time
7 see where you're coming from
8 had a similar problem
9 still think you should send
10 you might want to

3 Students match the phrases in **2** to categories a–c.

Answers
a 1, 3, 5, 7
b 2, 6, 8
c 4, 9, 10

Extra activity

Ask students to work with a partner and think of other phrases they might use for a–c in **3**. Write their suggestions on the board. See the following suggested answers.
a *I get your point, quite / absolutely / exactly, I know*
b *I see what you mean, we're going through the same thing here*
c *Why don't you …? Maybe you could try …?, What if you were to …?*

4 Students discuss possible responses to 1–4.

Possible answers
1 I know what you mean (It's quite hectic over here too).
2 I had a similar problem when I gave a presentation last week.
3 I know what you mean. I thought it was very confusing too.
4 I see where you're coming from – you might want to have a chat with Paul about it.

》 Refer students to the **Useful phrases** section on page 134 of the **Student's Book** for extension and revision.

5 Students think of a problem at work or choose one from the list and take turns to explain the problem and respond.

Possible answers
Problem 1: You might want to organize video conferences with them.
Problem 2: I can see where you're coming from. I think you should draw names out of a hat.

6 Students discuss their partners' reactions with the class.

Feedback focus

Focus on the correct use of phrases for showing understanding and on correct intonation. Check that students sound genuinely sympathetic.

Key word

Students match the sentences to the synonyms.
Answers: 1 c, 2 a, 3 b, 4 e, 5 d

ⓘ Refer students to the **Interactive Workbook Exercises and Tests** for revision.

Case study

Background

This *Case study* presents RM-Circuit and Isustain, two companies that are part of the multinational group, Parelect. RM-Circuit has redefined its work space and Isustain now want to improve their working environment. The topic enables students to consider the issues connected to redefining office space and implementing change. The *Task* enables them to discuss solutions to office space planning issues, and to practise giving a formal presentation.

Allow a few minutes for students to read the texts and look at the diagrams. Be prepared to answer any questions about vocabulary.

Discussion

1, 2 Students work in pairs and discuss the questions, referring to the diagrams and texts to support their ideas.

3 Students can discuss this question in pairs, before feeding back to the rest of the class. Write any ideas on the board.

Possible answers

1 Having two separate sites (one for HQ functions and general offices and one for the labs) could have a negative effect on communication between departments.

2 The new layout provides optimum communication between management and staff, the design is flexible so you can move people and work stations around easily, initial consultation with staff means their needs have been taken into account.

3 Ideas could include:
  - ergonomic principles (safety, comfort, ease of use, productivity and performance as well as aesthetics)
  - consideration of what staff do, where they do it, who they need to interact with
  - provision of space that allows easy communication with management, but that also respects privacy
  - management of the project (use of computer-aided designs, scheduling, cost, contractors, clear plans)
  - decisions on fittings and furniture, lighting, materials, colours, etc.
  - consultation with staff, as well as designers.

Task

1 Students work in groups and discuss their ideas for the new office space design for Isustain. They might like to draw a diagram illustrating their ideas.

2 The groups prepare their presentations. Refer students to the *Key expressions* in the *Business Communication Skills* section for help with language. Ask each group to assign sections of the presentation to each person. They might like to prepare PowerPoint slides or even CAD (computer-aided design) slides.

3, 4 Each group gives their presentation to the class. Everyone then votes on the best proposal.

Feedback focus

Give feedback on the content of the presentations as well as on the language and presentation skills. You might like to give short written feedback to each group, focusing on the main strengths and weaknesses.

One-to-one

Read the *Background* and follow the *Discussion* questions together. For the *Task*, let the student develop and then present his / her own ideas.

》 Unit 3 **Progress test** and **Speaking test**, pages 100–101.

4 | Risk

Unit content

By the end of this unit, students will be able to
- talk about different kinds of risk
- take part in a teleconference
- use pronouns for reference
- establish rapport and show interest.

Context

Life is full of risks for everyone. Getting out of the shower or opening champagne bottles should be done with care, and deciding whether to wear a helmet or not when riding a bike depends on your attitude to risk. In business, risk management has become a vital decision-making tool. Due to the fact that virtually every decision involves some element of uncertainty, and because there are risks inherent in most of the key issues facing companies today, the ability to understand risks and manage them effectively is an important ingredient for success. Risks are present whenever a company decides to expand into a new market, or to launch a new product. Similarly, companies are exposed to external risks, such as political or economic changes in the countries in which they operate, shifts in social behaviour, and new technology.

In this unit, students learn about different kinds of risk and are encouraged to discuss the various risks facing their own company. They have the opportunity to practise the language of managing discussions, checking understanding, and expressing opinions in the context of teleconferencing. They also review the use of pronouns as reference markers. In the *Case study* they look at the risks faced by food companies and discuss how to minimize them.

Starting point

Refer students to the three quotes and check they understand what they mean (first quote = risk-takers just do something and deal with problems as they come up; second quote = to achieve something important you have to take risks; third quote = if a risk pays off, it's more down to luck than judgement).

Students can discuss the questions in pairs before feeding back to the whole class.

Working with words

1 Discuss this question as a class and brainstorm risks faced by businesses on the board.

> **Possible answers**
> Investment in new products – may or may not be a commercial success.
> Investment in new technology – may be obsolete within a few years.
> Moving into new markets – cultural sensitivities, different working practices, local laws.
> Employing someone on the basis of one interview and their CV – they may not fit in.
> Takeovers – could lead to staff issues, differences in infrastructure and in shareholders' objectives, legal problems, etc.
> Giving credit to new customers – they may not pay on time, leading to cash flow problems.

Extra activity

Elicit what kind of risks we have to evaluate and manage in our daily lives, e.g. whether to leave home without your cycling helmet because you're late for work and can't find it, and so run the risk of being injured if you're knocked off your bike.

---

2 Students read the text individually, then discuss their answers in pairs. Compare answers as a class, and ask students if they agree with the points and if they would consider using such software for evaluating risks in their own professional or personal lives.

Watch out! Before they read, you might want to check that students understand the following.
adept = skilled
habitual = usual or typical
volatile = likely to change suddenly
let alone = never mind
assessment = evaluation
linear = following a regular pattern
sound = solid, reliable

Answers
risks in our everyday lives: We manage risks without thinking about it.
risks in the telecommunications sector: Shifts in taste move extremely fast, risk of being left behind by competitors.
the link between survival and change: Species most likely to survive is one most responsive to change, but change is no longer linear or predictable.
technology versus human skills: New software is impressive and allows you to view various risk factors at a glance, but as we can't be certain we've anticipated all possible eventualities, technology needs to be supported by intuitive opinions of an experienced risk manager.

Extra activity

Ask students to look at the text and find five nouns that collocate with risk (*management, assessment, factor(s), analysis, manager*) and two adjectives that collocate with risk (*possible, unnecessary*). Then brainstorm other collocations that they might know (e.g. *potential risks, inherent risks*, etc.).

3 Students match the verbs and verb phrases to the definitions. They can then check their answer in pairs.

Answers
1 predict, anticipate
2 evaluate, gauge (Note that *gauge* is used more often to judge people's feelings / attitudes.)
3 identify, recognize
4 weigh up
5 minimize
6 expose something / someone to
7 run the risk of
8 determine
9 accept

4 Students work in pairs and discuss what advice they would give. You might like to ask them to tick off the different verbs as they use them or hear them used.

5 21▷ Students listen and answer the questions. They can then discuss their ideas in pairs before feeding back to the rest of the class.

Possible answers
Speaker 1: CEO, risks = signing agreements, cutting prices, managing shareholders' money
Speaker 2: Sales Representative, risks = what deal to offer, who to follow up – risk of time-wasting
Speaker 3: Actuary (Risk Assessor), risks = potential risks in a company – both health and safety and external risks

6 21▷ Students listen again and note which speaker use the adjectives.

Answers
Speaker 1: over-cautious, reckless, bold, rash, imprudent, prudent, foolhardy
Speaker 2: sensible, cautious
Speaker 3: prudent, risk-averse*
* Note that *risk-averse* is not generally used to describe decisions / actions.

7 Students decide which adjectives in **6** have a positive and which have a negative connotation. Ask them to check their answers in pairs before feeding back to the rest of the class. When feeding back, point out that *risk-averse* could have a positive or negative connotation, depending on the context and the attitude of the speaker. If necessary, you could ask students to check in their dictionaries for exact definitions.

Answers
Positive connotation: sensible, cautious, prudent, bold
Negative connotation: imprudent, reckless, rash, foolhardy, risk-averse*
*risk-averse is considered negative in the audio, but it could also be perceived as positive in other contexts

8 This activity allows students to focus on the exact meanings of the adjectives in **6**. Students work in pairs. When checking their answers with the class make sure that they can pronounce the words correctly. If necessary ask them to mark the word stress on the adjectives of two syllables or more (see word stress marked in answer key).

Suggested answers
1 **Luis:** risk-a<u>ver</u>se, (over-)<u>cau</u>tious
2 **Anastasia:** <u>sen</u>sible, <u>pru</u>dent
3 **Victoria:** im<u>pru</u>dent
4 **Lothar:** <u>reck</u>less, rash, <u>fool</u>hardy, bold

9 Students work in pairs and discuss people they know. You might like to give an example to help them. Try to describe someone who has a very different attitude to risk from you. For example:
*I've got a friend who constantly speculates on the stock market and bets on the horses. He used his son's student loan to invest on the stock market – and made enough money for his son to cover his university costs. I'd never take that risk! He says he's **prudent**, because he studies the market carefully. I think he's very **bold** and maybe a bit **foolhardy**!*

When feeding back to the rest of the class, avoid asking students to talk about their own attitude to risk as they might not want to share this with everyone.

Feedback focus

Check that students are using the adjectives correctly, with appropriate positive or negative connotation.

Extra activity

Ask students to work in groups of two or three. Their task is to write a questionnaire to find out how risk-averse the class is. Each group should write five questions with a, b, or c answers. When they are ready they can circulate and ask their questions. They then collate the answers with their original group and summarize their findings for the class, using adjectives from **6**.

You could write the following example on the board to start them off.

You're on a skiing holiday. You've skied three times before in your life. Your friend, who's a very good skier, wants to take you on a black run, saying it'll be fun. Do you

    a accept without hesitation – you'll be safe with your friend and it'll be great?

    b say you'll think about it – maybe tomorrow, when you've had a chance to look at the slope?

    c say 'no way'?

Extension

Ask students to imagine they are in a job interview. One of the questions is:

- What risks are you exposed to at work and what is your attitude to them?

Give students ten minutes to prepare their answer, before presenting it to the class.

》 If students need more practice, go to **Practice file 4** on page 108 of the **Student's Book**.

10 As a lead-in, write the acronyms SWOT and PEST on the board and establish or explain that they are both tools for analysing a company and the environment it operates in. Elicit or explain what the letters in SWOT refer to (Strengths, Weaknesses, Opportunities, Threats), then refer them to the description of a PEST analysis. Elicit how SWOT and PEST are similar or different – a SWOT focuses on internal strengths and weaknesses as well as external factors (opportunities, threats), whereas a PEST concentrates only on external factors, which may represent either opportunities or threats.

Students then work in pairs to carry out their PEST analysis. If possible create pairs of students from the same company or from companies in a similar field of business. Explain that they should focus on the risks (or threats) to their business rather than the opportunities. Encourage them to use new words from this section where possible.

Pre-work learners

Elicit the names of some companies students know (e.g. a supermarket, a petrol company). They could be international or local companies. They can then prepare a PEST analysis for their chosen company.

---

11 Ask each pair to present their findings. You may prefer to deal with each point on the PEST analysis separately, i.e. all the pairs report on the political factors first, then the economic factors, etc. This may invite further discussion on the similarities between the different sectors or companies.

Feedback focus

Ask students to self-correct if you hear a target word being used incorrectly or the wrong word being used. Otherwise let the discussion flow freely.

ⓘ Refer students to the **Interactive Workbook Glossary** for further study.

Business communication skills

1 Students work in pairs to think of advice for participating in a teleconference for the first time. When they have finished, ask the class if there is anything in the guidelines in the *File* that they disagree with. If they take part in teleconferences themselves, ask which guidelines are most often not respected.

2 22▷ As a lead-in to the listening, ask students what risks traditional travel agents are facing today, and what they are doing about them, e.g. developing their own online sites in response to 'virtual' travel agents; offering new solutions to those tired of traditional packages, such as 'pick and mix' holidays, adventure tours, accommodation in local people's houses; offering more holistic holidays; offering 'green' holidays for people concerned about the environmental cost of the travel industry.

Ask students to listen with *File 10* in front of them so that they can tick the guidelines that are followed. Compare answers with the whole class.

Watch out! Before they listen, check that students understand the following.

pipe dream = a hope or plan that is impossible to achieve or not practical

carbon offsetting = calculating your carbon emissions and purchasing 'credits' from emission reduction projects

Answers

1 Everyone seems to be familiar with the agenda.
2 Jean-Luc and Khalid talk over people.
3 Nobody introduces themselves each time they come into the conversation. Jean-Luc doesn't identify everyone. Thomas, Joana, and Greta don't identify themselves, but they might have done before Extract 1. Khalid identifies himself.
4 Jean-Luc nominates Greta to speak.
5 Thomas checks he's understood correctly.
6 Thomas digresses. Jean-Luc keeps people to the agenda and encourages everyone to do the same.

3 Students categorize the phrases.

Answers

a 1, 7, 12
b 5, 8, 10
c 2, 11, 13
d 4, 6, 15
e 3, 9, 14
Note that 7 could also fit category d.

4 Discuss the differences with the whole class. You could then ask which style is closer to meetings held in students' own language.

Possible answers

A is more formal / tentative (*Could you …? / Am I right? / I'd be interested … just … / we seem …*) whilst **B** is much more direct / less formal.

5 23▷ Students listen and decide what the speaker really means. Stop the audio after each extract and elicit possible answers from the whole class.

Possible answers

2 You've said enough. Let Joana speak.
3 I don't agree
4 That's enough!
5 This is irrelevant.

6 Elicit an example from the whole class for the first item. Students then work in pairs to decide on possible answers.

Possible answers

1 X, could you talk us through this?
2 You're saying that …
3 X, I'd be interested to hear what you think about this.
4 Maybe we're digressing a little.
5 If I could just bring the conversation back to the agenda.
6 I'd like to draw things to a close.
7 Can I just ask everyone to sum up their views?

Culture question

Students can discuss these questions in pairs before feeding back to the rest of the class. You might like to raise the point that whether people interrupt or not can often depend on who is talking – you might be less likely to interrupt your superiors, even if they are talking about totally irrelevant issues. It may also be the case that there are far fewer interruptions in Eastern cultures, as decisions there are more often based on harmony and consensus, rather than argument and debate.

» If students need more practice, go to **Practice file 4** on page 108 of the **Student's Book**.

7 Students should work in groups with people from the same company or line of work. If this isn't possible, you should follow the activity in *File 11*. You may even choose to do both if you have time. Allow students time to prepare before they hold the teleconference and encourage them to use language from the *Key expressions*. If you have the possibility, you could use two real teleconferencing machines.

Pre-work learners

Write the following alternative topics on the board. Students work in groups and choose one topic to discuss in their teleconference. Ask them to identify three or four issues for their chosen subject. Allow plenty of time for students to prepare their ideas.

- *How to improve the health and fitness of people in your community.*
- *How to improve the education system in your country.*
- *How to improve the quality of TV programmes in your country.*
- *How to make your town more environmentally-friendly.*

Feedback focus

After the task, give positive feedback to students who included a lot of the target language. Note any phrases used incorrectly during the teleconference and ask students to correct them without looking at the *Key Expressions* list. You could also ask if they felt there was adequate turn-taking during the teleconference, or if the interruptions were excessive.

One-to-one

The student can be the moderator. Tell your student that you will play two roles (e.g. John and Peter), and make it clear when you speak which person you are, e.g. *This is John here. I'm having second thoughts about this.*

ⓘ Refer students to the **Interactive Workbook Email** and **Phrasebank** sections for further study.

Language at work

1 Write the words *this* and *that* on the board. Then write the following sentences on the board.
   - **This** *book here is mine.* **That** *book over there is yours.*
   - **This** *is Liz speaking. Is* **that** *Jorge?*

Ask students if they can explain when you normally use *this* and when you use *that*. (Answer: It relates to distance from the speaker – physically in these examples, but also metaphorically in others.) Then ask students to work in pairs, read the audio script, and identify the meaning of the underlined pronouns in the sentences.

> **Answers**
> 1 *That* refers to the comment the speaker has just made. *It* refers to the subject related to the comment.
> 2 *This* is the subject under discussion. *That* refers to last year when the solution was explored. *It* was the solution proposed.
> 3 *This* is the subject under discussion.
> 4 *This* is the proposal the speaker is about to make.
> 5 The first *that* refers to the point that has been reached in the discussion. The second *that* refers to what the speaker is saying.
> 6 *It* refers to the suggestion just made.
> 7 The first *it* refers to the decision-making process. The second *it* refers to the subject the speaker is about to talk about.

2 Ask students to refer to sentences 2 and 4 in **1**. Elicit the answers to the questions from the whole class.

> **Answers**
> 1 that
> 2 this

≫ Refer students to the **Language Reference** section on page 128 of the **Student's Book** for more information.

3 Students choose the correct answers. Ask individual students to read the sentences aloud. Point out that we normally stress *this* and *that*, but not *it*.

> **Answers**
> 1 That
> 2 That
> 3 It
> 4 that
> 5 this
> 6 It

Pronunciation

Write the following sentences on the board and elicit the difference in pronunciation of *that*.

> *That's interesting. I don't think that there's an easy solution.*

In the first case, *that* is stressed (strong form), because it's an emphatic pronoun. In the second, *that* is unstressed (weak form), so the vowel is pronounced as a schwa /ə/.

Now write the following sentences on the board and ask students to identify whether the strong or weak form of the words in **bold** would be used (answers are in brackets).

> 1 *Where do you come* **from**? *(strong)*
> 2 *He comes* **from** *Serbia. (weak)*
> 3 *What's it* **for**? *(strong)*
> 4 *It's* **for** *saving data. (weak)*
> 5 *Who do I send it* **to**? *(strong)*
> 6 *Send it* **to** *me. (weak)*
> 7 *Would you like* **some** *wine? (weak)*
> 8 *No, thank you, I've still got* **some**. *(strong)*

≫ If students need more practice, go to **Practice file 4** on page 109 of the **Student's Book**.

4 Students choose a topic and then discuss it in pairs. Encourage them to use reference markers in their conversations.

Pre-work learners

Write the following alternative topics on the board.

- *a current story in this week's newspaper*
- *a recent film you've seen*
- *celebrity gossip*
- *something happening in your town*
- *something happening in your place of study*

Feedback focus

Circulate and make a note of any incorrect uses of *it*, *this*, and *that*. Feed back on this after the activity.

Practically speaking

1 Students complete the activity in pairs. Discuss the possible answers with the whole class.

Watch out! You may need to give an example of g:
A   I work in publishing.
B   Publishing?
And an example of j:
A   Going down the Amazon was a real nightmare.
B   In what way was it a nightmare?

Possible answers
1 c, d, e, g, j
2 a, b, c, f, g, h, i, j
3 b, c, e, f, g, j

2 **24▷** Students listen and complete the table. Remind them to refer to the methods listed in **1**. Ask them to compare their notes before feeding back to the rest of the class.

Answers

Extract	Relationship	Methods	Phrases
1	1st meeting, colleagues in same company, different locations	e d	It's Steve, isn't it? I've seen your picture on the website. How was the journey?
2	old colleagues	b e h c	You're looking well. I thought I recognized that voice. I may be old, but you can't get rid of me that easily. And are you still enjoying it?
3	old colleagues	a e g	It must be two years or more since we last met. Wasn't it at that conference in … Oh yes, … it was really beautiful, … do you remember …? Someone said you'd had a difficult year. (Yes. I have had a few ups and downs.) Ups and downs?
4	colleagues who haven't met before	b e i	You're not the Janos that pulled off that big Integra deal, are you? Well, it wasn't just me. There was a whole team involved. And anyway, Pietro, I've heard quite a lot about you, too. You got the gold award last month, didn't you?
5	old colleagues	f j	Well, I'd been working … when senior management decided … So I've been … the job's pretty challenging. But I'm enjoying it. Challenging in what way?

》 Refer students to the **Useful phrases** section on page 134 of the **Student's Book** for extension and revision.

3 Refer students to the methods for establishing rapport earlier in **1** and give them a few minutes to think about their future life. Point out that their imagined future doesn't necessarily have to be completely perfect – they may have had some 'ups and downs'. Make sure you also prepare for the activity. When they are ready, ask students to circulate and talk to other people. After the activity, ask students which of them seems to have had the most successful / interesting / difficult five years.

Key word

Students match 1–7 to a–g individually. They can then compare their answers in pairs before feeding back to the rest of the class.
   Answers: 1 b, 2 a, 3 e, 4 d, 5 g, 6 c, 7 f

ⓘ Refer students to the **Interactive Workbook Exercises and Tests** for revision.

Case study

Background

This *Case study* presents a food company that is facing various risks as a result of changing consumer attitudes. Students have the opportunity to look at a PEST analysis to see an overview of the risks facing the company and they then find out how the company has dealt with these risks. The *Task* enables them to make recommendations on how a food company can limit risks when entering a new market, using language from the unit.

Allow time for students to read the *Company profile* and the texts and be prepared to answer any questions about vocabulary.

Watch out! You might want to check that students understand the following.

hash browns = chopped potatoes and onions, fried until they are brown (popular in USA)

croquettes = mashed potato shaped into a ball or tube, covered with breadcrumbs and fried

Alternative

Before they read the second text, you might like to elicit what political, economic, social / cultural, and technological challenges McCain might face in the near future. Note some key ideas on the board. Students can then read the PEST analysis and compare their ideas.

Discussion

1, 2 Students discuss the question in pairs, before feeding back to the rest of the class.

> **Possible answers**
> 1 The political emphasis on healthy eating and the subsequent cultural and social changes in attitudes to food choices are probably the most problematic factors.
> 2 Answers will vary.

3 25▷ Students listen and note the actions taken by the company. You could also ask the class which ideas they heard in the audio seemed the most attractive.

> **Answers**
> McCain is constantly adapting to changing market demands in order to answer the public's demand for tasty food and healthy products.
> • They organized an action plan to keep the public better informed about products including an education campaign in schools to explain why products are healthy.
> • They stress the use of simple, natural ingredients in their marketing.
> • They introduced the traffic light symbols to show their foods are healthy, with low levels of saturated fat.
> • They reduced the salt content in their products.
> • They emphasized the fact that their products will not result in chip-pan fires, as they are cooked in the oven.

Task

1 Students read the information. Ask them how AST's situation is similar to that of McCain (it also makes ready meals and is having to deal with food health issues).

2 Students work in pairs and discuss the questions.

3 Each pair from **2** joins up with another pair to make a group of four. Pair A and Pair B.

Students look at the *Files*. Each pair discusses questions 1–4 with reference to their own *File*. Circulate and give help with vocabulary if needed. Remind students that they're all working for the same consulting team.

4 When they have prepared their answers, they team up in their group of four. You could ask them to write an agenda and nominate a chairperson before the meeting. You could also decide to organize the meeting as if it were a teleconference. In this case, refer students to the *Key expressions* in the *Business communication skills* section before they have their meeting.

Ask all students to make notes recording what is discussed in the meeting.

Feedback focus

Write the following questions on the board.
- *Were all the participants in the meeting equally involved in the discussion? Why? / Why not?*
- *Did you reach an agreement on the advice you would give to the company? Why? / Why not?*

Ask students to answer the questions in their group before feeding back to the class and discuss how successful each meeting was.

Extension

For homework, students could either write up the minutes of their meeting, or they could write a report based on what ideas were recommended and what ideas were rejected and why.

One-to-one

You can do the first part of the *Case study* together, then one of you should look at *File 12* on page 138 and the other *File 56* on page 149. Let your student chair the meeting, with you playing the role of another consultant on the team.

» Unit 4 **Progress test** and **Speaking test**, pages 102–103.

5 | Teamwork

Unit content

By the end of this unit, students will be able to
- explore team relationships
- deal with conflict
- emphasize a point of view
- respond appropriately to feedback.

Context

Teamwork is important in our everyday lives. Most jobs involve an element of teamwork and your students are likely to have experienced working in both good and bad teams. Good teamwork is integral to the success of a project or a company. It can also increase levels of job satisfaction for employees, as it enables close working relationships to develop and each team member can feel they have a significant role to play.

In a successful team, ideas are shared freely, and all members of the team are committed to working towards a common goal and to giving each other supportive feedback. Clear leadership within the team is the key to success. However, problems can arise if there is a lack of strategy or focus. Poor communication between team leaders and their team can lead to de-motivation, whilst clashes of personality, working styles, or cultural differences can also cause divisions within teams.

Many businesses recognize how difficult effective team working is, and attempt to enhance their employees' collaborative efforts through workshops and training. Dr Raymond Meredith Belbin is a British researcher and management theorist, best known for his work on management teams. This unit includes a reading based on his research. He proposes nine team roles required for successful teams. In this unit, students have the opportunity to discuss team relationships in connection to these roles. They then focus on the language used when dealing with conflict and when emphasizing a point of view. In the *Case study*, they evaluate a teamwork problem and discuss ways to improve it.

Starting point

1, 2 Discuss the questions as a class. Write any ideas on the board.

> **Possible answers**
> 1 team members don't get on, they have different working styles, some people are unreliable, there may be a clash of objectives, some people don't participate enough
> 2 Answers will vary.

Alternative

Ask students to think of their favourite football team and ask them if it's a good team and why / why not. Then write the following quote on the board and ask students to discuss how far they agree with it.

> *'When a team outgrows individual performance and learns team confidence, excellence becomes a reality.'* Joe Paterno, American football coach, 1924

Then hand out large sheets of paper with the word *teamwork* on them. Ask students to work in small groups and brainstorm what *teamwork* means to them. When they have finished, ask students to walk around and look at other groups' ideas.

Working with words

1 Students read the text and compare the team roles with their ideas in *Starting point*.

Watch out! Before they read, you might want to check that students understand the following.
absent-minded = tending to forget things, often due to being unfocused / thinking about other things
boundless = without limits
thrive = prosper, make good progress

2 Students read again and answers the questions.

> **Answers**
> 1 **Plant:** + innovative and finds solutions, – not good at communication
> **Resource investigator:** + enthusiastic at the start, excellent networker, – loses momentum later on
> **Coordinator:** + able to see the bigger picture, good at delegating, – sometimes neglects own work
> **Shaper:** + motivates teams, pushes others hard, thrives on pressure, – can treat others unfairly
> **Team worker:** + good listener, – not good at making decisions
> **Completer Finisher:** + good attention to detail, – poor delegator, over-emphasis on minor details
> **Monitor Evaluator:** + logical, able to judge situations, – lacks drive, finds it difficult to relate passionately to work
> **Implementer:** + disciplined, performs at high level, – no deviation, finds it difficult to incorporate new ideas
> **Specialist:** + highly skilled and knowledgeable, – focuses on technicalities
> 2 Answers will vary.

Extra activity

Write the following adjectives onto card. Prepare a set for each pair in your class and mix them up. Ask the pairs to arrange the cards into two groups, one group for the positive adjectives, and one for the negative adjectives.

- **Positive**

  *thorough, tolerant, caring, prudent, supportive, attentive, helpful, enterprising, confident, humorous, *ambitious, open to change, understanding, fair, assertive, cheerful, flexible, persevering, energetic, *demanding, curious*

- **Negative**

  careless, opportunistic, arrogant, irresponsible, pushy, ruthless, controlling, bullying, confrontational, obsessive, uncaring, nosy, indecisive, interfering, lazy, passive, aggressive, nit-picking, absent-minded, moody

  *Note that these adjectives could also be considered to be negative.

When they have arranged the cards, ask students to check they understand the meaning of the adjectives. They should look up any unfamiliar words in a dictionary. As you circulate, check they can pronounce each one correctly. Then ask them use the adjectives to describe a team they have worked in to their partner.

Extension

If your students are interested in Belbin and his theories, refer them to the following website for more information: www.belbin.com

---

3 Students underline the adverbs and then check their answers in the text.

> **Answers**
> | | |
> |---|---|
> | 1 effectively | 5 unfairly |
> | 2 clearly | 6 closely |
> | 3 carefully | 7 objectively |
> | 4 hard | 8 positively |

4 Students work in pairs and share advice on how to have successful working relationships using the verb + adverb combinations from **3**.

> **Possible answers**
> If you want to be viewed positively, make sure you meet all your deadlines.
> It's important to express yourself clearly, otherwise there can be misunderstandings.
> If you are working with a difficult and demanding boss, you should always tread carefully with him / her.

Pre-work learners

Ask students to talk about successful relationships with people they're studying with. Alternatively they can refer to relationships they had with colleagues during work placements.

5 26▷ Students listen and identify the strengths and weaknesses of each person. Students can then compare their notes in pairs, before feeding back to the rest of the class.

> **Possible answers**
> 1 **Strengths:** ambitious, energetic, efficient, enthusiastic
>   **Weaknesses:** demanding, pushy
> 2 **Strengths:** thorough, quick, good product knowledge
>   **Weaknesses:** doesn't delegate
> 3 **Strengths:** methodical, thorough, reliable
>   **Weaknesses:** not open to change, can't move from brief, not flexible

6 Students decide which Belbin role best fits each of the speakers in **5**. Refer them to the text in **1** to remind them of the roles.

> **Answers**
> 1 Shaper
> 2 Completer-Finisher
> 3 Implementer

7 Students work in pairs and discuss which people they would choose to work with and why.

Pre-work learners

Write the following question on the board and ask students to answer it in pairs.

- *Which of the three people would you prefer as your future boss? Why?*

---

8 Students replace the <u>underlined</u> sections with a multi-word verb from the text in **1**.

> **Answers**
> 1 pay attention to
> 2 coping with
> 3 keep to
> 4 steer clear of
> 5 fall short of
> 6 focus on

» If students need more practice, go to **Practice file 5** on page 110 of the **Student's Book**.

9 Students work in pairs and describe their colleague / team leader using vocabulary from **3** and **8**. They can then discuss any similarities / differences.

Watch out! This could be a sensitive topic if students are from the same company, in which case you might like to avoid this activity.

10 Students work in pairs and take turns to ask and answer questions about recent projects. If your students haven't had much experience of teamwork, ask them to turn to the *File* and discuss the best combination of people for the team. Encourage students to use new vocabulary from this section where appropriate.

Feedback focus

Circulate and make a note of any good use of vocabulary. If appropriate, make a note of any errors. Provide feedback after the activity and write any mistakes on the board for the class to correct.

Extension

Write the following questions on the board and ask students to discuss them in small groups.

- *Should the Belbin team roles model be used in a company's recruitment process? Why? / Why not?*
- *Do you think it's realistic for companies to put teams together that include a balance of the Belbin roles?*
- *Have you ever had a bad team working experience? If so, what went wrong and why?*

ⓘ Refer students to the **Interactive Workbook Glossary** for further study.

Business communication skills

1 Ask students to read the *Context* relating to Duverger. Then ask them to discuss the questions in pairs, before feeding back to the rest of the class. Write their ideas on the board.

> **Possible answers**
> **What can go wrong:** wrong photograph or logo, typographical errors, wrong content / information, colours not right, wrong font, paper quality not right, wrong quantity, etc.
> **Why this might happen:** sample not carefully checked by someone in the company, sample not given, company changed mind about design, but this wasn't communicated to printer, rushed job, printer not reliable, etc.

2 27▷ Students listen and compare their ideas.

> **Answers**
> **What went wrong:** wrong logo – the logo includes a knife and they didn't want this.
> **Why:** Paul isn't happy because they didn't use their normal printer – they used one recommended by Riccardo; Riccardo suggests the initial artwork given to the printer wasn't up to scratch, and that perhaps the printer didn't have the latest version of the files; Paul says it was a rushed job because Riccardo's approval of prices wasn't given until late.

3 27▷ Students listen again and answer the questions.

> **Answers**
> 1 *J*
> 2 *J*
> 3 *R*
> 4 *P*

4 Student categorize the phrases. They can then compare their answers in pairs.

> **Answers**
> 1 d, e
> 2 f, i
> 3 c, h
> 4 a, b, g

5 Students work in pairs and have the conversations. Encourage them to use phrases from the *Key expressions*.

6 28▷ Students listen and answer the questions.

> **Answers**
> - Reprint the brochures or use the brochures as they are.
> - Riccardo is put in charge of speaking to the printer, organizing a reprint and changing the logo.

7 Students answer the questions.

> **Answers**
> a Jenny
> b Paul and Riccardo
> c Riccardo

8 28▷ Ask students to read phrases 1–10 and think about possible alternatives to the sections in *italics*. They then listen again and note phrases with similar meanings. Ask them to compare their answers in pairs before feeding back to the rest of the class.

Answers
1 how do you propose we deal with this issue
2 I'm sorry, but I can't just
3 I just don't understand how you could even
4 I see what you mean, but
5 I just won't be able to go ahead with
6 can we try to avoid
7 I'm prepared to overlook
8 look, would it help if I gave
9 I need to know we've got
10 can I leave you to

Extra activity

Write the following alternative phrases on the board. As a class, ask students to identify the difference in tone between the alternatives (answers are in brackets).

- **a** *What do you think we should do about …?*
  b *How do you propose we deal with …?* **(a** *is more informal)*
- **a** *Don't expect me to …*
  b *I'm sorry, but I can't just* **(b** *is more diplomatic)*
- **a** *I'm cancelling the launch …*
  b *I just won't be able to go ahead with the launch …* **(a** *is much more direct)*
- **a** *I don't want any setbacks …*
  b *Can we try to avoid any setbacks …?* **(b** *is much more diplomatic)*
- **a** *Why don't I give …?*
  b *Would it help if I gave …?* **(a** *is much more direct)*
- **a** *Would you be happy to liaise …?*
  b *Can I leave you to liaise …?* **(b** *is more direct)*

9 Students match the phrases they noted in **8** to a–c in **7**.

Answers
a 1, 6, 9, 10
b 2, 3, 4, 5
c 7, 8

» If students need more practice, go to **Practice file 5** on page 110 of the **Student's Book**.

10 Students work in groups of three and turn to their *Files*. When they are ready, they should discuss each situation and find a solution. Encourage them to use phrases from the *Key expressions*.

Feedback focus

Circulate and make notes of any errors. At the end of the activity, ask groups to feed back on their meetings. How did they deal with the conflict? Then write any errors on the board for the class to correct.

Culture question

Students discuss the questions in pairs. Answers will vary, although the discussion may include the fact that some cultures place a high value on consensus, and this often leads to an avoidance of conflict. Conversely, in many Western cultures it is expected that people will voice their opinions, even if this results in conflict.

(i) Refer students to the **Interactive Workbook Email** and **Phrasebank** sections for further study.

Language at work

1 29▷ Students listen and note how the speakers add emphasis to what they are saying.

Answers
1 adding words / phrases, intonation
2 adding words / phrases, intonation
3 word order, intonation
4 word order, intonation
5 adding words / phrases, intonation
6 adding words / phrases, intonation
7 word order, intonation
8 adding words / phrases, intonation
9 adding words / phrases, word order, intonation

2 Students match the sentences in **1** to the techniques. Ask them to <u>underline</u> any fixed phrases and adverbs of degree that add emphasis. Remind them that more than one technique could be used in each sentence.

Watch out! If students are unfamiliar with these techniques, you could refer them to *Language reference Unit 5* on page 128 of the *Student's Book* before they attempt this activity.

Answers
a 4, 6
b 1 (*The reason I say this is …*), 2 (*Which is why …*), 5 (*In which case …*), 6 (*What really concerns me is …*), 8 (*The thing that bothers me is …*), 9 (*Not only …, but also*)
c 3, 4, 7
d 4 (*really*), 6 (*so badly*), 2 (*just so*), 8 (*just*)

» Refer students to the **Language reference** section on page 128 of the **Student's Book** for more information.

3 Students work in pairs and add emphasis to B's replies.

Possible answers
1 In which case, wouldn't it be a good idea to sit down and sort this out properly?
2 Which is why I told you to book early.
3 What we must be clear about is that the contract must be signed by the 5th.
4 What I'd really like to know is what'll happen to the team if the project is abandoned.
5 Not only didn't they attend the meeting, but they also forgot to let us know.
6 It's the changes which make the job interesting.

4 Students add emphasis using the fronting technique.

Answers
1 How we go about this is what we need to think about.
2 Getting this right is absolutely crucial.

Extra activity

Ask students to work in small groups and write five more sentences using the fronting technique. The groups then compare their lists and decide which sentences would be particularly effective.

Extension

Ask students to bring in examples of emails in English they have been sent at work. In the next lesson, ask students to work in small groups and rewrite sections of the email, using techniques to add emphasis.

» If students need more practice, go to **Practice file 5** on page 111 of the **Student's Book**.

5 Students work in groups of three. Allow time for them to read their *Files* and to think about the techniques they will use to emphasize their points. When they are ready they should have the meeting, following the points on the agenda.

Feedback focus

Circulate and monitor the use of techniques for emphasizing. Give feedback on this at the end of the activity.

Practically speaking

1 Students work in pairs and discuss the questions. Ask students for examples of situations at work or home where they give or receive feedback or criticism.

Watch out! This could be a sensitive issue. How we react to feedback depends on how it is given, our personality, and how we feel about the person giving the feedback. If your students are all from the same company, you might want to discuss these questions fairly quickly as a class.

Possible answers
1 Feedback is part of the normal process of ongoing improvement and it can be positive or negative. Criticism tends to be negative, but it can also be helpful.
2 Feedback should be fair and specific. It should also be balanced – positive comments should also be made during a feedback session.
3 Answers will vary.

2 30▷ Students listen and answer the questions.

Answers
1 Conversation 3
2 Conversation 1
3 Conversation 2

3 30▷ Students match the phrases. They can then compare their answers with a partner before listening again to check.

Answers

a	3	g	3
b	1	h	1
c	2	i	2
d	2	j	2
e	3	k	3
f	3		

» Refer students to the **Useful phrases** section on page 134 of the **Student's Book** for extension and revision.

4 Students work in pairs and discuss appropriate responses to the feedback. Encourage them to use phrases from **3**.

Possible answers
1 Thanks for your support – it's good to know I'm on the right track.
2 Thanks! Though I have to admit, George and I worked on them together.
3 Look, you're entitled to your opinion, but I think it's just that you disagree with my findings rather than the quality of the report.
4 I'm sorry. I didn't realize that. I'll talk to them.
5 So how do you think we can improve it?
6 I see what you're saying, but the delay wasn't actually caused by us.

Extension

Ask students to walk around the classroom and practise the dialogues from **4** with different people.

5 Students work with a partner and read their *Files*. They then take turns to give feedback and respond.

Feedback focus

Whilst monitoring, pay particular attention to intonation. Do the students sound diplomatic / polite? Give feedback on this after the activity.

Key word

Students match phrases to suitable synonyms.
   Answers: 1 e, 2 a, 3 d, 4 c, 5 b

ⓘ Refer students to the **Interactive Workbook Exercises and Tests** for revision.

Case study

Background

This *Case study* focuses on Southwest Airlines and its attitude towards teamwork. Students read about how the teams work together to achieve a shared goal. In the *Task* they have the opportunity to evaluate the teamwork problems faced by a sandwich company. They then have a meeting to discuss various ways of resolving these problems, dealing with any points of conflict along the way.

Allow a few minutes for students to read the *Company profile* and the texts. Be prepared to answer any questions about vocabulary.

Watch out! Before they read, you might want to check that students understand the following.
pitch in = to join in and help with an activity

Discussion

1, 2, 3 Students can discuss the questions in pairs, before feeding back to the rest of the class. During feedback draw students' attention to the second text, where it says: *We ask for a warrior's spirit, a servant's heart, and a fun-loving attitude.* Ask students if they find this style of writing unusual and if this kind of imagery is used in their companies' literature. Remind them that this style of writing is not uncommon in American companies.

Possible answers

1 Good communication, clear goals, supportive and informal atmosphere, everyone pitching in, encouraging social activities so that people get to know each other outside work.

2 Pros are that everyone feels they have an important role to play and traditional hierarchies are broken down. Also, staff may be more motivated to work for the company due to the fact that they are made to feel part of a team with shared goals, they are encouraged to get to know each other, and they have the chance to work in other departments.
Cons could be that because everyone is pitching in, no one is there to oversee the entire process. This could be problematic if something goes wrong. It could also be difficult for people with families to join in with all the out-of-hours activities.

3 Answers will vary.

Pre-work learners

Write the following question on the board and ask students to discuss it in small groups.
   • *Would you like to work for Southwest Airlines? Why / Why not?*

Task

1 Students read the information about Alligator Sandwiches and the email. Ask them to make notes on the key problems. They can then compare their notes with a partner.

Possible answers

Staff no longer feel valued, managers have distanced themselves from store workers, managers are under pressure, there's been a rise in customer complaints, lots of staff are leaving.

2 Students work in groups of four and turn to their *Files*. Student D will chair the meeting. Allow students time to prepare for the meeting. They might like to refer back to the *Key expressions* in the *Business communication skills* section during the preparation stage. Before the meeting starts, remind students to listen carefully to what everyone has to say. Encourage them to make notes on the discussion. Allow about 20 minutes for the meeting. They should aim to reach agreement at the end.

3 Students report back to the whole class on what they agreed. If you had several different groups, you could discuss the implications of the different outcomes.

Feedback focus

Write the following questions on the board and ask each group to discuss them and to summarize their thoughts for the rest of the class.

- *Did all group members participate equally?*
- *Did the chairperson carry out his / her role successfully?*
- *Did your group reach a consensus? If not, why not?*

Then give any appropriate feedback on use of language.

Extra activity

Ask students to write up the minutes of the meeting, and email them to you. Provide feedback in the next lesson.

One-to-one

Your student can read the *Background* information, and then you can do the *Discussion* questions together. For the *Task* you could use roles B and C for a meeting. During the preparation stage, encourage your student to add any of his / her own ideas in the meeting. To guide your student during the meeting, write the following additional instructions on the board.

1 *Invite your partner to make his / her suggestions for improvement.*
2 *Check that you have understood each suggestion.*
3 *Keep the discussion on track.*
4 *Ask your partner to compromise if necessary and agree on at least two suggestions for improvement.*

» Unit 5 **Progress test** and **Speaking test**, pages 104–105.

6 | Progress

Unit content

By the end of this unit, students will be able to
- discuss factors for success
- evaluate ideas and solve problems in a brainstorming meeting
- use adverbs to show different attitudes
- use vague language to show uncertainty.

Context

In today's fast-moving business environment, it's becoming more of a challenge for companies to ensure that they continue to progress and grow. Their ability to do so depends on a number of factors. One of the most important of these is creativity. Many of the companies which became leaders in their field did so because of their ability to 'think outside the box' and come up with innovative products that captured the imagination of the market, e.g. Google with its wide range of search-related services, Skype with its concept of a free Internet telephone service, Sony with its novel vision of a portable music device that gave rise to the Walkman.

However, progress also depends on healthy financial performance, and with the emphasis on cost-efficiency, productivity, and shareholder value, today's companies have to balance the need for creativity with a more realistic economic view. This balance isn't always easy to achieve, since innovation and creativity require both time and money.

In this unit, students learn to talk about success factors and discuss the balance between creativity, profitability, and quality. They practise the language of putting forward, developing, clarifying, and evaluating ideas in the context of brainstorming meetings. They also look at the adverbs we use to indicate different attitudes and language for expressing vagueness. In the *Case study* they work on a rescue plan for a car manufacturer faced with possible bankruptcy after losing its way in the market.

Starting point

As a lead-in, write *Walkman* and *iPod* on the board (or draw them if you prefer). Ask students which companies they think of when they look at these items (Answers: Sony and Apple). Brainstorm everything they know about these companies on the board. Then ask them which of the companies is stronger now and why.

Possible answers: **Sony:** A Japanese company, founded in 1946. Introduced the Walkman in 1979 and this became an icon of pop culture. Latest Sony MP3 player offers music, radio, photo and video playback. In a constant marketing battle with Apple. **Apple:** An American company founded in 1976. Became a market leader with its launch of Apple Mac computer in 1984. Introduced the iPod in 2001 with a strong marketing campaign. iPod is seen by many as the ultimate fashion statement and some believe it has the edge over Sony on what its iPod provides (consumers can download music, photos, files, folders, etc. from their PCs).

1, 2 Students can discuss these questions in pairs before feeding back to the rest of the class. If they work, encourage them to also think about their own company and competitors in their field when discussing the questions.

Possible answers
1 Innovate, ensure best quality, benchmark against competitors, manage costs, maximize profit margins to be able to invest in new products, employ the best people, be flexible – offering different employment contracts, advertise widely.
2 Avoid complacency, seek to continuously improve, recognize mistakes and act on them quickly, avoid stretching company resources (financial or human), stay in touch with rapidly changing consumer tastes / demands and with new technology.

Working with words

1 Students read the text and answer questions 1–2. When eliciting their answers you can also ask what they think of the Creativity Lab.

Answers
1 Helps its customers develop innovative ideas, products, and services and facilitates their creative ideas through collaboration on projects.
2 She thinks that people need to look beyond technical training and find creative and innovative solutions. She also believes that creativity and success are products of a trial-and-error process where mistakes can be made and learned from.

2 Students work in pairs and match the phrases.

> **Answers**
> **1** c **2** d **3** f **4** e **5** a **6** b

Extra activity / Dictionary skills

To enable students to learn more about the origin of some of these phrases, write the following categories on the board.

- *trains*
- *planes*
- *plants*

Ask students to find phrases in **2** that are derived from language in these categories.
(Answers: *trains* = *get back on track*, *planes* = *get off the ground*, *plants* = *come to fruition*).
Then elicit other phrases in these categories that can be used to describe company / employee performance. You may like to encourage them to use dictionaries.
Examples: *trains* = *to get sidetracked, to get derailed, to run out of steam, to be on the wrong track, to go off the rails; planes* = *to take off, to make a soft landing, to crash, to nosedive; plants* = *to blossom, to thrive, to wilt, organic growth, a budding company, to branch out.*

3 Students replace the words. They can then compare their answers with a partner.

> **Answers**
> **1** try out
> **2** run into
> **3** figure out
> **4** look beyond
> **5** hit on
> **6** bounce around

4 Students look back at the text and find the nouns that collocate with the verb phrases.

> **Answers**
> **1** hit on + ideas
> **2** look beyond + their technical training
> **3** bounce around + ideas
> **4** try out + different things
> **5** run into + problems
> **6** figure out + ways to reduce costs

Watch out! Note that *try out, figure out*, and *bounce around* are separable so a noun / noun phrase can also separate the phrasal verb. For example, both *I'm trying different things out* and *I'm trying out different things* are possible. However, if a pronoun is used, it must separate the phrasal verb, e.g. *try it out*, not ~~try out it~~.

5 As a lead-in, ask students why they think writers often have problems meeting deadlines.

Ask them what they know about the company 3M. (Minnesota Mining and Manufacturing Company until 2002 - multinational conglomerate, produces adhesives, abrasives, electrical materials, inventor of Post-it notes, etc.) Students then read the quotation, and discuss as a class what the dilemma might be. Ask if they agree with George Buckley's views on creativity.

> **Possible answer**
> The quotation implies that under a strict quality control regime, coming up with new, innovative ideas would need to be measured against a set quota (*quota* = a fixed amount of something someone needs to achieve), but that this is problematic because it is impossible to predict when flashes of inspiration will occur.

6 31▷ Students listen and answer questions 1–4.

Watch out! Before listening, you might want to elicit the meanings of the following:
the bottom line = the amount of money that is a profit or loss after everything has been calculated
knock something into shape = to make something more acceptable, organized, or successful
an efficiency drive = an organized effort to be efficient
stifle creativity = to prevent creativity from happening

> **Answers**
> **1** How to run a profitable, efficient company while maintaining creativity and innovation.
> **2** There was a real emphasis on creativity because the company had built its reputation on innovation.
> **3** He shifted the emphasis to quality control, cost-saving, and efficiency using the Six Sigma strategy (which led to creativity being stifled).
> **4** A compromise solution which allows more room for creativity (aiming to get the balance right).

Extension

Ask your students what they already know about Six Sigma strategy (it's a business management strategy that was first introduced by Motorola in the 1980s and was designed to identify and remove causes of defects and errors in manufacturing companies). Ask them to find out more about the Six Sigma strategy before the next lesson including any advantages and disadvantages.

7 Students work in pairs and form collocations. Don't feed back on the answers yet.

8 31▷ Students now refer back to the text in **1** and then listen again to the interview to check their answers.

> **Answers**
> 1 b 2 a 3 b 4 a 5 a 6 a
> 7 a 8 a 9 b 10 a 11 b 12 b

Watch out! You might want to check that students understand the meanings of the following.
to cut into the bottom line = to reduce profits
to undergo = to be subjected to
to cause a stir = to create controversy
to shift = to change

9 Students work in pairs to put the collocations in the four categories. When they compare answers with another pair, ask them to justify their choices.

Watch out! Note that *impose targets* could be linked to profitability and / or quality.

> **Possible answers**
> **Profitability:** boost earnings, control costs, cut into the bottom line, outperform the competition, impose targets
> **Change:** shift the emphasis, cause a stir, undergo change
> **Creativity:** pursue ideas, explore a concept
> **Quality:** tolerate mistakes; demand precision, impose targets

» If students need more practice, go to **Practice file 6** on page 112 of the **Student's Book**.

10 Students work in groups and discuss a recent project. Encourage them to use some of the language in **2**, **3**, and **7** during their discussions. If students are not from the same team / company, you could ask them to compare and contrast different projects they have worked on.

Pre-work learners

Ask students to think about any projects they have been involved in. This could be
- a group project relating to their studies
- a group presentation they had to give
- organizing an event (e.g. a party, sports event, etc.).

Feedback focus

Listen out for collocations used by the different groups and make a note of who used them. When students have finished the activity, ask questions to the whole class relating to the collocations you noted. For example:
- Which group had an idea which took a long time to get off the ground?
- Who ran into problems?
- Who had a radical idea that caused a stir?

The groups that used those collocations can then explain briefly to the class what happened during their project, i.e. why it took a long time to get off the ground etc.

ⓘ Refer students to the **Interactive Workbook Glossary** for further study.

Business communication skills

1 32–34▷ As a lead-in, you could ask students to brainstorm ideas in pairs under the headings '*Problems faced by small shops*' and '*How small shops can fight back*'. Elicit answers from the class then refer them to the *Context*. Students then listen and answer questions 1–2.

Ask students to compare their answers in pairs before feeding back to the rest of the class.

Possible answers		
Ideas	**Pros**	**Cons**
1 Recycling of computer parts and maybe send them to developing countries	Gives company a more caring image.	Might not be cost-effective or practical.
2 Volunteer training programme in developing country	Rewarding experience for staff. Gives company a more caring image.	Might not be cost-effective or practical.
3 Specializing in energy-saving e.g. solar-powered laptops	Big money in energy-saving. Could open up market share, especially through website and company could gain competitive advantage.	Risky – too different from present business.
4 Sell recovered parts through brokers or even act as brokers themselves	Could be more competitive on service than brokers.	Not original – another company (Green PCs) already does this.

2 **32**▷ Students listen again to extract 1 and complete the sentences.

Answers
1 couldn't we consider
2 it's not clear to me what you mean by
3 Well, for example
4 I would have thought it would be possible to
5 Oh, I see, so you're thinking of, am I right
6 Thinking about it, we could even
7 I'm not totally convinced
8 I'm concerned about how
9 I can't help wondering whether
10 I would certainly need to know, before taking it any further

3 Students work with a partner and categorize the phrases.

Possible answers
a 1, 4
b 2, 5
c 3
d 6
e 7, 8, 9, 10

4 Students work in pairs and brainstorm alternative ways of saying sentences 1–9. Encourage them to consider the real meaning behind each sentence before they start to think of alternatives.

Possible answers
1 I doubt that it would be cost-effective.
2 I've got an idea about a wider policy on environmental issues, but I'm not sure it would work and I need input from other people on this.
3 Can you explain your ideas to us?
4 What I was thinking of was solar-powered laptops.
5 What if we were to sell recovered parts back to the manufacturers?
6 There's no reason why we can't set up as brokers ourselves, is there?
7 It's a good idea. It's got potential. Let's look into this further.
8 There are a lot of drawbacks to this idea, but we shouldn't abandon it completely.
9 Regarding marketing, I think it could be a really good idea.

Extra activity

Write the following sentence on the board. If you like you could draw a thought bubble around it.
  • *I think your idea is rubbish and it'll never work.*
Tell students that this is their opinion of an idea their boss / teacher has just had. Now ask students to work in pairs and brainstorm different ways of expressing their view more diplomatically. For example:
  • *I'm not sure how your idea will work in practice.*
  • *That's an interesting idea, but I think we need to explore it further.*
When feeding back to the class, make sure that students are also using polite intonation when expressing their opinions.

If students need more practice, go to **Practice file 6** on page 112 of the **Student's Book**.

5 Students work in groups of four. Ask them to read the information from HR before dividing the groups into two. Then allow each pair time to discuss the ideas in their *Files*. They should choose two to put forward at the meeting. Encourage them to consider the pros and cons of these two ideas and to think about how they will react if any disadvantages are mentioned during the meeting. Students should then return to their group of four and have the meeting. When they have finished, ask each group to summarize their decisions.

6 Ask students to work in groups of three or four. If students are choosing their own work-related scenario, ask them to focus on a problem which hasn't yet been resolved. One member of each group explains the problem and they all then brainstorm possible solutions. Remind students to make use of the phrases in the *Key expressions*.

Pre-work learners

Students can choose one of the two problems given. Ask them to develop the background of their imagined company a little more, e.g. what its area of activity is, what the product / service is, or what kind of employees are required.

Feedback focus

Make a note of three correct and three incorrect phrases students used during their discussion. After the activity, write them on the board and ask the class to correct where necessary.

Alternative

Ask students to work in groups of four. Write the following instructions on the board.

- *Find out which person in your group has had a work-related problem that they have already resolved.*
- *Write just the details of the problem on a piece of paper, then give it to another group.*
- *Look at the problem your group has been given and brainstorm a solution to it in your group.*
- *Present the problem and your possible solutions to the class.*
- *Find out who had the problem and if their solution was similar to any of your suggestions.*

Culture question

Ask students to discuss the question in pairs before feeding back to the class. Be aware that if students are from the same company, they may find the subject matter a little sensitive, especially if there are more senior managers present.

ⓘ Refer students to the **Interactive Workbook Email** and **Phrasebank** sections for further study.

Language at work

1 35▷ As a lead-in, write the following two sentences on the board and ask students to discuss in pairs if they are true or false (answers are in brackets).

1 *All adverbs end in -ly. (false, e.g. well / hard / just)*
2 *All adverbs qualify / describe a verb. (false, they also qualify adjectives)*

Students listen to adverbs being used and then match the adverbs to their uses individually before comparing their answers with a partner.

Alternative

Students could listen first with books closed and note down all the adverbs they hear, before matching the adverbs to their uses.

Possible answers

1	c	6	a
2	a	7	b
3	d	8	c
4	b	9	d
5	a	10	d

2 36▷ Students now listen to the pairs of sentences. You might like to pause the recording after each pair and allow the class time to discuss the difference in meaning with you.

Possible answers

1 **a** the speaker wants to add a bit more
  b the speaker is persuading others to listen
2 **a** the speaker wasn't expecting it to be a difficult year
  b the speaker expected it to be difficult, but not as difficult as this
3 **a** it was a surprise to the speaker
  b the speaker may be responding to another person who imagined the opposite would be true
4 **a** the speaker is emphasizing a comment - the speaker is convinced they can't get away with it
  b the speaker is softening a negative reaction

» Refer students to the **Language Reference** section on page 129 of the **Student's Book** for more information.

3 Students work in pairs to produce appropriate responses.

Possible answers

1 Can I just run through some ideas?
2 I'm not totally convinced the money is being well spent. I just feel that it could be better spent elsewhere.
3 Actually, there were far more people than we expected.
4 I just can't see why we're behind schedule.
5 Yes, I was - the proposal that was accepted was easily / obviously the best.
6 Actually, I would have gone for someone else.

Extension

Ask students to have the conversations again, but this time ask them to develop them further, using as many of the adverbs as possible. Write an example for the first conversation on the board.

B *Could I just run through some ideas?*
A *Well, it's not really convenient at the moment. Can it wait till later?*
B *Well, actually, it can't. I need an answer on this by tonight.*

4 Ask students to decide on their favourite and least favourite innovation. They should then explain their choices in pairs, using as many adverbs as they can.

Possible answers

My favourite innovation is MP3 players. It's easily the most convenient way to store your music because it's so compact and can store hundreds of songs.

My least favourite innovation is air conditioning. It's totally unnecessary in my country and it actually causes more problems than it solves – my skin and eyes become really dry and uncomfortable when it's on.

Alternative

You could ask students to note down the adverbs from **1** on slips of paper and place them face down in front of them. Students then talk about the innovations using the adverb they pick up.

Feedback focus

Circulate and note any mistakes made in the choice or placement of adverbs and write the sentences on the board for whole class correction after the activity.

» If students need more practice, go to **Practice file 6** on page 113 of the **Student's Book**.

Practically speaking

1 37▷ Students listen and answer the questions. Allow students time to discuss their answers in pairs before feeding back to the rest of the class.

Watch out! Check that students know the meaning of the following.
vague = not clear / without details

Possible answers

Conversation 1
1 tentative and vague, but tries to be helpful
2 he doesn't remember the details – too long ago

Conversation 2
1 not specific, but encouraging, although maybe a little lazy
2 no concrete ideas – wants to be encouraging, but doesn't want to do the work himself; probably hasn't studied the report in detail

Conversation 3
1 vague
2 she doesn't have the photos and is struggling to put her descriptions into words

Alternative

Before listening, you could refer students to the phrases already supplied in the table in **2** and ask them what we can predict about the context of each conversation.

Then ask students to listen to the conversations in audio 37▷ and compare their predictions with what they hear, before answering the questions in **1**. Possible answers could be as follows.

- **Conversation 1** Someone is in a difficult situation because they can't remember something.
- **Conversation 2** Someone is giving feedback to another person on something they've done.
- **Conversation 3** Somebody is trying to explain something they've seen or tasted.

2 37▷ Students listen again and add more phrases. You may like to point out / elicit how we can use *kind of* with a noun (*the kind of thing we're looking for*) and an adjective (*it was kind of minimalist*), and that we can replace *kind* with *sort* in both cases. They might also like to know that we use the expression *a hint of* to describe colour, taste, or your interpretation of someone's attitude (*a hint of irony*).

Answers

Conversation 1 I'm not quite sure now / I seem to remember / something like that / I'm trying to think

Conversation 2 it just needs a bit more / and so on / something along those lines / something like that

Conversation 3 it almost had a hint of / it was kind of … / you know, that sort of thing / a bit like that

Extra activity

Ask students to think about one of the following.
- their first English teacher (or lesson)
- the first room / flat they lived in as a student
- their first car
- the first boss they worked for

Then ask each student to give a brief, but vague description to the class. If you have a large class you could ask students to work in groups. Check that students are using the phrases for being vague correctly.

» Refer students to the **Useful phrases** section on page 135 of the **Student's Book** for extension and revision.

3 Students work in pairs. Allow them time to read the information about the situations before they have the conversations. Circulate and check they are using the phrases correctly.

4 Students work in the pairs. Each student chooses the subject they want to be asked about. Encourage students to ask fairly difficult questions (e.g. *What was the name of the trainer at the training session you went to last?).* Circulate and be ready to add a few 'difficult' questions of your own if students' memories seem a little too reliable.

Pre-work learners

Ask students to talk about a hotel or city they have been to, or they could also talk about one of the following childhood memories.
  • a house they lived in when they were younger
  • a holiday they had as a child
  • a relative they met only a few times

Key word

Students match 1–5 with a–e. Ask them to check their answers in pairs before feeding back to the rest of the class.
  Answers: 1 e, 2 b, 3 d, 4 c, 5 a

ⓘ Refer students to the **Interactive Workbook Exercises and Tests** for revision.

Case study

Background

This *Case study* gives an insight into the issues that companies need to consider when going through a period of rapid growth and expansion. Students discuss why MIG was so successful and then in the *Task* they move on to explore how Adamo Automotive can overcome the problems they encountered, due to rapid growth. During the discussion they have the opportunity to practise the language of brainstorming ideas, and vocabulary for discussing factors for success.

Allow a few minutes for students to read the *Company profile* and the texts and be prepared to answer any questions about vocabulary.

Discussion

1, 2 Students discuss the questions in pairs before feeding back to the rest of the class.

> **Possible answers**
> Answers will vary, although it's likely that having adequate financial resources and employing the right people will be considered most important.

Task

1 Students read the company history and discuss the company's key strengths in the 1990s in pairs before feeding back to the rest of the class.

> **Possible answers**
> • A long history of producing high-performance cars at an affordable price.
> • Highly skilled and motivated workforce.
> • Good profits, allowing possibilities for further investment.
> • Cars gained good reputation.

2 Students read the *Files* and discuss the problems faced by the company since the 1990s with a partner.

> **Possible answers**
> • Unsuccessful diversification moving away from its original market.
> • A top-heavy management structure that has been developed as the number of production workers diminishes.
> • Competition increased.
> • Poor reputation due to the unsuccessful Tera and Bos models.
> • Lack of cash means reduced possibilities for investment in creativity.

3 Students discuss the questions in their pairs and take notes in preparation for the brainstorming session.

4 Students join another pair and have the meeting. You might like to change the layout in the room to create a different (more creative!) atmosphere. You could push all the tables and chairs aside and give each group a large sheet of paper and some coloured pens so that they can record their ideas. Refer them to the agenda and point out that as it's a brainstorming session they shouldn't worry about putting forward any idea, however crazy it may seem. Students can refer back to the *Key expressions* in the *Business communication skills* section if they need to.

> **Possible answers**
> • stop all production of Tera and Bos and cut losses
> • change hierarchical management structure to a flat matrix structure, and get rid of excess management to improve company structure and cut costs
> • reduce the number of shift hours and save money by reducing salaries

Feedback focus

Ask each group to answer the following questions about their meeting.

- Were all ideas sufficiently clarified?
- Were ideas built on / developed by the other participants?
- Were all ideas evaluated in a fair and unbiased way?

Find out which groups had the most successful meeting and ask all groups to share their best ideas with the class.

Extension

Ask students to write a report (as consultants) for the company based on the findings of the brainstorming session. The report should include the following.

- Four ideas that were put forward.
- Two ideas that were rejected, and why.
- Two ideas that were accepted, and why.

One-to-one

Your student can read the *Background* and you can then answer the *Discussion* questions together. Have a brainstorming session together and then ask your student to write a report based on the findings as outlined in the *Extension* above.

❯❯ Unit 6 **Progress test** and **Speaking test**, pages 106–107.

7 | Learning

Unit content

By the end of this unit, students will be able to
- talk about training and learning
- use communication strategies on the telephone
- use participle clauses
- use 'the future in the past'
- express dissatisfaction.

Context

The topic of learning will apply to your students in different ways, depending on their previous learning experiences, whether they are pre-work or in-work – and, if so, the kind of organization they belong to. Learning was traditionally thought to end formally after school or university, but the concept of life-long learning is increasingly being embraced by both individuals and companies.

The concept of life-long learning suggests that you should always be open to new ideas, skills, or behaviours, and that learning opportunities are available for all age groups. Many companies promote life-long learning through internal training and through encouraging employees to develop their skills via distance learning and postgraduate programmes. Companies benefit from this by increasing the level of skill within their company, and staff benefit as they are more likely to get promoted and are more employable.

In this unit, students will have the opportunity to discuss their own experiences of learning and training in a variety of contexts: school, university, at work, in leisure time. The unit then moves on to address different approaches to staff training, with a focus on effective employee development. In the *Case study*, students are asked to discuss possible solutions to the problem of recruiting skilled workers.

Starting point

1, 2, 3 Students discuss the questions in pairs before feeding back to the rest of the class. During feedback, ask the students what opportunities they currently have for learning, and to what extent they use them.

Possible answers
1 Answers will vary.
2 Historical events: depending on teaching methods this is often about learning facts and figures. They can be memorized, and are not necessarily learnt within any meaningful context.
How to cook: this is likely to be 'learning by doing', making mistakes and getting better results each time.
How to negotiate: there are certain strategies that can be followed and learnt. Some people are natural negotiators, while others find it much more difficult.
How to balance work and private life: something many people, however long they have worked, find very difficult. Time-management courses can help people learn to prioritize their tasks.
3 Answers will vary.

Working with words

1 Ask students what the terms *learning organization* and *systems thinking* might mean. Write their ideas on the board. Then ask them to read the text and compare their ideas.

Watch out! Before they read, you might want to check that students understand the following.
nurture = to help somebody / something to develop and be successful

Answers
learning organization: an organization that can get the results it really wants by encouraging and enabling employees to achieve those goals in any way they choose
systems thinking: being able to see the organization as a whole

2 Students read the text again and answer the questions in pairs.

Answers
1 Getting greater commitment and involvement from employees and encouraging creativity could lead to more innovation and, ultimately, better results for a company. The focus on staff development could also mean that staff are less likely to leave, so teams will be stronger and recruitment costs lower.
2 Answers will vary.

Pre-work learners

Ask students to think about the kind of company they would like to work for. What learning opportunities would they want at work?

3 Students read the text and note the arguments for and against. They can then compare their answers with a partner.

Watch out! Before they read, you might want to check that students understand the following.
upheaval = a big change that causes a lot of confusion, worry, and problems
deferential = showing that you respect someone / something

> **Answers**
> **For:** usually leads to improved results, all staff are encouraged to be creative and take a holistic view of the business
> **Against:** can cause structural upheaval; requires a major change in thinking; the changes required may be unrealistic; it may be more difficult to organize training for staff as a whole, rather than the individual; management may still continue to impose values from the top; the workforce may still end up having to 'look up' to top management; individuals don't necessarily need to be involved in and aware of the overall running of the business, but should focus on their own work / contribution to the business

4 Students match the phrases in **bold** in the texts to the definitions.

> **Answers**
> 1 personal development plan
> 2 skills deficit
> 3 shared vision
> 4 performance management
> 5 employee participation
> 6 paradigm shift
> 7 structural change
> 8 collective aspiration

5 Students complete the sentences with the <u>underlined</u> phrases in the text.

> **Answers**
> 1 in the real world
> 2 the bigger picture
> 3 across the board
> 4 in the long run

Extra activity

Draw the following table on the board. Only write the words in **bold** (words from the texts). Ask students to work in pairs and complete the table in their notebooks. They should also <u>underline</u> the stressed syllables (see <u>underlined</u> sections in the table). Check their answers as a class. You could also ask students to rewrite sentences from the texts that include the words in **bold**, using a different form of the word.

NOUN (thing)	NOUN (person)	VERB	ADJECTIVE
<u>stra</u>tegy	**stra<u>te</u>gist**	have a <u>stra</u>tegy	stra<u>te</u>gic
organi<u>za</u>tion	<u>or</u>ganizer	<u>or</u>ganize	<u>or</u>ganized
ex<u>pan</u>se	/	**ex<u>pand</u>**	ex<u>pan</u>sive
ca<u>pa</u>city	/	be <u>ca</u>pable of	<u>ca</u>pable
cre<u>a</u>tion	cre<u>a</u>tor	**cre<u>ate</u>**	cre<u>a</u>tive
de<u>sire</u>	/	**de<u>sire</u>**	de<u>sired</u>
aspi<u>ra</u>tion	/	a<u>spire</u> to	a<u>spir</u>ing
<u>sys</u>tem	/	<u>sys</u>tematize	syste<u>ma</u>tic
<u>em</u>phasis	/	**<u>em</u>phasize**	em<u>pha</u>tic
<u>prac</u>tice	prac<u>ti</u>tioner	<u>prac</u>tise	<u>prac</u>tical
sug<u>ges</u>tion	/	**sug<u>gest</u>**	sug<u>ges</u>tive
en<u>cour</u>agement	/	**en<u>cour</u>age**	en<u>cour</u>aging
suc<u>cess</u>	suc<u>cess</u>or	suc<u>ceed</u>	suc<u>cess</u>ful
<u>rea</u>lism	<u>rea</u>list	<u>rea</u>lize	**rea<u>lis</u>tic**
sus<u>pi</u>cion	sus<u>pect</u>	sus<u>pect</u>	sus<u>pi</u>cious
partici<u>pa</u>tion	par<u>ti</u>cipant	par<u>ti</u>cipate	par<u>ti</u>cipative
impo<u>si</u>tion	im<u>pos</u>tor	**im<u>pose</u>**	im<u>pos</u>ing

6 Students work in pairs and discuss what advice they would give in each situation. Encourage them to use the vocabulary from **4** and **5**.

> **Possible answers**
> 1 They need an individual personal development plan.
> 2 There needs to be a shared vision so that all employees are aware of the bigger picture.
> 3 There needs to be a structural change in the company.
> 4 There's a skills deficit across the board.
> 5 There isn't sufficient employee participation.

7 38▷ Students listen and answer the questions. They can then compare their answers with a partner.

Watch out! Before they listen, you might want to check that students understand the following.
remit = the area of activity over which a particular person or group has authority, control, or influence
trigger = to make something happen

> **Answers**
> 1 Yes, to some extent, because they try to get employees thinking about the implications of their work in a larger context, rather than just the job itself.
> 2 Job-specific training and generic training.
> 3 Advantages: it can be quite responsive to employees' needs; they can provide a variety of training opportunities; training is more self-directed; staff take ownership of their learning and are therefore more committed.
> Disadvantages: a lot of different courses need to be run to cater to individual needs, which means that resources are not always used very efficiently.

8 38▷ Write the words *training* and *approach* on the board and elicit examples of adjectives that collocate with each, e.g. *job-specific training, bottom-up approach*. Students then listen again and make a note of the adjectives used.

> **Answers**
> job-specific training, generic training, bottom-up approach, decentralized approach, top-down approach, centrally-driven training, self-directed training, one-size-fits-all approach,

9 Students match the adjectives to the definitions.

> **Answers**
> 1 generic / one-size-fits-all
> 2 centrally-driven / top-down
> 3 bottom-up / decentralized
> 4 job-specific
> 5 self-directed

» If students need more practice, go to **Practice file 7** on page 114 of the **Student's Book**.

10 Students work in pairs and read the *File*. They can then discuss the questions. Encourage them to use vocabulary from this section where appropriate.

11 If possible, students from the same company should work together to discuss their ideas.

Alternative

If you have students from different companies, ask them to note down their ideas and answers, and then compare them with someone from a different company. Write the following questions on the board to guide their discussion.
- *Which approach do you think is best, and why?*
- *Would you like to work in your partner's company? Why? / Why not?*

Pre-work learners

If students have worked for an organization part-time, or on a temporary basis, they could refer to that experience. Otherwise, ask them to decide what sort of company they would like to work in, and how they would like their training to be organized.

Feedback focus

Circulate and monitor for correct use of the vocabulary in **4**, **5**, and **9**. Give feedback after the activity.

ⓘ Refer students to the **Interactive Workbook Glossary** for further study.

Business communication skills

1 39, 40▷ Ask students to read the *Context*, and brainstorm what decisions Kirsten would have to make when planning next year's training programme, e.g. details of training courses, names of relevant staff, dates for courses, who the training providers will be, face-to-face or distance learning, costs, etc. Students then listen and answer the question.

> **Answers**
> The main problem is that Kirsten thinks they don't have the expertise to run the training courses required. The eventual solution is that they decide to use outside trainers.

2 39, 40▷ Students listen again and complete the phrases.

> **Answers**
> 1 you say
> 2 clear about your last suggestion
> 3 run it by me
> 4 you're saying
> 5 not that
> 6 clarify exactly
> 7 their name
> 8 did you
> 9 to spell out
> 10 I'm saying is
> 11 mean that
> 12 quite sure
> 13 What I mean

3 Students categorize the phrases. They can then check their answers in pairs.

> **Answers**
> a 1, 7, 8
> b 2, 12
> c 3
> d 4, 11
> e 6, 9
> f 5, 10, 13

Extension

Write the following sentences on the board. Ask students to identify the repetition in each example (see words in **bold**).

- *It's not that **we don't have** the trainers. **We don't have** the expertise.*
- *That wasn't quite **what I meant to say**. **What I meant to say** was that we'll have to run this internally after all.*

Ask students why repetition is used in these examples (answer = to help the speaker communicate their point clearly and powerfully). Then write the following situation on the board and elicit a dialogue from students, including repetition (see suggested answer in brackets).

> *Situation: Idea for new product*
> *A Thinks B doesn't like it.*
> *B Likes the idea, but a competitor has already done it.*
> (*A So, you don't like the idea? B It's not what I meant, what I meant was that the idea itself is good, but it's already been done by the competition.*)

4 41▷ Students correct the mistakes. They then listen to check their answers.

> **Answers**
> 1 ~~relative~~ relevant
> 2 ~~outside the topic~~ off-topic
> 3 ~~recalls~~ reminds
> 4 ~~digress~~ digression
> 5 ~~at~~ to
> 6 ~~this way~~ the way

5 Students focus on the phrases in **4** and answer the questions.

> **Answers**
> a 1, 3, 6
> b 2, 4, 5

» If students need more practice, go to **Practice file 7** on page 115 of the **Student's Book**.

6 Students choose a topic and make notes on it.

7 Students work in pairs and have a telephone call using the topic they chose in **6**. They should follow the flow chart. Encourage them to use phrases from the *Key expressions*.

Alternative

Ask students to work in threes. Two students have the telephone call whilst the third student listens and ticks (✓) any phrases in the *Key expressions* that they use. They should also note any mistakes. They can then give feedback to the other students before changing roles and repeating the process.

Culture question

Ask students to discuss the questions in groups. Make sure they consider both business contexts and those with friends and family. You might want to discuss attitudes towards personal space. This tends to differ according to culture. In Latin cultures, people tolerate relatively small amounts of personal space, whereas in northern cultures it is likely to be bigger. Lack of awareness of these different preferences could cause misunderstandings.

ⓘ Refer students to the **Interactive Workbook Email** and **Phrasebank** sections for further study.

Language at work

1 42▷ Students complete the extracts. They then listen to check their answers.

> **Answers**
> 1 Faced
> 2 Working
> 3 Given the
> 4 Knowing how
> 5 Having discussed

2 Students match the phrases to the descriptions.

> **Answers**
> a knowing / working
> b given (the)
> c having discussed
> d faced (with)

3 Students look at the sentences and answer the questions. Ask them to discuss their answers in pairs.

4 Students look at the extract and answer the questions. They can then discuss their answers in pairs.

5 Students look at the examples and answer the questions. They can then discuss their answers in pairs.

Extra activity

Ask students to look at the tenses that are used in the sentences in **5**. What would the speaker have said when the plans were still OK? Write the first one on the board and discuss it as a class.

    1 *I was meeting Jim at 9.00 a.m. tomorrow.*
    I'm meeting Jim at 9.00 a.m. tomorrow. (the present continuous becomes past continuous).
    Answers: 2 We'll increase profits ... (*will* becomes *would*);
    3 I'm going to contact her this week ... (*am going to* becomes *was going to*); 4 They're supposed to call ... (*are supposed to* becomes *were supposed to*).

» Refer students to the **Language Reference** section on page 129 of the **Student's Book** for more information.

6 Students work with in pairs and turn to the *File*. They then discuss what the speaker might have said in each situation.

» If students need more practice, go to **Practice file 7** on page 115 of the **Student's Book**.

7 Students read the situations and think of their own examples. Allow time for them to make notes on what happened. They then take turns to explain to their partner what happened, using a participle clause and the 'future in the past' where appropriate. You can then ask students to describe their experiences to the rest of the class. Encourage the other students to ask questions to find out more.

Pre-work learners

Ask students to choose similar situations, but related to their studies, or private life.

Alternative

Ask students to write down some past intentions they had, but which didn't happen as planned (see the examples below). They can then share their experiences in pairs.

- *I **was going to** give up smoking, but **faced with** the prospect of working on a stressful project without cigarettes, I decided not to.*
- *After my last course finished, **I was going to** do 30 minutes of English homework a day, but **given** the fact that I had to do overtime I just didn't have time.*
- *I **had intended** to tidy my desk at the end of each day, but **having realized** how untidy I am by nature I didn't keep it up.*

Feedback focus

Monitor for correct use of the participle clauses and 'the future in the past'. After the activity, write any incorrect sentences on the board and ask the class to correct the mistakes.

Practically speaking

1 43▷ As a lead-in, ask students to think about a time when they weren't satisfied with something (e.g. at a meeting, on holiday, etc.). Then ask students to describe exactly why they weren't satisfied to the rest of the class. Elicit possible phrases the student could have used to express their dissatisfaction. Students then listen and answer the questions.

> **Answers**
> **1**
> **Conversation 1:** in a coffee break, probably at a training session
> **Conversation 2:** in an office / at work, discussing designs for a brochure
> **Conversation 3:** in a meeting
> **2**
> **Conversation 1:** They are bored by the speaker / trainer.
> **Conversation 2:** The second speaker doesn't find the design or wording suitable.
> **Conversation 3:** The second speaker doesn't feel the next topic is relevant to him, and therefore feels he cannot contribute.
> **3**
> **Conversation 1:** Similar, although the second speaker is more optimistic.
> **Conversation 2:** Yes, the second speaker persuades the first speaker to agree with her to some extent.
> **Conversation 3:** no

2 43▷ Students complete the extracts and then listen again to check their answers.

> **Answers**
> 1 much out of
> 2 doing my head in
> 3 testing my patience
> 4 reached my limit
> 5 lived up to expectations
> 6 was expecting something a bit more
> 7 it's just not up to scratch
> 8 not very happy with
> 9 can't really see the point of
> 10 finding it a bit frustrating
> 11 don't think this is the best use of

3 Students match the sentences to the categories. They can then check their answers in pairs.

> **Answers**
> **a** 7, 8
> **b** 5, 6
> **c** 1, 9, 11
> **d** 2, 3, 10
> **e** 4

4 Students <u>underline</u> the words the speaker uses to soften what they say.

> **Answers**
> 1 to be honest / I think / a bit of
> 2 really
> 3 I have to admit / really
> 4 I'm afraid / some

Extra activity

Write the following sentences on the board and ask students how they could be made less direct. Add their ideas to the board.
> 1 *This is terrible.*
> 2 *The talk was really boring.*
> 3 *Your report is far too long.*
> 4 *I hope you'll change your mind.*

Then ask students to look at their ideas on the board and identify which of the following methods they used to make the sentences less direct.

- using a softening phrase (e.g. *I'm afraid, to be honest*)
- using positive adjectives / verbs with 'not', rather than negative ones (e.g. *not enjoying* instead of *hate*; *not (very) interesting* instead of *boring).*
- making things sound 'smaller' by adding *some, really, rather, a bit,* etc.

5 Students work in pairs to make the sentences less direct.

> **Possible answers**
> 1 I'm afraid your performance this year has been somewhat / a bit below standard.
> 2 I have to admit that I'm not really enjoying the project I'm working on at the moment.
> 3 I'm sorry to tell you, but you need to rewrite rather a lot of your presentation.
> 4 I have to say that I feel that this meeting isn't hugely productive.
> 5 I'd like to know what the purpose is of our being here. There doesn't seem to be very much to do.

》 Refer students to the **Useful phrases** section on page 135 of the **Student's Book** for extension and revision.

6 Students read the situations and work in pairs to decide what phrases from **2** could be used. They should then have the conversations.

Extension

Ask students to look again at the situations in **6**. Then write the following questions on the board.

  1 *What would you say in these situations if you were talking to* **a** *your boss* **b** *an important visitor to your company?*

  2 *Is the language very different from what you would use with colleagues? If so, how?*

Possible answer for situation 1 (bad coffee in the coffee machine):

  1 To your boss: *I don't think the coffee's very good.* To an important visitor to your company: *I'm afraid I don't usually drink this coffee. I prefer to make my own.*

  2 The language used with the boss is likely to be less critical than the language used with a colleague. The language used with the visitor enables the speaker to hide what they really think – there is no open criticism and the visitor is left to deduce for themselves why the person doesn't drink the coffee at work.

Key word

Students match the phrases to the alternatives.

  Answers: 1 e, 2 f, 3 b, 4 c, 5 a, 6 d

(i) Refer students to the **Interactive Workbook Exercises and Tests** for revision.

Case study

Background

This *Case study* focuses on the skills deficit and how as a consequence companies in certain sectors are experiencing difficulties in finding sufficiently skilled employees. Students read about the problem and then have the opportunity to discuss how one company has dealt with it. The *Task* enables students to come up with a solution for another company facing a similar problem.

Allow a few minutes for students to read the *Company profile* and the texts. Be prepared to answer any questions about vocabulary.

Discussion

1, 2 Students discuss the questions in small groups.

Possible answers

1 The government needs to address the issue of basic subjects (maths, reading, writing) for pupils at primary schools. Education at secondary schools should include effective communication skills and IT training as part of the curriculum. Employees should also expect to take on training during their employment.

2 Leyland Trucks could offer placement schemes for undergraduates who would work at their company whilst continuing their studies. They could be given a conditional offer of a future job with the condition that they complete their studies successfully.

3 44▷ Students listen and compare their ideas in **2**.

Answer

Leyland worked in partnership with two colleges to design tailor-made courses for those staff with knowledge of the company, but lacking the required education and training.

4 Students work in pairs and list the advantages and disadvantages of Leyland's strategy.

Possible answers

Advantages: The staff already have knowledge of the business so can apply what they learn appropriately and immediately. The training that the staff receive is tailored to their needs, so it will be relevant and useful.

Disadvantages: Leyland is basing its future on staff without a higher-level qualification. They are ignoring / bypassing university students who may have the potential to gain engineering degrees. They are discouraging universities from catering for engineering undergraduates. Staff on training will need someone else to cover their work.

Extra activity

Write the following questions on the board and ask students to discuss them in small groups.

- *Which industries in your country find it difficult to recruit skilled employees? Why?*
- *Has this always been the case, or is it a recent trend / problem? What has caused it?*
- *Is your government trying to address any skills deficits? If so, how?*
- *How easy is it for you to find employment connected to your skills and qualifications?*

Task

1 Students read the text.

2, 3 Students work in pairs and read their information. If possible, put two Student As together and two Student Bs together. They can then help each other prepare for the telephone call. They might want to refer to the *Key expressions* list in the *Business communication skills* section.

Watch out! Check that Student Bs understand what *psychometric testing* is, i.e. tests that assess ability, aptitude, and personality.

4 Students now have the telephone call. Ask them to sit back-to-back so that the situation is more authentic. Encourage them to find out as much as possible about each other's suggestions, and to agree on the best suggestions.

5 Pairs now present their ideas to the rest of the class.

Feedback focus

Give feedback on the use of language. Write any mistakes on the board and ask the class to correct them.

One-to-one

Your student can read the *Background* information, and then you can do the *Discussion* questions together. For the *Task* you can each take a role and have the telephone call.

Extra activity

For extra writing practice, students could draft their suggestions in the form of an in-house proposal from the HR department to XM22's senior management team. This could list the pros and cons for various suggestions, and then give the final recommendation.

» Unit 7 **Progress test** and **Speaking test**, pages 108–109.

8 | Performance

Unit content

By the end of this unit, students will be able to
- discuss employer / employee expectations
- give an impromptu presentation
- use questions effectively
- deal with difficult questions.

Context

Performance in business is not only important for companies – it's also an essential part of an employee's career development. If employee performance is evaluated and enhanced through training and support, an individual is likely to be more motivated and driven. This will in turn be of benefit to the company itself.

Companies now recognize that improving employee satisfaction will enable them to retain their staff and improve performance across the board. Research has suggested that financial compensation is in fact relatively low on an employee's list of priorities and that more important issues include recognition, good teams and teamwork, having a sense of loyalty to the company, and being able to make a positive contribution to the company.

This unit approaches the topic of performance from two angles. Firstly, the issues of employee motivation and happiness are considered and students have the opportunity to discuss how this may affect the performance of an individual. The focus then turns towards staff performance in business situations, and in particular during impromptu presentations. Students have the chance to practise giving presentations under pressure with little or no preparation. They then focus on how to deal with difficult questions. The *Case study* examines the impact of management practices on employee and customer satisfaction. Students have the opportunity to draw up a plan for improvements for a company faced with this situation.

Starting point

1, 2 Discuss the questions as a class. Note any ideas on the board. You could then ask students to tell you about any rewards or forms of recognition in their companies.

> **Possible answers**
> 1 know-how from other companies in the industry, expertise in particular skills, specialist knowledge, language skills, enthusiasm, connections with important people in a field, etc.
> 2 being paid on commission, bonuses, a company car, the chance to work on another project, an opportunity to train further, promotion, staff parties, etc.

Working with words

1 Students make a list. They can then discuss and compare their ideas in small groups.

Pre-work learners

Ask students to think about how working will be different from studying. Write the following question on the board for discussion. *What do you expect will help you enjoy working for a company in the future?*

> **Possible answers**
> working with good people / teamwork, recognition for good work / being rewarded, being independent and allowed to take decisions, getting support from colleagues, being challenged, being paid well, having flexible working times, driving a company car, etc.

2 Students read the text and compare their ideas.

> **Answers**
> feeling part of a friendly and supporting atmosphere, having a say in what happens, enjoying 'a fun workspace', enjoyable work, gaining satisfaction from achievements, being able to relate to the values of the company, making a worthwhile contribution to the company, doing something good for the environment.

3 Students complete the phrases. They can then check their answers by referring to the text.

> **Answers**
> 1 a difference
> 2 recognition
> 3 part
> 4 a say
> 5 pride
> 6 a future

Dictionary skills

Ask students to work in pairs and to look up two nouns and two verbs in **3** in a monolingual dictionary. Ask them to find other phrases and collocations using these words. They should note them down, along with the meaning.
For example:
difference
a marked difference = a strong difference
tell the difference (between) = distinguish
a world of difference = very different
have our differences = to have disagreements
settle one's differences = to resolve disagreements
Then ask pairs to write example sentences for each phrase / collocation.

Extension

Ask students to close their books. Write the following sentences on the board and ask students to tell you which preposition should follow each one (answers are in brackets).
1 *make a difference (to)*
2 *gain recognition (for)*
3 *have a say (in)*
4 *take pride (in)*
5 *feel part (of)*
6 *see a future (for)*
Then ask students to write their own example sentence for each phrase.

4 Students match the combinations to the definitions.

Answers
a 2 **b** 4 **c** 5 **d** 1 **e** 3 **f** 6

5 Students work in pairs and discuss how satisfied they are at work, using vocabulary from **3** and **4**.

Pre-work learners

Write the following questions on the board and ask students to discuss them in pairs.
- *Do you take pride in the assignments you hand in? Why / Why not?*
- *Do you feel you'll be able to make a valid contribution to whoever employs you? How?*

6 45–47▷ Students listen and answer the questions.

Watch out! Before they listen, you might want to check that students understand the following.
prospective = expected, future
seek out = find
lateral moves = sideways moves to other departments, rather than just further up in the same department
strive = to make an effort

Answers
1 **Company 1:** De Beers = looks for people with qualities of enterprise, and who are able to take the initiative.
Company 2: Credit Suisse = looks for people with a combination of specialist knowledge and personality, with a strong team spirit, and who are able to build rapport and credibility easily.
Company 3: Orange = looks for people who can think on their feet, who learn fast, are flexible and adapt easily to new ideas; they also look for people who realize the importance of the customer, and who have a good sense of humour.
2 Answers will vary.

7 45–47▷ Students complete the combinations. They can then compare their ideas in pairs before listening again to check their answers.

Answers

1	out	7	on
2	in	8	to
3	from	9	to
4	up	10	to
5	up to	11	to
6	for		

8 Students work with a partner and replace sections of the sentences with a combination from **7**.

Answers
1 live up to expectations
2 I believe in the need
3 demonstrate an ability to
4 think on my feet
5 show a willingness to

» If students need more practice, go to **Practice file 8** on page 116 of the **Student's Book**.

9 Students think of examples from their own experience and then discuss them in pairs.

Pre-work learners

Ask students to talk about experiences they have had during their studies, whilst working part-time, or in their personal life.

10 Students can focus on their own company, or they can choose one of the company profiles in the *File* to work with. Put students into two groups. Ask each group to brainstorm ideas relating to their expectations.

11 Students now pair up with someone from the other group. They should imagine they are at a careers fair. They have an informal discussion and then decide how well-suited they are to each other.

Feedback focus

Circulate and monitor the use of the vocabulary from this section. At the end of the activity, ask students which pairs were most well-suited to each other and why. Give positive feedback to students who used vocabulary from **3** and **7** effectively.

ⓘ Refer students to the **Interactive Workbook Glossary** for further study.

Business communication skills

1 Ask students to read the *Context* about Ovanta. They should then work in pairs and discuss the questions.

> **Answers**
> 1 An impromptu presentation is one where there has been little or no advance preparation – someone may have asked you to give a short talk without any warning. This is particularly common in team meetings. Due to the lack of preparation, there won't usually be any visuals or handouts to support the presentation. The audience is likely to be smaller and the content will be less structured. There will be a lot of redundancy (*um, er,* repetition, etc.) and the aim is more likely to be related to informing or explaining, rather than being persuasive.
> 2 Answers will vary.

Extra activity

Write some simple topics on pieces of paper, and fold them in half. Topics could include: *My favourite restaurant; My plans for the future; My next holiday; Why I applied to work for this company; A recent business trip; A conference / training course I attended recently; A terrible day I had at work / college*, etc. There should be one topic per student. In turn, ask each student to take a piece of paper and give a two-minute talk on the topic (without any preparation). Discourage the others from interrupting during the talk. When they have all finished, ask the students which talk they liked best, and why. Then find out how difficult it was, and what made it easy or difficult.

2 48, 49▷ Students listen and answer the questions. They can then check their answers in pairs before feeding back to the rest of the class.

> **Answers**
> 1 b 2 a 3 b 4 a 5 b

3 48▷ Students listen again to the first part and complete the sentences.

> **Answers**
> 1 Where we are at the moment is
> 2 what I can tell you is that
> 3 I'd like to be able to, but unfortunately I can't
> 4 You'll appreciate that I still need to

4 48▷ Students listen again to the second part and complete the sentences.

> **Answers**
> 1 perhaps it would be a good idea if I just
> 2 I'd just like to sketch out
> 3 Let me just touch on
> 4 I think that's covered everything

5 Students categorize the phrases. They can then check their answers in pairs.

> **Answers**
> a all phrases from 4
> b all phrases from 3

6 Students work in pairs and turn to the *File*. Allow time for them to read the information. They then discuss what they could say to set the context and signal key points.

> **Possible answers**
> I'd like to be able to hand over the full report now, but unfortunately I can't because we're still waiting for all the questionnaires to come back in.
> Where we are at the moment is that we're still processing the feedback.
> Perhaps it would be a good idea if I explained some of the difficulties we've had.
> Let me just touch on the issue of 'effective questionnaires'.
> I'd just like to sketch out the general findings from the responses we've received so far.

7 Students work in pairs and brainstorm possible phrases for highlighting the main point. They then turn to the audio script and compare their ideas.

> **Answers**
> So, the first thing is …
> And I think you should be aware that …
> So that's one key point right there.
> … and I think this is a really important point …
> So, the main thing to remember is …

8 48, 49▷ Students listen again and note down the responses.

> **Answers**
> 1 I was coming to that. It's obviously a key area, and I have to admit that we haven't got as far as planning the specifics yet – we just haven't had the time.
> 2 That's a good point. I think so. Let me check, and I'll get back to you.
> 3 I can't remember exactly, but … off the top of my head, I think everyone had something to say. That's quite a significant factor, though … I can double check if you like?
> 4 Well, I don't have the exact figures, but what if I run through the rough numbers we've come up with so far?

➤➤ If students need more practice, go to **Practice file 8** on page 116 of the **Student's Book**.

9 Students work in pairs and take turns to respond to the questions.

> **Possible answers**
> 1 I have to admit, it has taken longer than expected.
> 2 I was coming to that. I don't have the schedule with me, but I think it's achievable in the time frame. Let me check after the meeting and I'll get back to you.
> 3 I was coming to that. We avoided any leading questions and most of them were multiple-choice.
> 4 I can't remember exactly, but off the top of my head I think it was 150.
> 5 That's a good point. However, I think the data will still be relevant. People don't tend to change their views on these issues overnight.
> 6 I was coming to that. Yes, we've already started planning the next research project. I don't have the exact details with me, but what if I asked Janice to email the initial plan to you after the meeting?

10 Students work in small groups. Allow time for them to think of their projects and to prepare the agenda. They should then take turns to give impromptu presentations.

Pre-work experience

Ask students to think of current study projects they are working on or any leisure activities they are involved in.

Feedback focus

Monitor for good use of the phrases in the *Key Expressions* and give feedback on this.

Extension

If possible, record the impromptu presentations to allow you to analyse students' fluency and use of language. In the next lesson, play each recording and ask students to note down any fillers used (small words and sounds used while a speaker is thinking, e.g. *um, er, like, you know*, etc.). It's often useful for students to hear themselves speaking and to see whether they are using one particular filler too often, as this will impede their level of fluency.

When students have a list of fillers they should match them to the following functions.

1 giving yourself thinking time
2 clarifying what you have said
3 giving an example
4 other

Then ask them to think of possible alternatives fillers for each category. Encourage them to try incorporating these alternative fillers into their language to improve their level of fluency.

For example:

1 Let me just think … / I'm sure you know, … / So perhaps I'll just …
2 What I mean is … / What I'm trying to say is … / Let me put it another way, …
3 So for example, … / Let me give you an example. / So, for instance, …

ⓘ Refer students to the **Interactive Workbook Email** and **Phrasebank** sections for further study.

Language at work

1 Students match the questions to the functions. They can then compare their answers in pairs before feeding back to the rest of the class.

> **Answers**
> a 1, 9
> b 2, 4, 7
> c 3, 8, 10
> d 5, 6

2 Students answer the questions.

> **Answers**
> **1** 1, 2, 9
> **2** 4, 6, 7
> **3** 4, 5, 6, 7, 10
> **4** 3, 8

3 Students answer the questions.

> **Answers**
> **1** 1, 6
> **2** 4, 5, 7
> **3** 2, 3, 8, 9, 10

>> Refer students to the **Language reference** section on page 130 of the **Student's Book** for more information.

4 Students work in pairs and take turns to ask questions. Encourage them to refer back to the question types in **1** to help them.

> **Possible answers**
> **1** Do you really think that is a good idea?
> **2** Phil, you've got the latest figures – would you mind talking us through them?
> **3** I assume you've all had a chance to look at the draft, have you?
> **4** Now, how can I put this …?
> **5** I don't know if you're familiar with the new software?
> **6** Do you think it was wise to show the findings to the client before checking with the boss?
> **7** I take it the research phase has been completed, has it?
> **8** Bob, can you give us an overview of your research trip?

Extension

Ask students to work in pairs. Each student should write eight questions that they would like to ask their partner, using various question types. They then take turns to ask and answer questions.

>> If students need more practice, go to **Practice file 8** on page 117 of the **Student's Book**.

5 Students work in groups of three. Each student should prepare some information about a recent project, making a few bullet points on paper (not full sentences). Give them about two minutes. When they are ready, Students A and B should start. Student C should take notes, writing down each question, who says it, and the function of the question. When they have finished, they should change roles and repeat.

Pre-work learners

Students should focus on a study project or another kind of project that they are working on.

Feedback focus

Ask students to give their feedback on the questions that were used in their groups. How many questions were asked? How many different functions were used? Were the questions suitably varied? Were the responses appropriate?

Practically speaking

1 As a lead-in, ask students why some questions are difficult to answer? Possible answers could be as follows.
- because you don't know the answer
- because the truthful answer may be unpopular
- because the truthful answer may give others a bad impression of you
- because you hadn't anticipated the question, so you hadn't thought about an answer

Students then discuss the questions in pairs.

> **Possible answers**
> **a** explain that you don't want to answer, try to delay giving an answer, give some possibly false information, admit that you don't know the answer
> **b** pretend that you don't know the answer, admit that you don't want to answer, refer the person to someone else

2 50▷ Students listen and tick the strategies.

> **Answers**
>
> | Strategies | 1 | 2 | 3 | 4 | 5 | 6 |
> | --- | --- | --- | --- | --- | --- | --- |
> | admit ignorance | | ✓ | ✓ | ✓ | | |
> | directly refuse to answer | ✓ | ✓ | | | | ✓ |
> | avoid the question | | | | ✓ | ✓ | ✓ |
> | distance yourself from the situation | ✓ | | ✓ | | ✓ | |

3 50▷ Students listen again and note down phrases. They can then compare their answers in pairs before feeding back to the rest of the class.

Answers
admitting ignorance: I'm afraid I don't know any more than you do; Sorry, I don't know what you mean; I'm afraid I'm not up to speed on …
directly refusing to answer: I'm sorry, but I can't answer that; I would prefer not to talk about it; I'm afraid I can't disclose that information – it's confidential.
avoiding the question: Well, it's not that straightforward; It's hard to say at the moment; I can't really comment.
distancing yourself from the question: I'm afraid I'm really not in a position to talk about that; It's not for me to say; It's nothing to do with me.

Extra activity

Write the following questions on the board. Ask students to discuss them in pairs, before feeding back to the rest of the class.

1 *Have you ever been asked a difficult question*
   • *in a job interview?*
   • *during a speaking exam?*
   • *in a meeting?*
   • *during a product presentation?*
   • *by your boss?*
   • *in front of your mother?*
   • *at a formal dinner?*
   • *in an appraisal?*
   If so, what was the question? Did you deal with it well or badly? Why?
2 *Which jobs demand an ability to deal with difficult questions well?* (Possible answers could include politicians, PR representatives, CEOs, teachers, etc.)
3 *Can you think of any examples of someone in the public eye who deals particularly well or badly with questions? Why?*

» Refer students to the **Useful phrases** section on page 135 of the **Student's Book** for extension and revision.

4 Students work in pairs. Allow time for them to read their information and to think about what questions they can ask, and how they'll answer their partner's questions. They should then take turns to ask questions and respond.

5 Students might like to swap pairs for this activity. Allow time for students to write two difficult questions. They then take turns to ask and answer.

Pre-work students

Ask students to choose a topic they'd be willing to discuss, e.g. their course, an exam, their plans after their studies, etc.

Feedback focus

Monitor and make a note of the phrases they use for asking and responding. When they have finished, ask them if they were able to ask appropriate and difficult questions? Were they able to answer the questions? Then give feedback on their use of language. Write any errors on the board for the class to correct.

Culture question

Ask students to discuss these questions in small groups. If they need help with the second question, suggest the following phrase.
I'd rather not answer that, if you don't mind.
This is usually suitable and effective in Western Europe.

Key word

Students match the phrases.
   Answers: 1 c, 2 a, 3 d, 4 e, 5 b

(i) Refer students to the **Interactive Workbook Exercises and Tests** for revision.

Case study

Background

This *Case study* focuses on the importance of rewarding staff and increasing customer satisfaction. Students find out about a company that succeeded in improving employee motivation and customer satisfaction through effective management strategies. The *Task* enables students to discuss ways of improving staff and customer satisfaction levels for another company.
Allow a few minutes for students to read the *Company profile* and the texts and be prepared to answer any questions about vocabulary.

Extra activity

Write the following questions on the board and ask students to discuss them in pairs (possible answers are in brackets) before feeding back to the rest of the class. Be prepared to help with vocabulary during the discussion where necessary.
   • *What are the disadvantages of working in a hotel?* (e.g. long hours, low pay, difficult customers, high staff turnover, limited promotion prospects, etc.)
   • *What are the advantages?* (e.g. discounts on accommodation, free meals, tips, opportunity to meet people from different cultures, flexible hours, opportunities to travel, etc.)

Discussion

1, 2, 3 Students can discuss these questions in pairs before feeding back to the rest of the class.

Possible answers

1 It has achieved radical improvements through new leadership strategies and management practices. These included ensuring all staff get appropriate training, giving employees the power to deal effectively with customer complaints, rewarding staff for outstanding customer service, etc.

2 Answers will vary. However, the idea of empowering staff by encouraging them to take the initiative in dealing with customer complaints, and in particular in giving them a significant budget to resolve these complaints, is certainly innovative.

3 Answers will vary.

Task

1 Ask the students to look at the graph and to discuss their ideas for improving the hotel in groups of three.

2 51 ▷ As they listen, ask the students to make notes on what problems the hotel is experiencing.

Watch out! Before they listen, you might want to check that students understand the following.
burst of optimism = sudden positive mood
scepticism = disbelief
regime = system
organic decrease = gradual or natural decrease, rather than a sudden or forced decrease

Possible answers

- motivation has dropped
- there's a lot of scepticism among staff about fitting into the new structure, especially within middle management
- skilled managers are moving to other hotels
- they are only just above break-even point
- growth is only about 1%
- competition is tough
- there are not enough repeat bookings
- customer satisfaction is at an all-time low

3 Students work in groups of three and plan their improvements for the Katisha hotel.

4 When the students are ready, ask each group to present their ideas to the class. Encourage the students who are listening to ask challenging questions.

Feedback focus

Focus on the quality of the plans. How realistic are they? Do they address all the problems outlined in the meeting? Which plan is the most likely to succeed? Give feedback at the end of all the presentations.

One-to-one

Your student can read the *Background* information, and then you can do the *Discussion* questions together. Listen to the meeting, and together note down the main points of concern. Use the Ritz-Carlton ideas as a starting point, and then try to elicit other ideas for addressing these problems. When your student has enough ideas, ask him / her to present the plan. Listen to the presentation and ask some difficult questions.

Extra activity

Ask students to write an in-house proposal from the HR department of GS International Hotel Group to Senior Management. This should list their suggestions, with details of how each suggestion addresses a problem experienced by the hotel.

» Unit 8 **Progress test** and **Speaking test**, pages 110–111.

9 | Resources

Unit content

By the end of this unit, students will be able to
- talk about resources
- discuss options and reach decisions
- use conditionals
- deal with misunderstandings.

Context

The topic of resources is fairly complex, due to the fact that the term can be interpreted in several ways. Generally speaking, 'resources' refers to a supply of something that a country, organization, or person can use. Your students will relate fairly easily to the concept of the 'natural resources' provided by the world around us (e.g. minerals), but they may be less familiar with the resources of an organization. The resources available to a company are generally divided into four categories: physical (e.g. buildings), financial (e.g. funds available), human (e.g. staff), and intangible (e.g. brands).

In today's business world, it is important for a company not only to manage its own resources effectively, but also to be seen to support the sustainability of natural resources. Many companies demonstrate their attitude towards managing resources (both natural resources and company resources) through Corporate Social Responsibility (CSR) projects. These usually involve working towards minimizing harm to the environment and benefiting local communities.

The first part of the unit looks at different resource types, and how they can be managed. *The Business communication skills* section gives students practice in evaluating options. They then focus on the use of conditionals and how to deal with misunderstandings. In the *Case Study*, students examine a CSR project run by Michelin. They then investigate other projects that a company in a similar position could take on, discussing the resources that would be needed, and what they could achieve in the short and long term.

Starting point

1 Draw a spider diagram on the board with two legs. Write *resources* in the middle, write *natural resources* on the left-hand leg, and *company resources* on the right-hand leg. Ask students to work in pairs or small groups and brainstorm examples for each category. Then write their ideas on the board.

Possible answers
natural resources: oil, gold, silver, copper, wood, cotton, coal, gas, water, wind, clay
company resources: employees, money, buildings, land, brands, equipment, loans and credit agreements

Watch out! Before doing this, make sure that students understand *intangible* – something that exists, but is difficult to describe, understand, or measure.

2 Students then work in pairs and match the resources types to the resource areas. You could also ask them to match their ideas for company resources in **1** to the four resource areas.

Answers
financial: ability to raise funds, existing funds
human: existing staff, changes to staff
physical: production facilities, IT
intangible: goodwill / reputation / brands

Working with words

1 Students can discuss the questions in pairs before feeding back to the rest of the class. They then read and check their ideas.

Watch out! Before they read, you might want to check that students understand the following.
embrace = to accept an idea, a proposal, a set of beliefs, etc., especially when it is done with enthusiasm
nurture = to care for and protect somebody / something while they are growing and developing
pledge = to formally promise to give or do something
roam = to walk or travel around an area without any definite aim

Possible answers
Marks and Spencer plc: specializes in food, fashion, and home furnishings. It has stores in over 30 countries, but not all stores worldwide sell the entire product range. Clothes in international stores are usually chosen to reflect trends in that particular country.
Natural resources: it will need to be careful about how much packaging is used for the food products and how much power, fuel, and water is used in stores. It will also need to consider how much fuel is used to transport goods, etc.
Company resources: it will need to ensure that employees are treated well, that products are sourced from ethical producers, that the buildings are clean and safe, and that money is invested in the right areas.

2 Students read the text again and match the headings to the paragraphs. They can then compare their answers with a partner.

> **Answers**
> 1 Responsibility and business
> 2 Being a responsible employer
> 3 Respecting customer opinion
> 4 Becoming a more responsible company
> 5 Just a PR tool?

3 Students match the noun phrases in **bold** to the definitions.

> **Answers**
> 1 corporate accountability
> 2 knowledge base
> 3 sustainability of resources
> 4 critical success factor
> 5 track record
> 6 competitive advantage

Dictionary skills

Ask students to work in pairs. Each pair should use a monolingual dictionary. Write the following tasks on the board.
* *Use the dictionary to find out which syllable is stressed in each word in* **3**.
* *Find all the weak forms /ə/ (schwas) in the words in* **3**.
(Answers (stressed syllables are in **bold**, schwas are underlined): **cor**p<u>o</u>rate <u>a</u>ccount**a**bility, **know**ledge base, sust<u>a</u>in**a**bility <u>of</u> re<u>sou</u>rces, **crit**ic<u>a</u>l s<u>u</u>**cess fac**t<u>o</u>r, track **re**cord, c<u>o</u>m**pet**itive <u>a</u>d**van**tage)
Then ask students to find five words in the dictionary that they don't know. Ask them to use the pronunciation information in the dictionary to help them practise saying the words. When they are ready, ask students to say their words for the rest of the class and give feedback on their pronunciation.

4 Students find the verbs in the text that collocate with *resources*.

> **Answers**
> deploy resources, allocate resources, maximize resources, optimize resources, utilize resources, put resources to good use, squander resources, mismanage resources

5 Students categorize the verbs.

> **Answers**
> 1 maximize, optimize, put to good use
> 2 squander, mismanage
> 3 deploy, allocate, utilize

Extension

Ask students to choose a large company they know (and / or their own company). Ask them to find out about its CSR programme for homework. They can then report back on this in the next lesson.

6 52▷ Students listen and answer the questions.

Watch out! Before they listen, you might want to check that students understand the following.
offset = to use one cost, payment, or situation in order to cancel or reduce the effect of another

> **Answers**
> 1 She's a shareholder, and wants to make his own decisions about donations and investments. She wants good long-term investments, and believes some CSR projects are not profitable in the long term.
> 2 CSR projects can really enhance the reputation and therefore the brand of a company.
> 3 Before signing an agreement, they ask for a cost-benefit analysis to ensure long-term project viability. They also make sure they can visit the site, and that they'll get reports and data relating to the project on a regular basis.

7 Students work in pairs and complete the sentences.

> **Answers**
> 1 cost-benefit analysis
> 2 drain on resources
> 3 long-term viability
> 4 return on investment
> 5 quantifiable data
> 6 assets
> 7 short-term profit
> 8 market value
> 9 bottom line

» If students need more practice, go to **Practice file 9** on page 118 of the **Student's Book**.

8 Students work in pairs. Allow time for them to read about the four projects. They should then discuss each project and think of the possible pros and cons for the employees, the customers, and the shareholders.

When they are ready, each group can summarize their discussion for the rest of the class. Ask students to decide which group of people benefits most from each project and why.

Possible answers
Project 1
Pros
current employees: improved knowledge base means each staff member will have improved their skills and therefore their career prospects
shareholders: maximizes use of human resources, and ultimately should result in an improvement to the bottom line and a good return on investment
customers: improved knowledge base of staff will mean a better service is provided
Cons
current employees: staff less comfortable with IT might struggle
shareholders: initial outlay of funds will affect the short-term profits
customers: staff might not be available when you need them – they'll be in training
Project 2
Pros
current employees: offers potential for promotion; reduces likelihood of having to do menial tasks
shareholders: putting local resources to good use could mean an improvement to the company's bottom line
customers: optimizing local resources – customers will see this as a benefit to the community (providing training and employment), so may be more likely to support the company
Cons
current employees: may feel their jobs are in jeopardy
shareholders: neither short-term profit nor return on investment is clear or guaranteed; could be seen as wasting or mismanaging resources: why not use current staff?
customers: may find themselves doing business with people with inadequate language skills
Project 3
Pros
current employees: benefits to health and fitness if staff walk or cycle to work
shareholders: increased market credibility due to clear concern for the environment
customers: will appreciate concern for the environment, and so may be more likely to support the company
Cons
current employees: some may live far from work and may not have access to public transport; will cause disruption during building works
shareholders: solar panels are very expensive – needs a cost-benefit analysis to decide if this has long-term viability

customers: product / service prices may increase due to costs of project
Project 4
Pros
current employees: current customer service staff may be offered alternative positions within the company
shareholders: increased market credibility due to clear concern for fair pay in developing countries
customers: may be more inclined to support the company
Cons
current employees: some will lose their jobs
shareholders: a cost-benefit analysis will be necessary to ensure long-term viability
customers: may have to deal with non-native speakers; accents and language issues may be problematic and this may be considered a mismanagement of resources

Feedback focus

Circulate and monitor their use of language. After the activity, give positive feedback on the correct use of vocabulary from **3** and **7**.

9 Students discuss the question in small groups. If they all work for different companies, they can share information about the projects and make suggestions together.

Pre-work learners

Write the following questions on the board. Ask students to work in groups of three or four and discuss the questions.
- *Do you know any companies that have started similar projects to those in 8? If so, tell your group what you know about it.*
- *Which of the projects would encourage you to work for a company that implemented them? Why?*

ⓘ Refer students to the **Interactive Workbook Glossary** for further study.

Business communication skills

1 Ask students to read the *Context* about Floralope and then discuss the question as a class.

Possible answers
Issues to consider include the availability of funds (financial resources), IT equipment and office / factory space (physical resources), trained staff and / or the possibility of recruiting them (human resources).

2 53–56▷ Students listen. They should check their ideas in **1** and answer the questions.

Watch out! Before they listen, you might want to check that students understand the following.
reputable = that people consider to be honest and to provide a good service
outlay = the money that you have to spend in order to start a new project

> **Answers**
> 1 The speakers discuss human, financial, and physical resources.
> 2 Staff will need training, but overall human resources are not problematic. There are some financial problems, but they think they can cope. Although the buildings are quite run-down, they agree it can support the new system.

3 53–56▷ Students listen again and answer the questions about the speakers' attitudes.

> **Answers**
> 1 Margit takes a positive lead – she directs the conversation through the various points on the agenda, using words such as *so, now, OK*, etc., and summarizes the conversation on a regular basis.
> 2 Judit seems quite negative throughout. She is very direct, and always focuses on the problems or difficult issues.

4 Students categorize the phrases.

> **Answers**
> 1 j, k, l
> 2 a, b, d, i
> 3 c, e, f, g, h

5 Students look at the phrases and answer the questions. They can then check their answers in pairs.

> **Answers**
> a using the auxiliary *do* emphasizes the contrast, helping someone to contradict a previous idea by pointing out the positive aspect
> b evaluating an option
> c 3, 6
> d 2, 4, 5

» If students need more practice, go to **Practice file 9** on page 118 of the **Student's Book**.

6 Students work in groups of four. Each pair within the group should turn to their *File* and discuss the advantages of their proposals. When they are ready, they should join with the other pair and have the meeting. Refer them to the *Key expressions*. They should also use the agenda to guide their discussion and should aim to reach a decision.

7 Students work in pairs and discuss the projects. If possible, students should work with someone from the same company. If they are from different companies, they can focus on each company in turn.

Pre-work students

Students should discuss the projects in relation to a company they know or the college / university where they are studying.

8 Each pair should now summarize their ideas for the rest of the class.

Alternative

Ask students to prepare a PowerPoint presentation to give to the rest of the group. Ask them to choose one of the projects in **7** and prepare their ideas under the following three headings.
1 Why is it a good idea for the company?
2 What resources would be necessary to implement the project?
3 How would the resources be managed?
Encourage them to keep the information on each slide fairly minimal, using bullet points only. They can give their presentations in the next lesson.

Feedback focus

Circulate and monitor how successful the meetings were. Make a note of any good use of the phrases from the *Key expressions* and give positive feedback at the end of the task.

ⓘ Refer students to the **Interactive Workbook Email** and **Phrasebank** sections for further study.

Language at work

1 Students read the sentences and underline the verbs.

> **Answers**
> 1 is, 'll be
> 2 check out, 'm, can find, will work
> 3 's, investing, don't have
> 4 'd invested, would have knocked down, had ... built
> 5 made, could ... train up
> 6 'd recruited, would have had
> 7 had, could use, could ... cope
> 8 hadn't invested, 'd be
> 9 work, can ... improve

2 Students work in pairs, and identify the conditional types.

> **Answers**
> zero: 3
> 1st: 1, 2, 9
> 2nd: 5, 7
> 3rd: 4, 6
> mixed: 8

Watch out! In sentences 2 and 9, *can* behaves in the same way as *will be able to*, so they are first conditionals.

Extension

Write the following sentences on the board. Ask students to identify the forms in each sentence (answers are underlined). Then ask them to identify the conditional type (answers in brackets).

1 *If interest rates go* up, *people save* more.
   Form = If + subject + present simple + subject + present simple. (= zero conditional)

2 *If I take* the job in marketing, *I will work* with Paul.
   Form = If + subject + present simple + subject + will + infinitive. (= first conditional)

3 *If we did* some research, *we could find out* what our customers want.
   Form = If + subject + past simple + subject + could / would / might + infinitive. (= second conditional)

4 *If I had listened* to my parents, *I would have studied* law.
   Form = If + subject + past perfect + subject + could / would / might + have + past participle. (= third conditional)

5 *If I hadn't spent* so much money on clothes, *I wouldn't be in debt now.*
   Form = If + subject + past perfect + subject + could / would / might + infinitive. (= mixed)

3 Students match the sentences in **1** to the categories. Then ask them to see if they can notice any patterns.

> **Answers**
> 1 1, 2, 9   4 7
> 2 5   5 4, 6
> 3 3   6 8
>
> **Students should notice the following:**
> • Zero conditionals are used to talk about facts.
> • First conditionals are used to predict the results of a likely future event.
> • Second conditionals are used to predict the results of a less likely future event, or to hypothesize / suggest.
> • Third conditionals are used to talk about past regrets or relief about things which didn't actually happen.
> • Mixed conditionals are used to express the present effects of a past decision / action.

>> Refer students to the **Language reference** section on page 131 of the **Student's Book** for more information.

4 Students work in pairs and take turns to discuss the situations using conditional forms.

> **Possible answers**
> 1 If we start cutting costs now, we might not go bankrupt / we may be saved from bankruptcy.
> 2 If we raise interest rates, consumer spending may drop.
> 3 If we hadn't hired Ian, those people probably wouldn't have left.
> 4 If I hadn't gone into this profession, I wouldn't be bored now.
> 5 If I was one of the ones relocated to Berlin, I'd be able to meet up with my friends more often. (less likely) / If I'm located to Berlin, I'll be able to …. (more likely)
> 6 If I can negotiate a good salary increase, we'll be able to go to the Caribbean!

>> If students need more practice, go to **Practice file 9** on page 119 of the **Student's Book**.

5 Students work in pairs and turn to the *File*. Allow time for them to read the information. They should then discuss what happened, using conditionals where appropriate.

> **Possible answers**
> 1 If we hadn't invested in new equipment, we wouldn't have been able to increase the membership fee.
>   If we had developed a competitive special offer in January, we wouldn't have lost potential customers to the competition.
> 2 If we had addressed the HR crisis, we would have more trainers now, and our current trainers wouldn't be overworked. We wouldn't have so many customers on our waiting list.
>   If we hadn't developed the local school partnership, we wouldn't have overweight teenagers on our fitness programme now.
> 3 (These answers can be in first or second conditional, depending on their likelihood).
>   If we can develop new membership packages, we'll increase member numbers.
>   If we start more initiatives with teenagers, we'll improve the gym's reputation and get new young members.
>   If we employ more trainers, we'll make more profit from tailor-made personal programmes.
>   If we renovated the pool, we'd have a better reputation and we'd be able to put our prices up.

6 Students make notes about the past year and next year. They then discuss their notes in pairs, using appropriate conditional forms. Encourage them to use the full range of conditional sentences to express their thoughts and ideas.

> **Possible answers**
> 1 If we hadn't won that contract, we wouldn't have had to work every evening and weekend.
> 2 If John hadn't left, he would be the first person I'd ask to help me!
> 3 If we give our staff more language training, they'll be able to deal more effectively with our international customers. If we were allowed to work from home, we would save time and petrol expenses, but we would still be able to communicate easily on the phone and by email.

Pre-work learners

Ask students to think about their past year of studies and their plans for next year.

Feedback focus

As you monitor the students, acknowledge good use of the conditional sentences. Make a note of any problems and deal with them at the end of the activity.

Extra activity

Write the following four prompts on cards. Prepare a set for every two students in your class. Ask students to work in pairs and take turns to interview each other using the prompts on the cards to form conditionals. Encourage students to ask further questions to find out more.
- chance to study abroad / take it?
- study something different / job now?
- any role in the company of your dreams / what? why?
- study again / what? why?

Example: *If you were given the chance to study abroad, would you take it?*

When they have finished, ask students to report back on what they found out.

Practically speaking

1 57▷ Students listen and answer the questions.

> **Possible answers**
> 1 polite = 1, 2, 4
> 2 less polite = 3, 5
> Intonation and language (usually longer phrases) help to identify politeness.

2 57▷ Students listen again and mark the sentences 1–5, according to the conversation they are heard in.

> **Answers**
> a 3   b 3   c 2   d 1   e 5   f 3
> g 4   h 4   i 5   j 2   k 5   l 5

3 Students work in pairs and answer the questions.

> **Answers**
> 1 Direct: a, b, e, f, i, k
> Less Direct: c, d, g, h, j, l
> 2 *Sorry; I was thinking ..., What I actually wanted to say ..., What I meant was..., It may seem ..., That's not exactly...*
> 3 You might want to be less direct when speaking to someone senior to you; when you know you've made a mistake; when you want to clarify something.
> You might want to be more direct when the mistake / misunderstanding has occurred more than once before; when the phone line is bad and you need to make yourself understood; when speaking to someone from a culture where they are more direct.

4 Students change the phrases to make them less direct.

> **Possible answers**
> 1 That's not exactly what I meant – I actually said ...
> 2 I didn't quite mean that, actually.
> 3 Actually, I'm not sure exactly what you mean.
> 4 (Sorry, but) I'm not really sure what you're talking about.
> 5 Actually, that's not exactly right.

Extra activity

Write the following sentence on the board. Then tell the students that you are going to say the sentence in three ways and they should decide which is the most polite.
- *That's not exactly what I meant, I actually said ...*

Say the sentence in the following three ways.
1 Say *exactly* and *actually* with very flat intonation.
2 Stress *exactly* and *actually* naturally to sound quite polite.
3 Exaggerate the stress on *exactly* and *actually*, with wide intonation, to sound very polite.

Refer students to the **Useful phrases** section on page 135 of the **Student's Book** for extension and revision.

5 Students work in pairs. Student A should complain about situations 1 and 2. Student B should misunderstand Student A. They then change roles to deal with situations 3 and 4.

Watch out! Remind students to think about their intonation. Do they sound polite?

Feedback focus

While monitoring the students, pay particular attention to their intonation. Give feedback after the activity.

Culture question

Students can discuss the questions as a class. You could also explore how different cultures value directness or indirectness. To generate discussion, write the following countries on the board. Ask students to decide which ones tend to value directness (D) and which tend to value indirectness (I). Can they add any other countries to the list?

(Suggested answers are in brackets, but these are only tendencies so handle this with sensitivity)
- *Portugal (I)*
- *Sweden (D)*
- *Holland (D)*
- *Indonesia (I)*
- *Britain (I)*

Key word

Students match the sentences to the uses / definitions.
Answers: 1 d, 2 a, 3 c, 4 e, 5 b

» Refer students to the **Interactive Workbook Exercises and Tests** for revision.

Case study

Background

This *Case study* presents a CSR project developed by the tyre manufacturer, Michelin. Given that the company is involved in an industry that is potentially damaging to the environment, it is making concerted efforts to try to counteract this by developing projects to benefit local communities. Students have an opportunity to discuss the project and its potential pros and cons. The *Task* then allows students to develop ideas for a similar project.

Allow a few minutes for students to read the *Company profile* and text. Be prepared to answer any questions about vocabulary.

Discussion

1, 2, 3 Students can discuss these questions in pairs.

4 58▷ Students listen and compare the information with their own ideas.

Answers
1 secure jobs, allowing people to learn more about the business, improved living conditions, gaining experience of managing a profitable project
2 It has a guarantee that a percentage of the rubber has to be sold to Michelin and this could be beneficial as demand for rubber is increasing and prices are rising. Indirectly, Michelin's image will be enhanced as the project will benefit the local community.
3 Production of rubber is still low so supply is limited. The project also provides rubber for its competitors.

Task

1 Students read about QP Plastics. They then work in groups and discuss ideas for CSR projects.

Possible answers
There could be a project focusing on education – students from universities and colleges could be offered work experience, literacy classes could be run for employees who struggle with reading and writing.
Alternatively, profits could be put into developing utilities – water sanitization and provision of generators for times when power supplies are unreliable.

2 Students choose a project from their discussion in **1**. They then discuss the project in more detail, answering questions 1–5.

3 Students now discuss resourcing for their project. Make sure they have made notes detailing their decisions.

4 Groups now present their projects to each other. Encourage students to ask questions and offer advice.

5 Students turn to the *File*. Ask them to discuss what the company should do. Then ask groups to explain their decision to the rest of the class.

Feedback focus

Give feedback on the project proposals. Have they considered all the issues? Does the plan sound feasible?

One-to-one

The student can read the *Background* and you can go through the questions in the *Discussion* section together. In the *Task*, brainstorm a list of possible projects for QP Plastics together. Then ask the student to prepare a presentation on how to implement one of the proposals.

» Unit 9 **Progress test** and **Speaking test**, pages 112–113.

10 | Leadership

Unit content

By the end of this unit, students will be able to
- talk about leadership styles
- give a briefing on change
- use the passive to distance and depersonalize
- express personal views

Context

Leadership is a topic that everyone can relate to. Even if someone hasn't had any leadership experience, they will have been led by good or bad managers at some point. It is important to note that there is a difference between the terms *leadership* and *management*. Whereas managers tend to have colleagues and work in teams, leaders are those who see the bigger picture, and have the vision and commitment to make radical changes. Leaders are usually creative and innovative, always looking for new solutions to problems, and it is often the managers who are called on to implement the leaders' ideas.

There are a variety of leadership styles, and your students may well have had different experiences, depending on their nationality, and the types of organization they have worked in. An autocratic style of leadership is one where the leader gives instructions to their subordinates. Conversely, a democratic leader will share the responsibility, involving others in the decision-making. A laissez-faire style involves minimal supervision, and allows employees to take the initiative and make decisions.

The first part of this unit allows discussion of different leadership qualities and examines which are typical in different national cultures. Students are then given the opportunity to practise a typical management task – giving an effective briefing to staff. They are also encouraged to use passive forms to help depersonalize the information. The *Case Study* is based on a cosmetics company in the Czech Republic. Students read about the leadership skills that the owner displayed. They then focus on a chocolate company on the verge of bankruptcy and discuss how the company could be led in the right direction.

Starting point

Discuss the first question as a class. Write the names of the people mentioned on the board and encourage students to describe the leadership qualities that they think each person has. They can then discuss questions **2–4** in pairs.

Possible answers
1 Answers will vary.
2 Answers will vary. Some may argue that skills can be learnt through experience, age, and management training courses. Others may believe that the skills are dependent on personalities and therefore cannot be learnt.
3 A leader is a person who leads a group of people, especially the head of a country, an organization, etc. They are more concerned with 'the bigger picture' rather than day-to-day events.
A manager is a person who is in charge of running a company department, a business, a shop / store or a similar organization. They usually work with teams and therefore need to be people-focused.
4 Leading a small team is more likely to be a managerial task (rather than the task of a leader). There is an emphasis on people – helping them work together and recognizing their individual strengths. It is also important that everyone in the team is focused on the same goal.
Leading an organization is connected to a leader rather than a manager. It is important to have an awareness of the overall goal of the organization and its context (environment, competitors, etc). Creativity is essential, as is the ability to communicate ideas effectively so that they quickly become reality.

Working with words

1 Students work in pairs and discuss the questions.

2 Students read the text and compare their answers in **1**.

Answers
1 Honesty and trustworthiness, conviction, passion, good interpersonal skills, decision-making skills (depending on culture), being flexible, being able to delegate, showing empathy, self-awareness, humility.
2 In Europe and Japan it is considered important to consult team members before decisions are made, whereas in China decisions are most often made by leaders.
Showing empathy is considered important in Europe and America and this may well become more important in emerging economies in the future.

Watch out! After students have read the text you might want to check that they understood the following.
overt = done in an open way and not secretly
trait = a particular quality in your personality

3 Students read the text again and match the adjectives and nouns from the text to the quotes.

> **Answers**
> | | | | |
> |---|---|---|---|
> | 1 | humble | 7 | conviction |
> | 2 | decisive | 8 | adaptable |
> | 3 | empathy | 9 | integrity |
> | 4 | self-aware | 10 | collaborative |
> | 5 | commitment | 11 | hands-off |
> | 6 | passionate | 12 | people-focused |

Dictionary Skills

Write the words from **3** on the board as indicated below. Ask students to indicate the stress on each word (see underlined sections below for the answers). Then elicit the noun form of each adjective, the verb form of *empathy*, *conviction* and *collaborative*, and the adjective from *commitment* (answers are in brackets). Ask them to check their ideas in a dictionary and to find out the word stress for the new words.

1 *humble (humility)*
2 *decisive (decision)*
3 *empathy (empathize)*
4 *self-aware (self-awareness)*
5 *commitment (committed)*
6 *passionate (passion)*
7 *conviction (convince)*
8 *adaptable (adaptability, adaptation)*
9 *integrity*
10 *collaborative (collaboration, collaborate)*
11 *hands-off*
12 *people-focused*

Extension

Write the following pairs of adjectives on the board. Ask students to match each pair of adjectives to an adjective in **3** with the opposite meaning (answers are in brackets).

1 *interfering, controlling (hands-off)*
2 *inflexible, rigid (adaptable)*
3 *hesitant, indecisive (decisive)*
4 *directive, top-down (collaborative)*
5 *apathetic, unenthusiastic (passionate)*
6 *autocratic, task-orientated (people-focused)*

4 Students work in pairs and read the *File*. They then prepare a short verbal report describing the leadership styles. You might like to write the following sentence starters on the board to help them.

Positive	Negative
He / She's quite / very …	*He / She's not very …*
He / She has …	*He / She lacks / has a lack of …*
He / She shows a lot of …	*He / She's not able to show …*

> **Answers**
> **Team leader A:** He / she's good at achieving results, and shows a lot of commitment. He / she is decisive, and is very good at delegating. However, he / she's not very good at consulting on decisions, and doesn't have much empathy. He / she also lacks self-awareness and is not able to demonstrate flexibility.
> **Team leader B:** He / she is very results-orientated and shows commitment. He / she can be trusted, and has a participative style. He / she is able to communicate well, and is very people-orientated. However, he / she lacks the ability to be decisive.
> Team leader B seems to show much better team-leading skills.

Extra activity

Write the following descriptions of teams on the board. Ask students to work in small groups and decide what kind of team leader would be best for each team and why.

- *Team 1: a team with lax discipline, high absenteeism, and a generally sloppy way of working – this has led to low levels of productivity.*
- *Team 2: a team where most participants work independently, only consulting each other when absolutely necessary. They stick closely to their remit, and get the job done on time, but the atmosphere at work is often fairly cold.*
- *Team 3: a team where participants try to get their tasks done as quickly as possible, though not necessarily doing them well. Cliques are forming within the team and there seems to be an atmosphere of back-stabbing and colluding, resulting in some team members withdrawing and not contributing as much as they could.*

5 Students work in pairs and discuss the questions.

Pre-work students

Encourage students with minimal or no work experience to talk about their experience of leaders and leadership styles in teams outside work / study places, e.g. teams in sports, music, clubs, etc.

6 59, 60▷ Students listen and answer the questions.

Watch out! Before students listen, you might want to check that they understand the following.
fuselage = the main part of an aircraft in which passengers and goods are carried
micromanage = to direct or control in a detailed way (negative)

7 59, 60▷ Students make phrases. Ask students to compare their answers in pairs. Then play the audio again so that they can check which combinations were used. Elicit additional possible combinations from students.

» If students need more practice, go to **Practice file 10** on page 120 of the **Student's Book**.

8 Students work in pairs and discuss the advice they would give. Encourage them to use vocabulary from **3** and **7**. You could then ask each pair to present advice for one of the situations for the rest of the class.

9 Students work in small groups and discuss their own leadership styles.

Feedback focus

Circulate and make a note of language used. Provide positive feedback on correct usage of the vocabulary from this section.

Culture question

Discuss the questions as a class. You might like to also discuss the second question in relation to the cultures within companies.

ⓘ Refer students to the **Interactive Workbook Glossary** for further study.

Business communication skills

1 61▷ Ask students to read about Nordica in the *Context*. Elicit what the problem is (the technology of the e-banking system is not fully integrated) and what the proposed solution is (to implement a faster, new single system). Students then listen and answer the questions.

2 61▷ Students listen again and note down phrases. Ask students to compare their answers with a partner. They can then work together to add any similar phrases.

3 Students work in pairs and choose one of the topics. Allow time for them to discuss their topic and make notes to help them with their introduction to a briefing. Encourage them to use phrases from **2** in their briefing. When they are ready, ask pairs to present their introductions to the class.

Feedback focus

After each presentation, ask the class the following questions, or write them on the board.
- *Did you feel involved?*
- *How did you feel about their approach (resentment / anxiety / solidarity / something else)?*

4 62▷ Students listen and answer the questions.

Watch out! You might want to check that students understand the following words in the questions and the audio.

dismissive = showing that you do not believe a person or thing to be important or worth considering

reassuring = making you feel less worried or uncertain about something

recoup = to get back an amount of money that you have spent or lost

Answers
1 They are concerned about timing and workload, getting the support to organize training for their teams, whether customers will be affected badly during the process, whether they will be asked to contribute from budgets.
2 He is reassuring. He acknowledges their concerns appropriately and explains how they will be dealt with. Where the solutions are less good, he focuses on the positive side, and tries to encourage them to do the same.

5 62▷ Before they listen again, ask students to read the incomplete sentences. Ask them to discuss in pairs how they think the sentences could be completed. Then play the audio and ask them to complete the sentences.

Answers
1 I'm slightly concerned about
2 I wonder if you have any information
3 I understand your concerns
4 I think we need to look at
5 As I understand it
6 I'm not very happy about
7 Can you give us an assurance that
8 That's a valid point
9 I really don't see this as a problem
10 My understanding is
11 I also have some concerns about
12 What assurances can you give us
13 I have some reservations about
14 Are there any guarantees that
15 I understand where you're coming from
16 Apparently
17 let's give this a chance to work

6 Students match the phrases to the categories.

Answers
a 1, 6, 11, 13
b 2, 7, 12, 14
c 3, 4, 8, 9, 15, 17
d 5, 10, 16

» If students need more practice, go to **Practice file 10** on page 120 of the **Student's Book**.

7 Students work in pairs and read the situations. Before they begin their discussion, ask them to brainstorm any potential problems relating to each situation and any additional positive points. Then ask them to take on A and B roles, and discuss the situations. Encourage them to use the phrases from **5**.

8 Each student should think of a possible change in their company. They then take turns to explain the change, whilst the other student takes notes and lists any concerns.

Pre-work students

As a class, brainstorm changes that could be made at the students' college / university. Use the following ideas if necessary.
- Increase / introduce tuition fees so that college / university facilities can be improved.
- Force students who miss more than four classes in one subject to leave the college / university.
- Abolish coursework – exams will form 100% of assessment.
- Introduce a strict fining system on overdue library books.

Students then work in pairs and choose one of the ideas. They then prepare to present it to another pair. Then put two pairs together. Students should take notes and then make a list of concerns when listening to the other pair. They can then move on to activity **9** using these notes.

9 Students now tell each other about the concerns they listed in **8**, using phrases from **5**. Their partner should respond to the concerns.

Feedback focus

Circulate and make a note of any errors and any good use of the phrases from **5**. Give positive feedback to students who used phrases from **5** appropriately and correct any mistakes if necessary. Then ask students if their partner responded appropriately to their concerns and if not, how they could improve.

ⓘ Refer students to the **Interactive Workbook Email** and **Phrasebank** sections for further study.

Language at work

1 Students look at the sentences and underline the passive forms.

Answers
1 was taken
2 has been agreed
3 've been given
4 will be coordinated, 'll be briefed
5 is proposed
6 's been suggested, will be recouped
7 've been told, need to be shared around
8 has already been made.

2 Students work in pairs and discuss the questions

Answers
1 was taken = past simple passive
has been agreed = present perfect passive
've been given = present perfect passive
will be coordinated / 'll be briefed = future passive
is proposed = present simple passive
's been suggested / will be recouped = present perfect passive / future passive
've been told / need to be shared around = present perfect passive / present simple passive (infinitive)
has already been made = present perfect passive
2 Answers will vary, although the following are likely.
  a all, but especially 4 and 5
  b 3
  c 4
  d 1, 2, 5, 6, 7, 8

3 Students look at the sentences and answer the questions.

Answers
1 b
2 *me* in the active sentence becomes *I* in the passive – it becomes the subject of the passive sentence
3 no, because *suggest* does not take an indirect object, so *I* cannot be the subject here

» Refer students to the **Language Reference** section on page 132 of the **Student's Book** for more information.

4 Students work in pairs. They take turns to use the verbs to report the information in the sentences.

Possible answers
1 I / we have been informed that …
2 It has been agreed that we should cut back on …
3 It has been proposed that the department is / be restructured …
4 We have been instructed by Head Office to reduce our spending by 5%.
5 It has been decided that bonuses will be paid …
6 We've been persuaded to take part in a new system trial.

Extension
Ask students to choose one of the ideas in **4** and write an email to their staff about it.

» If students need more practice, go to **Practice file 10** on page 121 of the **Student's Book**.

5 Students work in pairs and turn to the *File*. Allow time for them to read the memo. Ask them to underline the sections of the memo that would need to be depersonalized in a briefing meeting. Students should then think about how they would rephrase those sections in a briefing meeting. The following sections are most likely to need rephrasing.
  * *We have approved …*
  * *All members of staff at team leader grade and below will have to spend a minimum …*
  * *We want all individuals to set up and schedule … / agree with their line manager …*
  * *We will not allow extra time for work you don't complete.*
  * *We expect that staff will cover for absent colleagues.*
Then ask pairs to give a short briefing to the rest of the class, rephrasing information where necessary.

Extension
Ask students to work in pairs and use the memo to help them write a briefing for staff in email format, rephrasing where necessary. Students then swap emails with another pair and write an email in reply, expressing their concerns. Pairs then swap emails again and write a response, dealing with the concerns.

Feedback focus
Before the students give their briefings to the class, divide the students into two groups. Group A should listen and comment on how willing they think staff would be to participate in the job-shadowing initiative, based on the way the information is presented. Group B should listen and note down any correct and incorrect use of reporting verbs (*tell, inform, agree, decide*, etc.). After each briefing, elicit comments from the two groups.

Practically speaking

1 Students work in pairs and answer the questions.

Answers
Answers will vary.

2 63▷ Students listen to the conversations and answer the questions.

Answers

Conversation 1: They are discussing a new assessment system. They are probably chatting over coffee after a meeting.

Conversation 2: They are talking about one of the speaker's experiences in Kenya, and why they liked it. It could be part of an appraisal meeting between a manager and an employee, or it may be colleagues talking.

Conversation 3: They are talking about dealing with attitudes and using a team-building weekend as an example. They could be at a meeting bringing together people from different departments of a big company.

3 63▷ Students read the extracts. Before they listen again, ask them to see if they can complete the sentences. They can then listen again and check their ideas.

Answers
1 to be honest with you
2 personally speaking
3 I have to say
4 to tell you the truth
5 To be perfectly honest
6 Honestly
7 Personally
8 I look at it like this
9 my attitude is

» Refer students to the **Useful phrases** section on page 135 of the **Student's Book** for extension and revision.

4 Students work in pairs and answer the questions.

Answers
1 In each case, the speaker's opinion follows. The phrases are used to let the listener know that you are expressing a personal opinion, or revealing your true thoughts. Sometimes they soften the tone, or indicate that a negative response will follow.
2 Speaker A uses the following phrases.
What did you think of ...?
Such as?
You're not in favour of ...?
It must have been challenging at times?
How does it feel to be back at the centre of things?
I heard some people thought it was a waste of time.
What do you mean?
So ...?

5 Students work in pairs. Ask them to decide who is A, and who is B for each situation. Allow time for them to read the situations and form an opinion about the details. When they are ready, they should take turns to ask for and give their personal views.

Feedback focus

When students have finished, write the following questions on the board.
- *Did you have a chance to express your opinion?*
- *Were you prompted appropriately?*
- *How easy was it to ask questions to find out your partner's opinion?*
- *Did you use many of the phrases from 3?*

Elicit answers to the questions from the whole class and discuss any ways in which they could improve.

Key word

Students read the sentences and answer the questions.
Answers: a In sentence 1 *even* emphasizes that something hasn't happened. In sentence 3 *even* emphasizes a comparison; b In sentence 2 *even* can be replaced by *nevertheless*. In sentence 4 *even if* can be replaced by *despite the fact that*.

Extra activity

Ask students to work in groups of three. Write some topics on individual cards, making sure they will be suitable for your group. For example:
- the state of the economy in your country
- the last film you saw / book you read
- the royal family in the UK
- the future of your company / college / university
- your first boss / your first English teacher
- your best / worst assignment
- your dream job

Give each group a set of cards, face down. Students then take turns to take a card and begin talking about the topic. The other students should listen, and ask questions to prompt the speaker to give their opinions. They can then also express their own opinions.

ⓘ Refer students to the **Interactive Workbook Exercises and Tests** for revision.

Case study

Background

This *Case study* looks at the success of a Czech cosmetics company, Ryor, through the leadership qualities of its owner, Eva Štěpánková. It focuses on four specific decisions that she took, all of which resulted in improvements for her company. Students discuss the leadership qualities she displayed, and how she overcame various problems. In the *Task* they discuss what decisions are needed to help a company with similar problems to Ryor.

Allow a few minutes for students to read the company profile of Ryor and the information about Eva Štěpánková. Be ready to answer any questions students may have about vocabulary.

Discussion

1, 2, 3 Students can discuss the questions in pairs, before feeding back to the rest of the class.

Possible answers

1 passion, commitment, conviction, adaptability, decisiveness
2 She has remained committed to her product and company, even when times were difficult, because she was convinced that the products were good enough to keep the company alive. This led to her taking the risk of borrowing money to build a new factory, continuing despite stiff competition from hypermarkets, rejecting designs she wasn't happy with, and moving production back to the Czech Republic from Slovakia.
3 Answers will vary. Students might discuss the fact that good leaders usually have a loyal team of managers who implement their ideas. It could therefore be argued that it's possible to be successful without good people management skills, however the managers themselves would still need to be 'managed' effectively.

Task

1 Students read about Maximum Cocoa. You might want to ask them to brainstorm solutions to each of the problems at this stage.

2 Students work in groups of four. They then turn to the *Files* in their pairs and prepare their briefings. Refer students to the *Key expressions* in the *Business communication skills* section to help them with the preparation.

3 Students now join with the other pair in their group. They then have two meetings. Pairs take turns to give their briefing and respond to concerns. The other pair should take notes and then express their concerns.

One-to-one

Your student can read the *Background*, and then you can do the *Discussion* questions together. In the *Task* use roles A and C only, and carry out the meetings as described.

Feedback focus

Focus on the language that students use during the meetings. Give feedback on their use of passive forms and on the phrases they use to express and respond to concerns. Put any incorrect sentences on the board and ask the class to correct the mistakes.

Extra activity

Ask students to explain their chosen solution in an email addressed to *All staff*. Students can then exchange emails and respond to each other, raising any concerns. The first student can then write a follow-up email to provide assurances. You can then collect all the emails and provide feedback in the following lesson. Focus on common errors. You could also prepare a worksheet with a list of sentences from their emails. Students can then work in pairs to correct the mistakes.

» Unit 10 **Progress test** and **Speaking test**, pages 114–115.

11 | Values

Unit content

By the end of this unit, students will be able to
- talk about values
- reach an agreement
- use inversion for emphasis
- raise a difficult point.

Context

A company's values provide guidelines that can inform company decisions and activities. There is a growing trend in the business world not only to make the values of a company explicit to all staff, but also to use these values as a PR device. By publicizing their values, companies underline their corporate aims and help to build up trust amongst their customers.

Publicly-stated values are used to inform procedures and behaviour at all levels of the company. Indeed, many staff are now given training relating specifically to these values. Appraisal systems can also include adherence to company values as part of the performance objectives. Basing these measures on publicized values could be seen to strengthen the foundations of a company.

In the first part of this unit, students look at the language used to describe company values. They also have the opportunity to discuss what factors might affect public perception of these values. Students then move on to focus on the language used in negotiations and how to use inversion to emphasize a message. The *Case study* focuses on an organization that helps companies to reduce and offset carbon emissions. Students then negotiate an environmental plan for a company.

Starting point

1 Ask students to work in pairs to come up with a definition of the term *values* (it's important this is in the plural).

> **Possible answers**
> *values* = beliefs about what is right and wrong and what is important in life

Watch out! Students may mention the following meaning.
value = how much something is worth in money
This is also correct, but this is not the focus of the unit. You might like to discuss the connection between this definition and the definition of *values* (i.e. both are related to the importance you place on something).

2, 3 As a lead-in to these questions, elicit what the values of a company could include. You could find out the values of a well-known company by researching on the Internet before the lesson. Then write the values on the board and ask students to explain what they think each value means in practice (e.g. offering excellent customer service, building good relationships with clients, employees, and wider society).

Students can then discuss questions **2** and **3** in pairs.

> **Possible answers**
> **2** A company needs values so that it has a set of rules / rationale on which to base its decisions. It will also be able to use these values as a PR tool. Without clear values, companies are not able to be consistent; staff will be unable to perform effectively, and customers may be confused.
> **3** Answers will vary.

Working with words

1 Students work in small groups or pairs and discuss the questions. You could introduce a competitive element to the first question, giving points to each group for correct answers.

> **Answers**
> **1** Ikea = Sweden, Starbucks = USA, Skoda = former Czechoslovakia, now owned by German company VW, Microsoft = USA, Tata = India, Shell = UK / Holland, Gap = USA, Nestlé = Switzerland
> **2** Answers will vary. Positive associations will relate to what your students know about employee welfare in these companies, the health and safety precautions, how they are involved in communities, etc. Negative associations will relate to any stories they know about companies that treat their employees badly, etc.

2 Students read the values statements and answer the questions. Ask them to compare their ideas with a partner. They then turn to the *File* to check their ideas for the first question.

> **Possible answers**
> 1 The first statement is from Microsoft and the second is from Tata.
> 2 Similarities = integrity, excellence, and responsibility are present in both statements.
>   Differences = the second statement focuses more on social aspects than the first, particularly in connection with the idea of responsibility, e.g. it refers to the importance of caring, showing tolerance and understanding, and supporting communities, whereas the first statement focuses more on accountability.
> 3 Answers will vary. Discussions could include the fact that the second statement conveys a more collectivist attitude, whereby the well-being of the entire community is considered important, not just the well-being of the clients. This tends to be a more prevalent attitude in Eastern cultures, whilst the more individualistic messages in the first statement are linked to Western cultures.

Watch out! Students may not be familiar with Tata and its activities. It is an international business group based in India with operations in seven business sectors. If students wish to find out more about it, direct them to the website. www.tata.com

3 Students match the phrases.

> **Answers**
> 1 e 2 g 3 d 4 b 5 f 6 c 7 h 8 a

4 Students work in pairs. They read the statements again and discuss them in relation to their own company.

Extension

Students might not know what the values of their company are – ask them to research this for the next lesson.

Pre-work learners

Ask students to look at the two company statements and decide which company they would prefer to work for, based on the values statement. Encourage them to give reasons.

5 Students work in pairs and choose a company from **1** or another well-known company. They then write a values statement for their chosen company, using vocabulary from **3**. The rest of the class guess the organization from the statement.

Extension

Ask students to research the values of their chosen company for homework so that they can compare them with the statement they wrote in class. They can probably find information on this on the company's website. Ask them to be prepared to share their findings in the next lesson.

6 64▷ Before they listen, ask students to look back at the companies in **1** and to focus on the American companies. Ask students what their attitudes are to these American companies (positive / negative) and why. Students then listen and answer the questions.

> **Answers**
> 1 Recent American foreign policy is thought to be controversial, there have been several corporate financial scandals, it has a poor environmental record, it has lost its moral authority.
> 2 Fewer people are buying American brands.
> 3 Other economic factors could be the reason and European brands are also suffering from lower sales.

7 Students match the adverb + adjective combinations to the statements.

> **Answers**
> 1 increasingly difficult
> 2 relatively stable
> 3 significantly different
> 4 unexpectedly rapid
> 5 potentially disastrous
> 6 appreciably more hostile
> 7 profoundly worrying
> 8 irretrievably damaging

8 Students decide which adverbs in **7** could be replaced, keeping the same meaning.

> **Answers**
> *noticeably* = could replace *significantly / appreciably*
> *comparatively* = could replace *relatively*
> *considerably* = could replace *significantly / appreciably*
> *surprisingly* = could replace *unexpectedly*

>> If students need more practice, go to **Practice file 11** on page 122 of the **Student's Book**.

9 Students work in pairs. Allow time for them to read their *Files* and prepare their explanation. They then take turns to explain the situations using vocabulary from **7**.

Watch out! Before they read the *Files*, you might want to check that students understand the following.
abide by = to accept and act according to a law or a rule
robust = strong; able to survive; being used a lot and not likely to break

Extension

Ask students to write a formal email from the head of PR to senior managers in the company they focused on in **9**, summarizing the situation.

10 Students work in pairs and prepare a statement. Remind them to focus on what's important for a new employee and encourage them to use vocabulary from this section. When they are ready, ask each pair to read out their statement to the rest of the class.

Pre-work learners

Students work in pairs and choose either Company X or Company Y from **9**. Ask them to think about the core values that the company might have, based on the information in the *File*. Then ask them to prepare a short values statement for the company.

Feedback focus

When the students read out their statements, divide the rest of the class into two groups. Group A should note any good use of language, or any possible errors. Group B should listen and decide if they would like to work for that company. Discuss the feedback as a class after each statement.

ⓘ Refer students to the **Interactive Workbook Glossary** for further study.

Business communication skills

1 As a lead-in to this section, ask students to think of all the cosmetics companies they know (e.g. L'Oréal, Bodyshop, Avon, Estée Lauder, etc.). Find out which products your students use and if they have had any bad experiences with any cosmetic products. Then ask students to read the *Context* about Alanas Pharma. They can then read the email to find out about the problem and the possible consequences.

> **Answers**
> The problem is that the new factory in South Korea can't meet demands.
> The company won't be able to meet its deadlines. Laura and Andrew may not have enough stock for the launch in Berlin.

2 65▷ Students listen and then discuss the questions.

Watch out! Before they read, you might want to check that students understand the following.
backlog (of work) = a quantity of work that should have been done already, but has not yet been done
pushy = trying hard to get what you want in a way that seems rude

> **Answers**
> 1 The factory has had too many orders and therefore can't meet the deadline.
> 2 Laura
> 3 If they don't have the product for the launch, the launch cannot take place. If the product launch is delayed, this may cause irreversible damage to the company's sales / reputation, etc.

3 Students categorize the phrases.

> **Answers**
> 1 d, f
> 2 b
> 3 a, c, e, g

4 66▷ Students listen and then discuss the questions in pairs.

> **Answers**
> 1 Publicizing products, but supplying them to customers after the exhibition; speeding up delivery so that products arrive on the last day and then have the launch party on the last day; use a different (local) supplier; use just samples instead.
> 2 Andrew is negative about all suggestions, except his own (use a different supplier); Laura is more willing to consider the other suggestions.
> 3 Answers will vary.

5 66▷ Students listen again and complete the phrases.

> **Answers**
> 1 out of   6 stay firm
> 2 just won't   7 make do
> 3 consider   8 possibly do
> 4 the question   9 say to doing
> 5 to budge   10 be willing

6 Students look at the phrases in **5** and answer the questions.

> **Answers**
> a 3, 7, 9
> b 1, 2, 5, 6, 8
> c 4, 10
> d 7

7 67▷ Students listen to the final part of the conference call and answer the question.

> **Answers**
> 1 Answers will vary, but probably the answer is 'yes'. Accepting the idea of 500 samples of each cream being sent directly to Berlin is a good compromise. However, Andrew is least likely to be happy.

8 67▷ Students listen again and note down phrases for reaching an agreement.

> **Answers**
> That sounds feasible.
> Are we all agreed?
> Yes, I'll go along with that.

Extension activity

Write the following tips for negotiating on the board. Ask students to work in groups and decide if they think the tips are true or false, and why. Elicit their ideas, encouraging them to give reasons.
   1 *Always start high with your prices and only reduce them if necessary.*
   2 *Don't allow the other person to talk much.*
   3 *Express your emotions – if you feel angry, show it.*
   4 *Make the first move.*

You can then discuss the following suggested answers with the whole class.
   1 True: this gives room for negotiation and helps both sides feel that they have benefited.
   2 False: let the other person talk; you should listen – this will give you more information and allow you to react in a way that will get you what you want.
   3 False: stay calm and rational throughout to convey a professional image and help you get what you want.
   4 False: let the other person set the agenda and then react, e.g. if they ask you how much you will charge for a service, ask them how much they would pay – this usually means you will get a higher amount.

9 Students work in pairs. Allow time for them to read their *Files*. Refer them to the *Key expressions* and encourage them to think of arguments to support their position. When they are ready, ask them to discuss the situation and find a solution.

Feedback focus

Monitor and give feedback on the use of phrases from the *Key expressions*. After their discussions, ask each pair to tell the class who benefited most from their solution and why.

>> If students need more practice, go to **Practice file 11** on page 122 of the **Student's Book**.

10 Students work in pairs. Ask them first to think of a problem or change they'd like to make at work. They should then discuss their ideas and makes notes on how to present their proposal. They then swap their notes with another pair, read those notes, and think about their objections to the other pair's proposal.

Pre-work learners

Write the following changes on the board. Ask pairs to choose one of them or to come up with their own idea. They should then prepare their proposal, thinking about how the change would affect students / teachers.
   • *All subjects will be taught in English.*
   • *One-to-one lessons will be introduced and every student should have one per week.*
   • *Students will negotiate every syllabus with the teacher in the first lesson.*

11 Pairs join to form groups of four. They then discuss each proposal and negotiate a solution.

Culture question

Students can discuss the questions in pairs before feeding back to the rest of the class. Answers will vary, but discussions may focus on the fact that in some cultures group harmony takes precedence over individual performance and therefore the negotiating style is likely to be influenced by this. These cultures are referred to as *collectivist* (e.g. Japan, Indonesia, Venezuela).

ⓘ Refer students to the **Interactive Workbook Email** and **Phrasebank** sections for further study.

Language at work

1 Students compare the sentences and answer the questions.

Alternative

If students find this difficult, elicit standard word order in English for statements and questions. Write the following examples on the board to clarify.
*Statements = **subject** then <u>verb</u>, e.g. **One of our contractors** <u>has</u> just trebled their order.*

*Questions = <u>verb</u> then **subject**, e.g. <u>Has</u> **one of our contractors** just trebled their order?*
Then ask them to look again at the sentences in **1** and answer the questions.

Answers
1 Subject / verb word order. Inversion gives the sentences in B the same form as a question: the subject, *One of our contractors*, changes places with the auxiliary verb, *has*.
2 The first and second in B.
3 The third sentences in A and B are both conditionals.
4 To emphasize something and / or in a more formal context.

» Refer students to the **Language Reference** section on page 132 of the **Student's Book** for more information.

2 Students read the text, <u>underline</u> the sentences that use inversion, and try to rewrite them. They can then compare their answers with a partner.

Possible answers
Not only are staff required = Staff are required to formally request … and …
Under no circumstances will staff be paid overtime = Staff will not be paid overtime under any circumstances …
Were a member of staff to take on … = If a member of staff took on …

3 Students rewrite the sentences using an inversion.

Answers
1 At no time will we be …
2 Were you to join the union, …
3 Under no circumstances will we negotiate …
4 Had we known about the consequences, we wouldn't …
5 Not only did you ask us to cut costs, but you also asked us to …

» If students need more practice, go to **Practice file 11** on page 123 of the **Student's Book**.

4 As a lead-in, ask students the following questions.
- What health and safety rules are there at your place of work / study?
- Are they sufficient?
- Would it be a good idea to tighten the rules?
- Why / Why not?

Then ask them to work in pairs and create a formal statement, using ideas from the list or their own ideas. Ask them to include inversion where possible. When they are ready, ask each pair to make their announcement to the rest of the class.

Possible answers
Had the fire doors been kept closed as they should be, we would have had a more realistic practice during last week's drill.
Under no circumstances can any employee or student drive or cycle on company premises.
At no time can any hot food or drink be taken into the conference hall.
Were employees to follow the advice about not carrying heavy loads, we wouldn't have had so many employees with back problems.

Pre-work learners

Ask students to imagine that they are the staff / management of their school or college. They should work in pairs to prepare an announcement on any health and safety regulations that students have recently been ignoring.

Feedback focus

Monitor for correct use of inversion and correct intonation / word stress. Give feedback where necessary.

Extra activity

Students work in groups. Write the following rules / situations on the board. Tell students that they are flight attendants and they need to make three announcements to passengers about 1–3. They also need to speak to one of the passengers about the situation in 4. Ask them to prepare what they would say, using inversion where possible. See suggested answers in brackets.

1 *Drink lots of water and avoid drinking too much coffee and alcohol.* (Not only should you try to drink lots of water during the flight, but you should also avoid drinking too much coffee or alcohol.)
2 *No sharp instruments (e.g. knives) in hand luggage.* (Under no circumstances are sharp instruments allowed to be brought onto the plane in hand luggage.)
3 *No smoking.* (At no time are you permitted to smoke during the flight.)
4 *Situation = a passenger with medication was not allowed to take it onto the plane because he didn't show you a letter from his doctor. He is now complaining about this.* (Had I seen your letter from the doctor, I would have allowed you to bring your medication on board.)

Practically speaking

1 **68**▷ As a lead-in, write the following situations and questions on the board. Ask students to discuss them in pairs.

- *Shared an office with a noisy / untidy colleague.*
- *Had a colleague who was always late for meetings with you.*
- *Received bad quality work from a colleague.*

1 *Have you experienced any of these situations?*
2 *Did you say anything about it to the person involved? If you did, what did you say and was it effective? If not, why not and what happened?*

Students then listen and answer the questions.

> **Possible answers**
> 1 extract 1: she speaks very loudly on the phone
>   extract 2: he must dress more smartly for the situation that's coming up
>   extract 3: the report isn't good enough
>   extract 4: she is not happy with the package that goes with the new job (i.e. salary, etc)
>   extract 5: they haven't given enough information
> 2 In all extracts, the person raising the point sounds apologetic and respectful, and is quite careful with their choice of words. The other people respond in different ways: in 1, she is understanding and apologetic; in 2, he is a bit offended and rather defensive; in 3, she is a bit upset; in 4, they seem open to discussion; in 5 he is very defensive.

2 **68**▷ Students listen again and complete the sentences.

> **Answers**
> 1 I don't mean to sound rude
> 2 this is a bit delicate, don't take offence
> 3 please don't take this the wrong way, the thing is …
> 4 quite sure how to put this
> 5 respect, I have to say that, The fact is

3 Students read the phrases and then rewrite them to make them less direct.

> **Possible answers**
> 1 Look, this is a bit delicate. Please don't take offence, but I'm afraid your design isn't very good. I was thinking I could ask someone else to do it instead. What do you think?
> 2 I'm sorry, I don't mean to sound rude, but do you think you could try to control your laugh a bit? It's a bit loud, and it might be disturbing some of the others.

> 3 Listen, we'd be delighted if you took on this job, don't get us wrong. But, you see, the thing is, I have to say that the price really does seem rather high. I'm afraid we just wouldn't be able to pay quite that much.
> 4 Oh, have you got a minute? Well, you see, the things is, I know you've put in an awful lot of effort and have really tried hard. But, well, it's just that over the last year your performance hasn't really improved very much. And it's got to the point that we won't be able to give you an increase in pay until there are some significant improvements.
> 5 I don't mean to sound rude but, well, I was wondering if I could ask you not to leave dirty mugs around? Do you think you could put them in the kitchen, and perhaps even wash them up?

Extension

Ask students to work in pairs and to look at their rewritten sentences in **3**. They should think of a suitable response to each one (see possible ideas below). Then ask them to practise the dialogues using these ideas.

1 Well, actually, I'd rather have another go. May I? / Sure. Who do you have in mind? / Oh, really. What exactly don't you like about it?
2 I'm sorry. I didn't realize. / I have got quite a loud laugh. Sorry. / Oh, it's this really funny email. I'll forward it to you.
3 How much can you pay? / Well, then I'm sorry. We can't do it.
4 What specifically do I need to do? / That's strange. I've been getting really positive feedback recently.
5 Oh, sure. Sorry. / Well, actually, they're not mine. / I suppose so. Is someone else going to throw away the pizza boxes?

» Refer students to the **Useful phrases** section on page 135 of the **Student's Book** for extension and revision.

4 Students work in pairs and read the situations. They then take turns to raise the difficult points. The other student should respond appropriately.

Feedback focus

Circulate and monitor students' use of language. You should also check that they're using polite intonation. Provide feedback at the end of the task.

Key word

Students read the phrases and match each to the appropriate meaning of *mean*.
Answers: 1 e, 2 c, 3 a, 4 d, 5 b

ⓘ Refer students to the **Interactive Workbook Exercises and Tests** for revision.

Case study

Background

This *Case study* focuses on a company that helps other companies to offset or reduce their carbon emissions. It also encourages discussion of offsetting versus reduction. In the *Discussion* section, students discuss their own thoughts on these issues. The *Task* then allows students to consider how a mobile phone company can best reduce its carbon footprint.

Allow time for students to read the *Company profile*, the glossary, and the texts. Be prepared to answer any questions they may have about vocabulary.

Discussion

1, 2, 3 Students discuss the questions in pairs, before feeding back to the rest of the class.

Answers
1 Answers will vary.
2 Companies use environmental strategies to let the public know that they are conducting their business with respect for the environment. This is likely to enhance their reputation.
3 Answers will vary.

Extension

Ask students if they have ever calculated their own carbon footprint. Tell them that several websites will do this for you if you type in your data, e.g. daily commute, flights per year, electricity consumption, recycling habits, etc. Ask students to calculate their carbon footprint for homework. Students can compare their results in the next lesson.

Task

1 As a lead-in, ask students what sources of carbon emission might be relevant to a mobile phone company. Students then read about Corutel and compare their ideas.

2 Students work in groups of four. Each pair within the group should read their notes and prepare for the meeting. Be ready to help with vocabulary where necessary.

3 Students now join the other pair and have the meeting. Encourage them to compromise where necessary. Refer them to phrases for negotiating in the *Business communication skills* section if they need more support. When the meeting is finished, they should work together to write up their action plan.

One-to-one

Read the information in the *Background* and go through the questions in the *Discussion* together. In the *Task* the student should be Student A and you should be Student C. Read your notes and have the meeting.

Feedback focus

Ask students to comment on how their group members behaved during the negotiation. Were they willing to negotiate / compromise? Were they polite? Was the outcome acceptable to all participants?

Extra activity

Ask students to think about their own place of work or study. What activities currently cause high carbon emissions and what could be done to reduce these? Ask students to draft a proposal focusing on key areas, e.g. electricity, recycling, transport.

» Unit 11 **Progress test** and **Speaking test**, pages 116–117.

12 | Persuasion

Unit content

By the end of this unit, students will be able to
- talk about how we are persuaded and influenced
- sell an idea
- use discourse markers
- give and respond to compliments.

Context

Over two thousand years ago, the Greek philosopher, Aristotle, defined persuasion as the ability to convince others to adopt your ideas. Today it's an increasingly important concept, and one your students will relate to on several levels. As consumers they will be constantly subjected to persuasive messages through advertising. They are also likely to have observed politicians using highly-refined persuasive techniques. They will have had to use persuasive techniques themselves, both in their working lives and in their personal relationships. They may have had to sell their company's service / products to customers, and may have even been involved in developing persuasive publicity for their company.

Effective persuasive techniques are becoming more and more important in the business world, for both individuals and for companies. A person's powers of persuasion can often contribute directly to their ability to achieve goals. Someone with strong persuasive techniques can speak logically, fluently, and confidently, and if they are effective, they are convincing and trustworthy, and understand the needs and motivations of others. This makes it far easier for them to get what they want out of a situation.

The first part of this unit looks at persuasion in advertising, and how techniques vary according to the culture of the target market. Students then focus on the language for selling an idea and how to use spoken discourse markers to punctuate their speech. The *Case study* enables students to examine a company's plans for expanding into a new market. They then have the opportunity to conduct a SWOT analysis and to give a presentation to the company stakeholders.

Starting point

1, 2 As a lead-in, ask students to brainstorm a list of decisions they have to make (both in their personal lives and their working lives), e.g. where to go on holiday, buying a car, buying gadgets, buying clothes, voting, where to advertise, office location, etc. Write their ideas on the board. Students can then work in pairs to discuss the questions, before feeding back to the rest of the class.

> **Answers**
> Answers will vary.

Extension

Write the following words on the board.
- *children*
- *teenagers*
- *adults*
- *old people*

Then write the following questions on the board and ask students to discuss them in pairs.
- *Which of these groups would be most easily persuaded / influenced? Why?*
- *Which age group would be the hardest to persuade / influence? Why?*
- *Does a person's personality affect how easily they are persuaded? Why? Give examples.*
- *Does the amount of money a person has affect how easily they are persuaded / influenced? Give examples.*

Working with words

1 As a lead-in, elicit different kinds of advertising, e.g. word-of mouth, posters, radio / TV commercials, leaflets, etc. Students then work in pairs and discuss the question, before reading the text to compare their answers.

> **Answers**
> Advertisers generate demand for products / services using images and messages. They exploit consumers' desires to belong and to gain social status.

Watch out! Before they read, you might want to check that students understand the following.
conform = to behave and think in the same way as most other people in a group or society

2 Students work in pairs and think of examples of adverts for each category. They can then discuss their examples as a class.

3 Students make phrases and then match them to the definitions.

Answers
1 to promote consumption of
2 to reinforce an association between
3 to generate a demand for
4 to tailor something towards a need
5 to appeal to
6 to hold out for
7 to pick up on
8 to tap into
9 to live up to
10 to buy into
11 to be taken in by
12 to play on
13 to put across

Pronunciation

Write the following phrases on the board and ask students to identify any weak forms, i.e. schwas /ə/ (see <u>underlined</u> sections for the answers). Note that the final prepositions in these phrases (*to, for*) will be weak when used in full sentences.

reinforce <u>an</u> <u>a</u>ssociation between
tail<u>o</u>r something t<u>o</u>wards <u>a</u> need

Then ask them to look at the other phrases in **3**. Students should work in pairs and <u>underline</u> the weak forms in these phrases.

   Answers: *pr<u>o</u>mote the consump<u>ti</u>on <u>of</u>; gen<u>e</u>rate <u>a</u> demand f<u>or</u>; hold out f<u>or</u>; <u>a</u>ppeal t<u>o</u>; live up t<u>o</u>; play on; be tak<u>e</u>n in by; buy int<u>o</u>; pick up on; put <u>a</u>cross; tap int<u>o</u>.*

4 Students work in pairs and look at the advertisements. They then use vocabulary from **3** to discuss them.

Answers
1 appeals to adults wanting a tempting dessert, taps into concerns about health
2 appeals to young people, generates the demand for colourful and fashionable clothes, and taps into the fear of being left out
3 appeals to adults who wish to be seen as sophisticated and glamorous, picks up on the idea of 'his' and 'hers' watches

Alternative

If students find this difficult, write the following phrases on the board.
This is trying to …
This image is aiming to …
I think an advert like this would …
Then ask them to look at the advertisements and to try to complete the sentences.

Extension

Bring in a selection of magazine adverts (or ask students to bring them to the next lesson). Give each pair one advert to discuss (they shouldn't show them to any other students). When they're ready, collect all the adverts / pictures, and stick them up around the room. Pairs then take turns to explain the message behind their advert to the rest of the class without saying which product it is. The others have to guess.

5 69▷ Students listen and answer the questions.

Watch out! Before they listen, you might want to check that students understand the following.
to get on = to be successful in your career
to keep up with = to move, make progress, or increase at the same rate as somebody / something else
aspirational = wanting to achieve success in your career, and / or to improve your social status and standard of living
imperative = a thing that is very important and needs immediate attention or action

Answers
1 Because Americans are very competitive, advertisers have to focus on persuading customers how they will benefit from the product in terms of health, social status, youthfulness etc.
2 Denmark is less competitive, and the Danes are far less materialistic and showy than the Americans, therefore fewer luxury items are sold. Russia and China haven't had the choice of many products until recently, so advertisers focus more on pointing out the main product facts and features.

Extra activity

Ask students to work in pairs and discuss what could be said about advertising in their culture(s). They should then share their ideas with the rest of the class.

Extension

Find out from your students what adverts are currently popular or high profile in their country. Write a list of examples from students on the board. Then ask students to describe their reactions to them. Do they think these adverts would be effective in Russia, China, Denmark, or America?

6 Students complete the sentences.

Watch out! You might want to check that students understand the following.

USP = a Unique Selling Proposition – a statement that identifies what makes a person, product, or organization different from competitors.

> **Answers**
> 1 exploitative
> 2 USP
> 3 aspirational
> 4 materialistic
> 5 motivational
> 6 status anxiety
> 7 market penetration
> 8 consumer profile

Extra activity

Draw the following table on the board. Ask students to copy it into their notebooks. They should then complete the table in pairs. Ask them to identify the word stress.

Verb	Noun	Adjective
		exploitative
		motivational
		aspirational

> **Answers**
>
> | Verb | Noun | Adjective |
> |------|------|-----------|
> | exploit | (2) exploitation; exploit(s) | exploitative |
> | motivate | motivation | motivational |
> | aspire (to) | aspiration | aspirational |

When students have checked their answers as a class, ask them to work in pairs and formulate sentences using the words.

Watch out! Note that *exploit* (a brave, exciting, or interesting act, often used in the plural) is very different from *exploitation* (a situation in which somebody treats somebody else in an unfair way, especially in order to make money from their work).

>> If students need more practice, go to **Practice file 12** on page 124 of the **Student's Book**.

7 Students work in pairs and discuss the questions.

>> Refer students to the **Interactive Workbook Glossary** for further study.

Pre-work students

Students can describe a company they know well. Alternatively ask students to do some research for the next lesson. They should choose one company, and find out how it markets itself. Does it have different adverts in different countries? Ask them to bring examples to the next lesson, and to be prepared to talk briefly about what they found.

Feedback focus

Allow the discussion to flow freely. Give positive feedback to students who make effective use of the vocabulary from this section.

Business communication skills

1 Students read the *Context* about Ranjit Shetty. They then work in pairs and discuss the questions.

> **Possible answers**
> 1 reach a wider customer base, keep products up-to-date, keep customers happy and maintain success
> 2 very, otherwise they won't be willing to make them work

2 70–73 ▷ Students listen and answer the questions.

> **Answers**
> 1 In the long term the business will dry up and the company might go bankrupt.
> 2 More companies invest in multimedia advertising now than in print advertising; this will also help them gain new customers and get a higher position in the market.
> 3 He has appointed an in-house specialist; that person's assistant will take over his work; they have external investment for the plan and have employed an outside consultant.
> 4 because they are acting ahead of time

Watch out! Before they listen, you might want to check that students understand the following.

genuine = real; exactly what it appears to be; not artificial

ring alarm bells = to cause people to start to feel worried and suspicious

brutally = violently and cruelly

solely = only; not involving somebody / something else

guru = a person who is an expert on a particular subject or who is very good at doing something

3 70–73 ▷ Students listen again and answer the questions. They can then compare their answers in pairs before feeding back to the rest of the class.

> **Answers**
> 1 assertive, upbeat, enthusiastic
> 2 invites audience members to speak, uses rhetorical questions, addresses the audience directly, uses word stress and intonation, shocks the audience (when talking about the competition), uses visuals, keeps pace fast, uses tripling (lists of three points) (*We're committed, we're motivated, and we believe in what we do.*), uses positive language / vocabulary, speaks with enthusiasm

4 Students match the categories to their explanations. You might want to check that students understand *on board* (working together). If it helps, you could use an image of a ship, where all passengers are <u>on</u> the ship / on board, going somewhere together to help students to remember the meaning.

> **Answers**
> 1 b 2 d 3 a 4 e 5 c

5 Students match the phrases with the categories in **4**.

> **Answers**
> a 5 b 2 c 1 d 3 e 3
> f 5 g 2 h 1 i 4 j 4

6 Students work in pairs and decide which phrases could be used. They then take turns to practise giving the presentation.

> **Answers**
> **slide 1:** phrases for establishing the need for change
> **slide 2:** phrases for building the argument
> **slide 3:** phrases for acknowledging different points of view
> **slide 4:** phrases for asking for commitment / reinforcing the message

⟩⟩ If students need more practice, go to **Practice file 12** on page 124 of the **Student's Book**.

7 Students work in pairs. Give them time to think of an idea and to prepare a presentation to convince the rest of the class. Encourage students to think about why the idea is a good one and how they will support their argument (e.g. how colleagues will benefit). They should also be ready to show awareness of any problems it may cause, and try to get their audience's commitment. Refer them to the *Key expressions* during the preparation stage.

Pre-work students

If your students have no work experience, they can base their ideas on a company they know well. Alternatively they can develop an idea for where they study. If they are finding it difficult to think of an idea, write the following examples on the board.

- *Introduce a one-semester exchange programme with a British / American / Australian college or university.*
- *Start a mentoring system: older students have one-to-one sessions with newer students to help them with their learning and with managing their workload.*

Extension

If possible, record the presentations and listen / watch the recording before giving feedback.

Feedback focus

Ask the class to give feedback after each presentation. They should think about answers to the following questions.
- *Was the presentation effective?*
- *Did they convince the audience that it's a good idea?*

ⓘ Refer students to the **Interactive Workbook Email** and **Phrasebank** sections for further study.

Language at work

1 74 ▷ The focus here is on discourse markers (words and short phrases to help clarify the speaker's message, and to give signposts to the listener). They are used structurally to give clarity to information, and can be considered as 'lexical grammar' items. They are very common in native-speaker English and using them effectively will increase the fluency of learners at this level. Before they listen, ask students to look at the sentences. Can they think of any phrases that go in the gaps? Students then listen and complete the sentences.

> **Answers**
> 1 to tell you the truth
> 2 After all
> 3 Admittedly
> 4 mind you
> 5 Of course
> 6 Basically
> 7 As a matter of fact
> 8 Obviously
> 9 Quite honestly
> 10 so to speak
> 11 as I was saying
> 12 Anyway

2 Students categorize the phrases. Remind students that the discourse markers may have more than one function.

> **Possible answers**
> **a** to tell you the truth, as a matter of fact, admittedly, quite honestly
> **b** after all, mind you, as I was saying
> **c** after all, basically, obviously, of course
> **d** so to speak
> **e** anyway, mind you

Pronunciation

To help students use discourse markers effectively, write the following on the board and ask students to identify which words or parts of words are stressed (answers are in brackets).

to tell you the truth (to tell you the <u>truth</u>)
after all (after <u>all</u>)
admittedly (ad<u>mitt</u>edly)

Then ask them to listen to all the sentences in **1** again and to mark the stress.

> Answers: *of <u>course</u>, <u>bas</u>ically, as a matter of <u>fact</u>, <u>ob</u>viously, quite <u>hon</u>estly, so to <u>speak</u>, as I was <u>say</u>ing, <u>any</u>way.*

Extension

Ask students to work in pairs and to think of other discourse markers to add to each category. Then ask pairs to share their ideas with the rest of the class.

> Possible answers: a to be (perfectly) honest, truthfully; b so; c fundamentally, what matters (is), it goes without saying (that); d as it were; e right (then), so, by the way, well

>> Refer students to the **Language reference** section on page 133 of the **Student's Book** for more information.

3 Students work in pairs and discuss the questions.

> **Possible answers**
> **1** They are more likely to be used in spoken English.
> **2** We use discourse markers to 'punctuate' spoken language. They act as signposts to indicate what a speaker is thinking, the way conversation is going, when a change of pace / direction is taking place, and so on. They aim to help both the speaker and the listener.
> **3** Answers will vary.
> **4** Answers will vary.

Extension

Ask students to listen to some authentic spoken English for homework (they could listen to the radio or listen to interviews with famous people on the Internet, etc.). Ask them to listen and note down any discourse markers they hear. Which discourse markers do they hear most often? Do different people use different discourse markers? Why? Ask them to be prepared to discuss their findings in the next class.

>> If students need more practice, go to **Practice file 12** on page 125 of the **Student's Book**.

4 Students work individually. They should choose one category of news, and prepare to talk about it. They should then work with a partner and describe the news using appropriate discourse markers.

Feedback focus

Circulate and monitor. Make sure they use the discourse markers appropriately. Discourage them from using too many, as this can sound unnatural.

Extra activity

For homework ask students to find a short news item in a newspaper or business magazine. They should prepare to talk about it in class next time, explaining their reaction to it and giving their opinion. Encourage them to use discourse markers naturally when doing so.

Practically speaking

Watch out! This section deals with compliments. If you have students from cultures where this can be a sensitive issue, approach it with caution. It is also important to note that the language students will hear is very British – language used in other English-speaking countries, and specifically in the USA, may be different.

1 75▷ As a lead-in, ask students if they have complimented anyone, or been complimented by anyone today, or in the past few days. If so, what was the compliment about? What was said? Then ask students to listen and answer the questions.

> **Answers**
> **1** 2, 3, 6
> **2** 1, 4, 5
> **3** 3, 4, 6

2 75▷ Students listen again and answer the question.

Answers
In 3 the compliment is fine, but the response is not appropriate; it could sound boastful, as she obviously has enough money to afford expensive shoes.
In 4 the compliment is rather strong, so it might have caused embarrassment.
In 6 the compliment is inappropriate.

3 Students decide which phrases are used to give a compliment and which are a response.

Answers
compliments: 1, 2, 5, 6, 7, 8, 11, 12, 14, 15
responses: 3, 4, 9, 10, 13

Watch out! Note that 15 (*you have very nice …*) could often be inappropriate, so warn students to avoid using this phrase unless they are certain it won't cause offence.

» Refer students to the **Useful phrases** section on page 135 of the **Student's Book** for extension and revision.

4 Students work in pairs, taking turns to compliment each other. Encourage them to use the phrases from **3**.

Extra activity

- Give each student three slips of paper. They should write down three topics that someone could be complimented on, each on a different piece of paper. Encourage them to make the compliments interesting, but not embarrassing, e.g. clothing, a new haircut, a presentation, participation in a meeting, a new brochure, etc.
- Ask them to swap their papers with another student.
- Ask students to mingle and find another student to talk to – they should choose one of the compliment topics, give the compliment and hand over the corresponding piece of paper. They will then receive a compliment and should respond appropriately. Each student will now have two of their original pieces of paper, plus another topic that they can then use with other students.
- Allow the activity to continue for a few minutes. Then ask students to return their seats. Ask the class how they felt during the activity. Were there any awkward moments? Why?

Culture question

Students can discuss these questions in small groups. Answers will vary, although the following issues may arise. It is safe in most cultures to comment generally on someone's well-being. It's usually best to avoid commenting on specific parts of the body (especially to women), e.g. eyes, smile, legs, hands, etc. In some cultures people find it difficult to accept compliments (they make them feel uncomfortable). In Arabic cultures, commenting positively on a possession can prompt the host to *give* you that possession.

Key word

Students match the phrases to the definitions.
 Answers: 1 e, 2 a, 3 d, 4 b, 5 c, 6 f

ⓘ Refer students to the **Interactive Workbook Exercises and Tests** for revision.

Case study

Background

This *Case study* investigates the expansion plans of an international property company, FJR Immo. Students focus on the steps the company will take to ensure the stakeholders accept their plan. In the *Task* students draw up a SWOT analysis and then prepare a presentation to sell their idea to the stakeholders.

Allow time for students to read the *Company profile* and the text.

Watch out! Before they read, you might want to check that students understand the following.
to be on the up = increasing or improving
in the pipeline = something which is being discussed, planned, or prepared, and will happen or exist soon
a rare commodity = an unusual asset

Discussion

1, 2, 3 Students can discuss these questions in pairs.

Possible answers
1 By focusing on specific industrial sectors (IT) and by using good local agents.
2 They might think the staff are too inexperienced; or that they don't have enough information about the country they want to expand into; or that the investment is too expensive.
3 Answers will vary.

4 76▷ Students listen to the conversation.

> **Answers**
> **plan of action:** to focus on the KPIs, to work with local agents, to do a SWOT analysis, to read the information on Brazil

Watch out! After the listening, you might want to check that students understood the following.
off-the-record = something that is not (yet) official and that is not to be mentioned publicly
be up against somebody / something = facing problems or opposition
tackle = to make a determined effort to deal with a difficult problem or situation

Task

1 Before students read their *Files*, ask them to look at the SWOT analysis grid. What information can they fill in already? For example:

Strengths: they already know some local agents
Weaknesses: they are a young, inexperienced company; it's a new market

Students work in groups of three. Each person reads a different *File*. Allow time for them to read the information. Be ready to answer any questions they may have. Students then work together to fill in the SWOT analysis form with the information.

> **Possible answers**
>
> | Strengths | Opportunities |
> |---|---|
> | They already know some local agents. | The points listed in the Brazil fact file are all positive; however, many of them are projections and predictions, and are not necessarily guaranteed. |
> | **KPIs:** Customer satisfaction should remain high if they continue to work with industries where they have experience. | |

Weaknesses	Threats
The staff and company do not have much experience. Brazil is new territory for them, so they are not familiar with the customs and business practices.	The issues mentioned under *Doing business in Brazil* could cause problems: it would be important for the staff to be fully aware of the cultural differences, and to take great care not to offend, as well as to respect how the Brazilians do business. Making a mistake could jeopardize the project.
By focusing on IT companies all their eggs are in one basket.	
KPIs: Dealing with local staff and suppliers could initially be difficult (even though they know agents).	Additionally, if the IT industry suffers a downturn, the company will be affected.
Short-term return on profit may not be good; longer term it may be more reliable.	

2 Students work in their groups and prepare the presentation. Encourage students to use language from this unit, specifically the phrases from the *Key expressions*, as well as the discourse markers. Students should decide who will deliver which section of the presentation.

3 Groups take turns to give their presentations. As they do, the other students should act as stakeholders.

One-to-one

Your student can read the *Background*, and then you can work on the *Discussion* questions together. For the *Task*, use all the *Files*, but read each one together in turn, filling in the SWOT analysis form as you do so.

Make sure you give your student time to prepare their presentation. When they give the presentation make sure they cover all four points. Act as a stakeholder and ask questions to clarify.

Feedback focus

During the presentations, make a note of any good use of language and any mistakes. After the presentations, ask the class to give feedback on the content of each presentation. Did the presentation convince them (as stakeholders) that expansion in Brazil is a good idea? Then give positive feedback on the use of language and write any mistakes on the board for the class to correct.

Alternative

If giving presentations is an important skill for your students, they could spend more time preparing their presentation at home, perhaps using PowerPoint slides. Make sure that they use the slides as prompts only and that they don't read out long passages.

Extra activity

If your students need extra writing practice, ask them to prepare a report to present their idea to the stakeholders. Write the following headings on the board to guide their writing.

1 ***Executive summary*** *– a summary of the main points and conclusions of the report to give the reader a very quick overview of the entire situation.*
2 ***Introduction*** *– the sequence of points that will be examined in the report.*
3 ***Findings*** *– the relevant facts / issues.*
4 ***Conclusion*** *– what you think about the facts and how you interpret them.*
5 ***Recommendations*** *– practical suggestions to deal with the situation and ideas for making sure future activities run smoothly.*

» Unit 12 **Progress test** and **Speaking test**, pages 118–119.

Complete the missing words in these sentences.

1 This area around the docks is certainly u_____.
   A lot of new flats have been built, and it seems like new restaurants are opening every day!

2 John always says exactly what he thinks. That isn't normally a problem, but I think we need someone less o_____ and more diplomatic for this negotiation.

3 This candidate is certainly very s_____, which is good. We need someone who is confident.

4 John is always so relaxed and never gets irritated with his colleagues. Having such an e_____ person in the department has had a positive influence on the team.

5 This is so t_____! It's taken me three hours so far to enter all the information onto the database.

6 The site is too o_____. I don't think we would get much passing trade. We need to open the restaurant in the centre of town.

Complete these sentences with phrases from the list.

> build relationships   give you an insight
> form an opinion   keep your eyes open
> weigh up the pros and cons   manage unknowns

7 You can't _____ about someone if you hardly know them.

8 When you travel abroad, you should always _____ and take notice of the way people in that culture interact with each other.

9 You can't foresee exactly what's going to happen, so part of the skill of being a good leader is to be flexible and ready to _____.

10 To _____ with people, you have to be open and trusting.

11 A three-week trip to Japan will certainly _____ into their culture, but you would have to live there to be able to really understand it.

12 It's important to _____ before making a decision.

Complete these conversations with phrases a–j. Write the letters in the spaces.

a I gathered from
b I'm a bit reluctant to
c I wouldn't go so far as
d We can't go wrong
e outweigh the cons
f The major advantage
g I'm sure you'll agree
h not 100% convinced
i I'm not saying
j it's just that

A How did the meeting go?
B ¹³___ to say that they're ready to sign, but it was positive. ¹⁴___ what they said that they're not happy with their current suppliers, so we're in with a chance.
A We're onto a winner here. ¹⁵___. We've got a great product, at the right price. I'm sure they'll make an order soon.
B Well, ¹⁶___ open the champagne yet.
C What do you think of the possible new site for our offices?
D ¹⁷___ is that because it's out of town, it's so much cheaper.
C The rent may be cheaper, but I'm just ¹⁸___. I'm worried about the commute for staff.
D But ¹⁹___ that the offices are bigger and more modern.
C True. ²⁰___ that there aren't lots of positive points, ²¹___ I think we should think it over carefully before we decide.
D OK. But I think the pros definitely ²²___.

Choose the correct answer from the words in *italics*.

23 I *had planned / have planned* to go to Spain on holiday, but I broke my leg, so I couldn't go.

24 I *'ll be finishing / 'll have finished* the report by Friday.

25 I *was talking / talked* to Gaston when we were cut off.

26 The negotiations *could be / could have been* easier, to be honest – in fact they were pretty intense.

27 I *shouldn't have ordered / shouldn't order* so much stock. There's so much here – we'll never sell it.

28 I *'ve been buying / 've bought* the tickets. We just need to book the hotel now.

29 I *try / 've been trying* to get in touch with Mr Anderson, but his line's always busy.

30 Can you phone the factory and find out what *will be happening / is happening*?

Result _____ / 30 marks

Role cards

Copy this page and cut out the role cards for the students. Students should do both role-plays.
Then use the *Speaking test results* forms to evaluate each student's performance. You can then cut out
the results and give them to the students.

Cut along this line

Student A

1 You are a manager at an IT company and you think the
company should expand to a second site and rent offices in
the up-and-coming docks area. Tell another manager about
the idea.

- Introduce yourself.
- Report why you like the the docks area (looks modern,
  would give the company a young image, would be good
  for employee morale).
- Report the opinions of the estate agent (need to decide
  now – offices are being sold and rented quickly).
- Try to persuade Student B that this move is a good idea.

2 Listen to Student B explain why he / she prefers a new
out-of-town business park.

Express doubt about his / her idea.

- it's depressing (lots of concrete)
- it's quite far out of town

Student B

1 You are a manager at an IT company. Listen to another
manager explain why he / she thinks the company should
expand to a second site and rent offices in the up-and-
coming docks area.

Express doubt about his / her idea.

- it's unreasonably expensive
- it's noisy (more suitable for restaurants and flats)

2 You prefer a new out-of-town business park. Tell
Student A about your idea.

- Introduce yourself.
- Report why you like the new business park (near the
  university so would be easier to recruit young IT
  specialists for internships etc., nice setting – lots of
  trees).
- Report the opinions of the estate agent (rent is
  reasonable, with reductions for the first year).
- Try to persuade Student A that this move is a good idea.

Cut along this line

Speaking test results

Cut along this line

Student A

Can the student ...	Didn't do this (0 points)	Yes, but with some mistakes (1 point)	Yes, did this very well (2 points)
introduce him / herself?			
report a personal observation?			
report information from another source?			
express doubt?			
be persuasive?			

Result _____ / 10 marks

Student B

Can the student ...	Didn't do this (0 points)	Yes, but with some mistakes (1 point)	Yes, did this very well (2 points)
introduce him / herself?			
report a personal observation?			
report information from another source?			
express doubt?			
be persuasive?			

Result _____ / 10 marks

Cut along this line

Complete these sentences with words from the list.

stay	stick	stand	come	cling	keep	move

1 You have to _____ up for your beliefs.

2 He's trying to _____ on to his job, but I think they're going to fire him.

3 I'm ready to _____ on to something new in my life.

4 We'll need to improve our career development if we want to _____ ahead of the competition.

5 Have you _____ up with any new recruitment ideas?

6 If you want to be promoted, you have to _____ in with the right people.

7 It's difficult to _____ up for somebody if you know they're in the wrong.

Replace the words in bold with the correct word. The first letter is given.

8 My brother works for the family business, but I didn't want to follow such a **standard** path.
c_____

9 She decided to move **laterally** to get away from a difficult boss.
h_____

10 It's taken me about a year to **progress** into my role.
g_____

11 He's reached the **point** where he just has to move on.
s_____

12 It's time to look for another job to **extend** my horizons.
b_____

13 When he moved to the subsidiary he felt he'd taken a step **behind**.
b_____

Complete this conversation with the missing words.

A So, let's get [14] s_____. The purpose of today's meeting is to discuss ways of improving our performance evaluations. Philippa, would you like to [15] r_____ us through your findings?

B Yes, sure. Now, I know not all of you are [16] k_____ on this idea, but what's clear is that many of our line managers need further training.

C Sorry, can I just [17] c_____ in here? [18] W_____ this be the right time to talk about the management course we ran earlier this year?

A Can I suggest we [19] c_____ back to that when Philippa's finished? Philippa, go [20] a_____.

B Thanks, David. The best course I've found was a weekend course, and I was [21] w_____ if our line managers would be prepared to give up one Saturday some time in the next three months. I'll [22] m_____ on to the details of the course in a moment, but could you answer that question first?

Complete these sentences with the correct tense of the verbs in brackets.

23 If only I _____ (be) there to see his face when they told him about the crisis in Paris!

24 What do you think _____ (happen) if we hadn't made that decision?

25 I'm so glad we _____ (have) time to discuss recruitment at yesterday's meeting.

26 If they _____ (think) about it earlier, we wouldn't have had that problem.

27 It _____ (might / be) better if you hadn't paid them in advance, but maybe it wouldn't have made a difference to the quality of the work anyway.

28 The directors _____ (should / not / react) like that.

29 The training course went very well in the end. It's just as well we _____ (not / cancel) it.

30 Suppose you _____ (go) ahead with the plan, we'd probably have gone bankrupt.

Result _____ / 30 marks

Role cards

Copy this page and cut out the role cards for the students. Students should do both role-plays. Then use the *Speaking test results* forms to evaluate each student's performance. You can then cut out the results and give them to the students.

Cut along this line

Student A

Your company has lost many of its best employees to competitors. You are a senior manager. Meet another senior manager to discuss the problem.

- Start the discussion. State a past mistake and the consequences. (The company concentrated on satisfying customers, and the needs of the staff were neglected.)
- Deal with the interruption and clarify your views. (Not enough IT training for staff to do their jobs properly, which led to stress and dissatisfaction.)
- Ask for clarification of Student B's views.
- Interrupt your partner. Respond with reservations. (Increasing salaries would be too expensive. A bonus would be better.)

Student B

Your company has lost many of its best employees to competitors. You are a senior manager. Meet another senior manager to discuss the problem.

- Student A will start. Interrupt and ask for clarification.
- Listen to the clarification and respond with reservations. Then state another past mistake and the consequences. (IT training isn't the answer. Problems are due to the lack of performance evaluations which led to a lack of career development opportunities.)
- Clarify your views. (New staff were employed instead of promoting internally. Increasing salaries and benefits would boost morale and solve the problem.)
- Deal with the interruption. Give your opinion and decide on future action.

Cut along this line

Speaking test results

Use these forms to evaluate the students.

Cut along this line

Student A

Can the student ...	Didn't do this (0 points)	Yes, but with some mistakes (1 point)	Yes, did this very well (2 points)
state past mistakes and consequences?			
interrupt / ask for clarification?			
deal with interruptions?			
put forward an idea?			
express reservations?			

Result _____ / 10 marks

Student B

Can the student ...	Didn't do this (0 points)	Yes, but with some mistakes (1 point)	Yes, did this very well (2 points)
state past mistakes and consequences?			
interrupt / ask for clarification?			
deal with interruptions?			
put forward an idea?			
express reservations?			

Result _____ / 10 marks

Cut along this line

Complete these sentences with words from the list. Change the form if necessary.

option	put in place	enter	carry out
procedure	means	transform	implement

1 We're _____ a very busy period now, so we need people to work overtime.

2 _____ extensive research is essential before redesigning the workplace.

3 What's the exact _____ for the fire drill?

4 They are _____ a new expense accounts system and it should be much better.

5 The _____ to the office is spectacular! It looks so much better now.

6 Our boss has a lot of new ideas, but as you can see from our current sales figures, we haven't got the _____ to see them through.

7 I would like to work flexible hours, but they don't give us the _____ to do so.

8 Senior management have established new rules for getting promoted, and HR now have to _____ them.

Choose the correct answer from the words in *italics*.

9 The sales team will get a big bonus this year. They achieved all their *targets / progress*.

10 The idea of an inter-departmental sports competition has certainly generated a lot of *performance / enthusiasm*. Fifty people have signed up already!

11 We anticipated that there would be a lot of *problems / growth* during the project, but we didn't think it would be quite that bad!

12 Regular team meetings have enabled staff to exchange *productivity / information* about their schedules and workloads.

13 We need the latest sales figures to help us measure the *progress / special requirements* of the company.

Complete these sentences with phrases from the list.

Just to digress for a second
Perhaps here I should explain what I mean by
Now, I don't know if you're familiar with
Just to fill you in on some of the background
I'd like to start by

14 _____ saying how excited we are to be collaborating with you on this project.

15 _____. The idea for the project came about after a chance visit to one of our customers, whose office space has been totally redesigned.

16 _____ their design concept, but this slide outlines the key points.

17 _____ a 'career nomad'. It's when employees move from one company to another, or even one career to another.

18 _____, I'd like to congratulate the divisional golf team, who won the tournament at the weekend.

Correct the two mistakes in these sentences. (2 points per sentence)

19 I know what you are meaning, things aren't looking good – I think they are making people redundant sooner or later.

20 I know this is a tricking time for you, but everyone is expected working overtime next week because we're really busy.

21 You might best want to word this letter differently, so it's a little more diplomacy.

22 This time tomorrow you are flying to New Mexico – it might be worth to try to check in online today.

23 I can see where you're going from, but everyone's exhausted. By the time we finish, we will be working on this project for eight hours.

24 They think that the reaction to the takeover will have been quite aggressive. We'll have to wait until tomorrow to find out for certainty.

Result _____ / 30 marks

Speaking test

Role card

This Speaking test has only one role card because each student has to give an individual presentation. Copy this page and cut out the role card for the student. Then use the *Speaking test results* forms to evaluate the student's performance. You can then cut out the results and give them to the student.

Cut along this line

Student A

Prepare a five-minute presentation on one of the topics in the list.

- recent changes in my company and their impact
- how to boost morale in a company
- my predictions for the future world economy
- how to improve your work / life balance
- my hobby

When giving your presentation, you should

- outline your presentation and give background information
- signal the different sections of your presentation
- refer to something you'll say later or that you said earlier
- ensure your audience understands
- finish appropriately

Cut along this line

Speaking test results

Use this form to evaluate the student.

Cut along this line

Can the student ...	Didn't do this (0 points)	Yes, but with some mistakes (1 point)	Yes, did this very well (2 points)
outline the presentation / give background information?			
signal the sections of the presentation?			
refer to something that will be said later / was said earlier?			
ensure the audience understands?			
finish appropriately?			

Result _____ / 10 marks

Cut along this line

Complete these sentences with words from the list.

> run   weigh up   minimize   determine
> expose   anticipate

1 It's important to _____ problems so you're ready for them when they happen.

2 We have to _____ all the pros and cons.

3 You _____ yourself to risk every time you step out of your front door.

4 If we don't do something now, we _____ the risk of going out of business.

5 You'll have to identify the causes. Then you can _____ what action to take.

6 If we do safety checks, we'll _____ the risk of accidents.

Choose the correct answer from the words in *italics*.

7 I don't like investing in new markets. People say I'm *over-cautious / bold*.

8 Our profits have been low recently, so it wasn't very *imprudent / sensible* to employ another member of staff.

9 I'm nervous whenever I'm in the car with him. He's a really *risk-averse / reckless* driver.

10 I thought buying all those shares was a good idea, but now they've fallen by 50% it seems rather *bold / rash*.

11 Insurance companies are by nature *risk-averse / rash*, so they won't insure you if they think you'll cost them money.

Each sentence contains one mistake. <u>Underline</u> it and write the correct word.

12 I'd be interested to hearing what you think about this.

13 I'm beginning to have serious thoughts about this.

14 If I could just digress the conversation back to the agenda …

15 Sorry, Ariane. Could you leave Jason answer that question?

16 I'd like to drag things to a close.

17 Can I just ask everyone to resume up their views?

Complete these dialogues with the missing words.

A Am I [18]r_____ in saying that we all want to go ahead with this?

B Yes, I think we all agree on that.

A So what do you think of the project?

B Well, personally, I still have serious [19]r_____.

A I really think we have to invest now.

B With [20]r_____, Brian, I think you're being too hasty.

A I think we need to come back to this another time.

B Yes, we're not [21]g_____ anywhere. We're just going round in circles.

A So, can we make a decision?

B Yes, I think we have some kind of [22]c_____ here.

Two people are discussing a new project. Complete the conversation with *this*, *that*, or *it* and an appropriate form of the verb *to be*, if necessary.

A We've spent an hour talking about the project. I think we need to move on.

B Yes, I know you've never liked the idea and you think [23]_____ a complete waste of money.

A No, [24]_____ not fair. Maybe [25]_____ my opinion a year or so ago, but I've realized since then it's not as risky as I thought.

B Well then, my next question is [26]_____: when are we going to give it a try?

Look at the conversation below. Match phrases 27–30 in *italics* with categories a–d.

  a paying a compliment
  b recalling past events in common
  c picking up on a word to extend the conversation
  d being modest about achievements

Jack Pete! How are you? After all this time! It must be ten years since we last met.

Pete Yes, [27]*wasn't it at the conference in Rio*? ___

Jack That's right. I remember it well! So, how are you doing?

Pete Fine, thanks.

Jack By the way, I saw your picture on the inside page of the conference brochure – [28]*what you've done for your company is really fantastic*. ___

Pete [29]*It wasn't just me*. I work with a great team. ___

Jack [30]*Talking of teams*. How did you manage to get Pete Tomlin on board? ___

Result _____ / 30 marks

Speaking test

Role cards

Copy this page and cut out the role cards for the students. Students should do both role-plays. Then use the *Speaking test results* forms to evaluate each student's performance. You can then cut out the results and give them to the students.

Cut along this line

Student A

1 Your company produces televisions. You are discussing the risks of moving all your production to China.
- Ask about B's recent trip to Shanghai.
- Check you've understood: 'factory sites' are sites for building a new factory, not pre-existing factories?
- Express doubts about low labour costs in Shanghai being long-term.
- Listen to B's opinion, then get conversation back onto the main topic. Ask B when a decision has to be taken on factory sites.
- End the meeting and summarize what's been said.

2 You work for a pharmaceutical company. You are discussing the risks of launching a new slimming tablet.
- When invited, talk about the recent clinical trials: positive results with minimal risk to health.
- Confirm what B says, but point out slight risk of addiction if tablet used for too long.
- Listen, then suggest alternative = anti-ageing tablet developed a year ago, but never launched.

Student B

1 Your company produces televisions. You are discussing the risks of moving all your production to China.
- When invited, talk about your recent trip – your Chinese partner has found two available factory sites.
- Confirm what A says. Point out that there is also a lot of skilled low-cost labour available.
- Listen, then suggest alternative option = cut costs in existing factories by increasing automation.

2 You work for a pharmaceutical company. You are discussing the risks of launching a new slimming tablet.
- Ask A to talk about results of recent clinical trials.
- Check you've understood: no long-term health risk?
- Express doubts about launching an over-the-counter drug that could be addictive.
- Listen to A's opinion, then get conversation back onto the main topic. Ask A if marketing study has been done based on prescription-only use of slimming tablet.
- End the meeting and summarize what's been said.

Cut along this line

Speaking test results

Use these forms to evaluate the students.

Cut along this line

Student A

Can the student …	Didn't do this (0 points)	Yes, but with some mistakes (1 point)	Yes, did this very well (2 points)
invite someone to speak?			
check understanding?			
express doubts?			
keep to the main topic?			
end the meeting and summarize?			

Result _____ / 10 marks

Student B

Can the student …	Didn't do this (0 points)	Yes, but with some mistakes (1 point)	Yes, did this very well (2 points)
invite someone to speak?			
check understanding?			
express doubts?			
keep to the main topic?			
end the meeting and summarize?			

Result _____ / 10 marks

Cut along this line

Cut along this line

Photocopiable © Oxford University Press

Complete these sentences with two words from the list. Change the form of the verb where necessary. (2 points per sentence)

express	do	treat	view	work
tread	clearly	thoroughly	unfairly	
closely	positively	carefully		

1 He is not a good manager. He _____ his employees very _____, favouring one over another.

2 The presentation wasn't very good – I really didn't understand what he was going on about. He seems incapable of _____ himself _____.

3 This is an excellent report. I think you've really _____ it _____, focusing in detail on all the problems in the department.

4 You need to _____ quite _____ with John this morning. He's had some bad news from Head Office, so he's not in a good mood.

5 We've got subsidiaries all over the world. We have to make sure we offer the same style of service so it's essential that we _____ very _____ with all our counterparts.

6 He's a hard worker, but he isn't always _____ very _____ by the team because he tends to be pushy when the senior managers are around.

Complete these sentences with the missing preposition.

7 Coping _____ a full-time job and a family can sometimes be stressful.

8 You should steer clear _____ any confrontation at this stage. It won't help.

9 If you had paid closer attention _____ what he said, you'd understand how the new software works.

10 The sales team fell short _____ their targets again this quarter. Perhaps the targets are just too unrealistic.

11 There are five presentations this afternoon, so it's important you keep _____ the schedule.

Complete the missing words in these sentences.

A Can I just make sure I've [12]u_____ this correctly? You sent the invoice for McLaren to Linux and the invoice for Linux to McLaren?

B Yes, but it was the temporary secretary's fault.

A Look, you're entitled to your opinion, but can we try and stay [13]f_____ on the facts? How do you propose we [14]d_____ with this issue now? I don't know if you're [15]a_____, but McLaren pay thirty percent more than Linux for the same services!

B Look, [16]w_____ it help if I called Linux and McLaren and just asked them to send back the invoices without opening them?

A To be [17]h_____, I just don't understand how you could even [18]c_____ doing that – it would look so unprofessional!

B Well, I'm often in contact with the receptionists from both companies. I'm [19]p_____ to call them, explain we've sent them some confidential documents by mistake and offer to go and pick them up.

Re-write these sentences using the words / phrases in brackets to add emphasis.

Example: *The people in the marketing department are the ones that make the most noise. (it's)*

It's the people in the marketing department who make the most noise.

20 Why did they get rid of Tom? He was a very valuable team member. (what I'd really like to know)

_____

21 The new finance manager has stopped all new recruitment and there's talk of redundancies. (not only …, but also …) _____

22 We're a successful team because we get on so well together. (the reason) _____

23 We have to finish this project before Friday, so we're all working overtime at the moment. (which is why)

_____

24 The financial data for this quarter is a real worry. (what)

_____

Result _____ / 30 marks

Speaking test

Role cards

Copy this page and cut out the role cards for the students. Students should do both role-plays. Then use the *Speaking test results* forms to evaluate each student's performance. You can then cut out the results and give them to the students.

Cut along this line

Student A

1 You are overseeing a project and you've been having problems with your designer (Student B) and have arranged a meeting to discuss this. Your concerns are:
   - One team member (John), has said that designs are often late and are not of a good standard.
   - John also says that Student B doesn't seem interested in the project at all and that he / she doesn't always turn up for important update meetings.

During the meeting
   - express your first concern diplomatically
   - express your second concern more directly
   - respond to B's offer and finish the meeting appropriately.

2 You're having problems with a team member (Brad). Your team leader (Student B) has arranged a meeting to discuss this. During the meeting
   - listen and disagree – Brad is always interrupting you in meetings and he has too many impractical ideas
   - listen to the second point and offer a compromise – you'll reconsider his ideas if he stops interrupting you.

Student B

1 You're the designer on a project and you're having problems with a team member (John). Your team leader (Student A) has arranged a meeting to discuss this. During the meeting
   - listen and disagree – John is disorganized. There have been a lot of last-minute changes to the designs
   - listen to the second point and offer a compromise – you've been away a lot, but you'll arrange to meet John for an update if he makes a decision about the design.

2 You're a team leader. Two people in your team (Student A and Brad) don't get on. You have arranged a meeting with Student A to discuss this. Your concerns are:
   - Student A and Brad are always arguing – bad for morale. Brad says Student A never takes his ideas on board.
   - Students A has been in the company far longer than Brad so he / she has to resolve the problem.

During the meeting
   - express your first concern diplomatically
   - express your second concern more directly
   - respond to A's offer and finish the meeting.

Cut along this line

Speaking test results

Use these forms to evaluate the students.

Cut along this line

Student A

Can the student …	Didn't do this (0 points)	Yes, but with some mistakes (1 point)	Yes, did this very well (2 points)
express concerns diplomatically?			
express concerns directly?			
disagree?			
offer a compromise?			
finish a meeting appropriately?			

Result _____ / 10 marks

Student B

Can the student …	Didn't do this (0 points)	Yes, but with some mistakes (1 point)	Yes, did this very well (2 points)
express concerns diplomatically?			
express concerns directly?			
disagree?			
offer a compromise?			
finish a meeting appropriately?			

Result _____ / 10 marks

Cut along this line

6 | Progress test

Complete these sentences with appropriate prepositions.

1 We've run _____ big difficulties in our Far East market.

2 We should look _____ the same old solutions and try and find a really novel way of doing this.

3 We thought the idea would really take off, but in the end it just fell _____ the wayside.

4 One way companies try to stay _____ _____ the competition is by spying on them.

5 Let's bounce _____ a few ideas and see what we come up with.

6 It's a great product, but without adequate marketing support it'll never get _____ the ground.

7 The project manager's been ill, but now he's here I think we'll get _____ _____ track pretty quickly.

8 It's not easy to think _____ the box when you're surrounded by unimaginative people.

9 They're trying to figure _____ why the press conference went so badly.

Complete the conversation with the missing words.

A It's not ¹⁰c_____ to me what you mean by 'further training'.

B Well, I was thinking along the ¹¹l_____ of a course in creative thinking for all line managers.

A That's not such a bad idea. But I can't help ¹²w_____ if it's really going to be effective.

B So you're suggesting that some of our managers are hopeless cases?

A Well, not exactly, but I'm ¹³c_____ about how some of our more senior managers will respond to that kind of course. You can't teach an old dog new tricks!

B Well, ¹⁴s_____ we were to offer a half-day seminar in the company to start off with? Then we could evaluate who is or isn't responding well to the method.

A Yes, I quite like that idea. And there'd be nothing ¹⁵s_____ us from pulling out the plug after that first session, would there?

B Well, no, I guess not. It's certainly ¹⁶w_____ thinking about.

Match verbs from A to nouns in B to answer these questions.

A	cause demand undergo control outperform
B	change precision costs the competition a stir

17 What does a political scandal normally do?

18 What does a good quality manager do?

19 If you are the best company in your field, what do you do?

20 What's the key to good financial management?

21 What don't many employees like to do?

Complete these dialogues with an adverb from the list.

obviously surprisingly just totally actually

A You've never been there, have you?
B ²²_____, I have. I went last year.
A So that was the situation at the end of the year.
B Sorry, could you ²³_____ run through the figures for the last quarter again?
A So what do you think?
B Well, I can't say I'm ²⁴_____ enthusiastic about the idea
A They didn't ask a single question after my presentation.
B No, they didn't, ²⁵_____. I wonder why.
A I thought he handled the negotiation very well.
B Yes, it's ²⁶_____ not the first time he's done something like that.

Complete the conversation with phrases from the list.

It's difficult for me to explain really
It just needs a bit more
I'm trying to think how
you're on the right track

About your proposal for how to make our company more innovative, I'd say ²⁷_____ and it's definitely what we're looking for, but I disagree with some of the ideas you have. ²⁸_____ I could help you – maybe you could talk to my partner, as he's spent a lot of time on this. ²⁹_____, but I feel you've focused too much on creative ideas. ³⁰_____ on technical training really.

Result _____ / 30 marks

Speaking test

Role cards

Copy this page and cut out the role cards for the students. Students should do both role-plays. Then use the *Speaking test results* forms to evaluate each student's performance. You can then cut out the results and give them to the students.

Cut along this line

Student A

1 You want to improve morale in your company and you think you could do this by improving employees' health and fitness.
   • Put forward your idea to B.
   • Clarify your idea – you'd like to introduce healthy menus in the canteen and put up posters with tips for healthy living in the offices.
   • Evaluate your partner's idea and give a positive or negative reaction.

2 Listen to B's idea for making the company more innovative.
   • Ask B to clarify the idea.
   • You like the idea.
   • Build on the idea – suggest that you offer creativity development seminars, or bonuses to employees who come up with interesting ideas for the company.

Student B

1 Listen to A's idea for your company.
   • Ask A to clarify the idea.
   • You like the idea.
   • Build on the idea – suggest that employees could finish early on Fridays and sports activities could be organized, e.g. football games or running.

2 You'd like to make the company more innovative and bring out the creative side of people in the company by offering them time during work to develop this.
   • Put forward your idea to your A.
   • Clarify your idea – you'd like to create a space or room that's brightly painted, with games, paper, pens, etc. Employees could go there and share creative ideas.
   • Evaluate your partner's idea and give a positive or negative reaction.

Cut along this line

Speaking test results

Use these forms to evaluate the students.

Cut along this line

Student A

Can the student ...	Didn't do this (0 points)	Yes, but with some mistakes (1 point)	Yes, did this very well (2 points)
put forward an idea?			
ask for clarification?			
clarify an idea?			
build on an idea?			
evaluate an idea?			

Result _____ / 10 marks

Student B

Can the student ...	Didn't do this (0 points)	Yes, but with some mistakes (1 point)	Yes, did this very well (2 points)
put forward an idea?			
ask for clarification?			
clarify an idea?			
build on an idea?			
evaluate an idea?			

Result _____ / 10 marks

Cut along this line

Choose the correct answer from the words in *italics*.

1 Can you bring your *personal development plan* / *performance management* so that we can review your targets and objectives for next year?

2 We have to ensure that we all have a *structural change* / *shared vision*, otherwise we won't all be focused on achieving the company goals.

3 Due to the serious *skills deficit* / *structural change*, we'll be introducing extensive in-house training.

4 Our employees are far more committed if they're personally involved in their own development, so we're focusing on *centrally-driven* / *self-directed* training.

5 We take a *bottom-up* / *top-down* approach to training, using information from appraisals and focusing on individual needs.

Complete this conversation with phrases a–h. Write the letters in the spaces.

a	have you heard	e	you're saying
b	run it by me again	f	do you mean that
c	spell out	g	by the way
d	it's a bit off-topic	h	what was the name

A I didn't quite follow. Could you ⁶___?

B Well, I was thinking we could send two or three members of staff abroad.

B So ⁷___ that we send them to England to do a language course?

A Well, yes. Or Ireland. For a month or so.

A ⁸___ we'll just pay for the courses and let them go? What about their projects?

B I don't see why not – if we choose the right time.

A Could you ⁹___ some of the details?

B Well, they do three months training here, and then go abroad. Then they come back and continue as before. Academy International in Dublin has a great reputation.

A Sorry, ¹⁰___ again?

B Academy International.

A Didn't Sue go on one of their courses? Oh, ¹¹___, have you heard that she's thinking of applying for Fran's job and … actually it doesn't matter – ¹²___ right now.

B That reminds me – ¹³___ that Fran was actually forced to retire early?

Re-write these sentences using a word from the list.

faced	given	knowing	having

14 As a result of seeing how our sister organization works, I'd like to suggest a few structural changes.

_____

15 Because there is a shortage of people with these qualifications, we need to consider other attributes in potential staff. _____

16 If we were up against similar circumstances again, we wouldn't accept the offer.

_____

17 I realize you've worked really hard, and you deserve credit for it. _____

Re-write these sentences with a tense expressing 'the future in the past', using the information in brackets. (2 points per sentence)

18 I'm supposed to meet the visitors from Germany at the airport this afternoon. (Harry went in my place)

_____

19 Elke has joined the team and I think she'll be a great addition. (Elke is very lazy and hasn't fitted into the team)

_____

20 I'm going to finish the report before I leave the office today. (couldn't finish it – had a long phone call)

_____

21 The company intends to review the pay scale in June. (no review due to bad financial results)

_____

Complete the missing words in these sentences.

22 This workshop is not the best u_____ of my time.

23 The noise in this office is doing my h_____ in.

24 She hasn't lived up to e_____ so far.

25 I have to leave. I've just about reached my l_____.

26 This leaflet is not up to s_____. We need a redesign.

Result _____ / 30 marks

Speaking test

Role cards

Copy this page and cut out the role cards for the students. Students should do both role-plays. Then use the *Speaking test results* forms to evaluate each student's performance. You can then cut out the results and give them to the students.

Cut along this line

Student A

1 You are the training manager at the Montenegro branch of an international company. Call your colleague in London to suggest a presentation skills course for your staff.
   • two-day course
   • in May or June (date to be finalized by Friday next week)
   • 12 participants (could push this to 15)
   • use hotel conference rooms in town – good rates offered
   • When asked, recommend a wonderful hotel in Kotor on the coast for their next trip and offer to send details.

2 You work for an international company in Zurich. Your colleague organizes team-building weekends. They call to tell you about a new venue. During the conversation
   • check the facts
   • check that you've understood everything
   • ask for clarification if necessary
   • digress and ask for a recommendation for a good Swiss restaurant in Zurich for friends visiting next month – then get back to the main topic.

Student B

1 You work in HR at Head Office in London. The training manager from the Montenegro office calls to discuss a possible presentation skills course for his / her staff. During the conversation
   • check the facts
   • check that you've understood everything
   • ask for clarification if necessary
   • digress and ask A to recommend a hotel for your next trip to Montenegro – then get back to the main topic.

2 You organize team-building weekends for an international company in Zurich. Call your colleague to suggest the Bernese Alps as the venue for the next event.
   • weekends between November and March
   • activities (e.g. Nordic walking) plus corporate training
   • accommodation in chalets – max 45 people
   • full board, instructor fees, and all activities included
   • When asked, recommend a traditional Swiss restaurant in Zurich and offer to send a link to the website.

Cut along this line

Speaking test results

Use these forms to evaluate the students.

Cut along this line

Student A

Can the student ...	Didn't do this (0 points)	Yes, but with some mistakes (1 point)	Yes, did this very well (2 points)
check facts?			
check understanding?			
ask for clarification?			
digress?			
get back to the main topic?			

Result _____ / 10 marks

Student B

Can the student ...	Didn't do this (0 points)	Yes, but with some mistakes (1 point)	Yes, did this very well (2 points)
check facts?			
check understanding?			
ask for clarification?			
digress?			
get back to the main topic?			

Result _____ / 10 marks

Cut along this line

Complete this job advertisement with the correct prepositions.

Career opportunities in conservation

Want to make a difference ¹ _____ the world you live in? Look no further! Caspar International is looking for a dynamic and motivated graduate to fill the post of trainee Marketing Assistant for its busy operations in South East Europe. The prospective candidate will be able to think ² _____ their feet in unpredictable situations and easily build ³ _____ rapport with a variety of clients. The successful applicant will gain recognition ⁴ _____ any positive client feedback and will be rewarded with an incremental salary and discretionary bonuses.

Correct the two mistakes in these sentences. (2 points per sentence)

5 Working for Caspar International would enable me to take my skills and experience to the test and I would give pride in the fact that I would be working for a company with such a great reputation.

6 I would like to have part of an organization that can really achieve something and I can really see a forecast for myself in this sector.

7 The budget? Yes, I was going to that – where we are in the moment is that we're staying just within budget.

8 Let me just touch over the question of resources – perhaps it will be a good idea if I go over the resource plans now.

9 I'd just like to sketch up my plans for the research project – I'd also like to be able to tell you who'll be helping me with the project, but fortunately I can't.

10 I don't have the exactly figures, but I know that the sales potential exists – let me check the data and I get back to you.

11 Out the top of my head, I think last month's sales figures were £11,000, but I can check double if you like.

Complete this conversation with questions based on the phrases in *italics* and the prompts in brackets.

Potential investor ¹² _____?
should I invest / your company (wh- question)

Entrepreneur Because we have a unique product and we'll offer you a great return on your money.
¹³ _____? *show you / product* (modal auxiliary)

Potential investor That might be a good idea, yes.

Entrepreneur Here it is. It's an electric potato peeler.

Potential investor ¹⁴ _____?
you think / unique product (question tag to challenge speaker)

Entrepreneur Well, yes our research showed that there isn't anything else like it on the market.

Potential investor ¹⁵ _____?
sure about that (question tag to challenge speaker)

Entrepreneur Yes – this is 100% unique.

Potential investor ¹⁶ _____?
assume / already / speak / retailers / about stocking your product (statement question)

Entrepreneur Yes, actually we have. We've had a lot of interest.

Potential investor ¹⁷ _____?
I / look / your business plan (modal auxiliary)
¹⁸ _____? *much money / look for* (Wh / how question)

Complete these dialogues with phrases a–e. Write the letters in the spaces.

a I'd love to tell you   d I'm afraid I
b Sorry, I'm not up   e It's hard
c I'm sorry, I'm really

A And what are the criteria for evaluation?
B ¹⁹___ can't reveal the details on that.
A Do you know how many other people applied?
B ²⁰___, but I don't know any more than you.
A When do you expect the project to finish?
B ²¹___ to say at the moment.
A So when did Mike take over as project manager?
B ²²___ to speed on all the developments.
A Do you know how Sally got on at the interview?
B ²³___ not in a position to talk about that.

Result _____ / 30 marks

Speaking test

Role cards

Copy this page and cut out the role cards for the students. Students should do both role-plays. Then use the *Speaking test results* forms to evaluate each student's performance. You can then cut out the results and give them to the students.

Cut along this line

Student A

1 You are in a monthly department update meeting. You are asked to talk about the new parking facilities. Give a short impromptu presentation to your colleagues.
   • introduce the topic (new underground car parking – still being built)
   • signal intention (you want to talk about the what will happen when car park is finished)
   • highlight the key points (150 permits available, although the staff totals 280 –only for those unable to get here on public transport; for emergency parking for deliveries / conferences apply to HR 48 hours in advance)
   • answer questions (parking available soon - you don't know exactly when; permits available from HR from next month)

2 Student B will tell you about the new employee exchange system. As appropriate, interrupt and ask your questions.
   • Is it for everyone?
   • Can staff choose where they go?

Student B

1 Student A will tell you about the new company parking facilities. As appropriate, interrupt and ask your questions.
   • When will the car park be finished?
   • When are permits available from HR?

2 You are in a monthly department update meeting. You are asked to talk about the new employee exchange system. Give a short impromptu presentation to your colleagues.
   • introduce the topic (new employee exchange system – still in planning stage – will allow staff to work for short periods in company locations around the world)
   • signal intention (you want to talk about what staff need to do to be involved)
   • highlight the key points (will start from 1st January; only one person per department can go every year)
   • answer questions (only for staff who have been at the company for more than two years; staff must state three preferences of where they would like to go)

Cut along this line

Speaking test results

Use these forms to evaluate the students.

Cut along this line

Student A

Can the student ...	Didn't do this (0 points)	Yes, but with some mistakes (1 point)	Yes, did this very well (2 points)
introduce the topic?			
signal intention?			
highlight key points?			
answer challenging questions?			
ask challenging questions?			

Result _____ / 10 marks

Student B

Can the student ...	Didn't do this (0 points)	Yes, but with some mistakes (1 point)	Yes, did this very well (2 points)
introduce the topic?			
signal intention?			
highlight key points?			
answer challenging questions?			
ask challenging questions?			

Result _____ / 10 marks

Cut along this line

Complete these sentences with a phrase from the list.

> quantifiable data   drain on resources
> knowledge base   track record
> return on investment

1 We don't know what that company's _____ is for this kind of work.

2 I'm sorry, but I need more _____ – your proposal doesn't include any actual figures.

3 We've hardly started this project, but already it's proving very expensive – it's a real _____.

4 I'm afraid I'm not prepared to put up the money for this unless there's going to be a decent _____.

5 We don't need to outsource this. The _____ we have within the company is more than sufficient.

Complete the missing verbs in these sentences.

6 The project failed because we m_____ our resources.

7 Have you a_____ sufficient resources to the project?

8 We're so wasteful. We must stop s_____ our resources.

9 How can we best u_____ our resources?

Complete these sentences with words from the list.

> consensus   perspective   picture
> points   position   strategy   viability

10 So the general _____ is that we should go ahead?

11 We need to look at this from a long-term _____.

12 It's all fine, but we need to look at the bigger _____.

13 Are there any other _____ we need to consider?

14 Yes, but we need to bear in mind the long-term _____ of all this. Will it still be working ten years from now?

15 Look, we can't give up now. We're in a really strong _____. I really think we could win this tender.

16 We need a clear _____ to move the business forward.

Complete these sentences with the correct form of the words in brackets.

17 If we'd thought about this before, we _____ (not / experience) so many problems now.

18 You'll be able to finalize the plans by the weekend if you _____ (set up) a meeting for Thursday.

19 If we could use the same contractors as last time, then it _____ (be) easy to get started.

20 _____ (provide / we / do) the interviewing in pairs, it shouldn't take more than two afternoons.

21 Had I known the system would be out of date within a year, I _____ (not / invest) so much in it.

22 Unless he _____ (become) more professional since I last saw him, we won't get a reply.

23 If we _____ (not / already / spend) all the budget, we'd have the funds to put an advert in the paper.

24 Well, if we targeted school-leavers, we _____ (be able to) focus far more on technical skills.

Put the words below in *italics* in the correct order to complete these sentences.

25 No, not three thousand. Three hundred!
   didn't / sorry / clear / if / I / that / make.
   _____

26 Actually, *lines / of / was / I / more / the / thinking / along* employing staff locally to do the job.
   _____

27 *meant / I / was / what* that we should outsource IT.
   _____

28 No, *I'm / not / what / exactly / that's / saying.*
   _____

29 Send half a dozen staff members to Belgium?
   meant / what / that's / really / not / I.
   _____

30 *actually / wanted / say / I / was / what / to* that we've already got the green light on this project.
   _____

Result _____ / 30 marks

Role cards

Copy this page and cut out the role cards for the students. Students should do both role-plays. Then use the *Speaking test results* forms to evaluate each student's performance. You can then cut out the results and give them to the students.

Cut along this line

Student A

1 You are a senior manager. Your business is going well, but because of staff increases, space in your city centre offices is limited. Parking is becoming impossible.
  • tell a staff member (Student B) about the problem
  • explain why it's important to act
  • present, discuss, and evaluate each option
  • reach an agreement

Options
  • Move to offices in the 'Garden City' area, 12 km from town – shopping and sports centre nearby, good transport connections, lots of green areas.
  • Outsource IT to Malta – technical and English language skills are high there, and staff are cheaper.

2 You work in a restaurant. Your manager (Student B) will tell you about the current situation.
  • listen to the explanation and options
  • discuss and evaluate the options (you see good food as essential for everyone and you love gardening)
  • reach an agreement

Student B

1 Your manager (Student A) will tell you about options for solving current workspace problems.
  • listen to the strategy and options
  • discuss and evaluate the options (you live near the town centre, you have friends in IT)
  • reach an agreement

2 You are the manager of Four Quarters of the Moon, a vegetarian restaurant. Due to rising oil and food prices worldwide, the prices of many of your imported supplies have increased dramatically.
  • tell a staff member (Student A) about the problem
  • explain why it's important to act
  • present, discuss, and evaluate each option
  • reach an agreement

Options
  • Reduce importing, and use much more fresh local produce.
  • Put up prices – focus on re-branding to attract clientele with more money.

Cut along this line

Speaking test results

Use these forms to evaluate the students.

Cut along this line

Student A

Can the student ...	Didn't do this (0 points)	Yes, but with some mistakes (1 point)	Yes, did this very well (2 points)
set the context of a problem?			
explain options?			
discuss options?			
evaluate options?			
reach agreement?			

Result _____ / 10 marks

Student B

Can the student ...	Didn't do this (0 points)	Yes, but with some mistakes (1 point)	Yes, did this very well (2 points)
set the context of a problem?			
explain options?			
discuss options?			
evaluate options?			
reach agreement?			

Result _____ / 10 marks

Cut along this line

Choose the correct answer from the words in *italics*.

1 She promised to be heavily involved in the project, but she doesn't put in much effort. She's not *empathetic / committed / people-focused*.

2 He can never make his mind up, and can't ever provide a definite answer. He's not *self-aware / adaptable / decisive*.

3 She seems to prefer working independently – she's not very good at working with the rest of the team. She's not *adaptable / collaborative / passionate*.

4 One minute he's shouting at someone, and the next he's locked himself in his room! He just has no idea of how this affects other people. He's not *self-aware / passionate / collaborative*.

A company director is talking about his work. Choose the correct answer from the words in *italics*.

Well, first, I'd say it's crucial to build a culture ⁵ *with / of* trust, because without this no one will be fully committed to the project. Basically, it's up to me to gently exert influence ⁶ *through / over* my staff and in so doing, to encourage them to achieve their own goals. I also have to avoid the temptation ⁷ *to / of* do the jobs myself – effective delegating is really important! In terms of feedback and progress I always try to be consistent ⁸ *for / in* my expectations.

Rewrite the phrases in *italics* using the words in brackets. The meaning should stay the same.

9 *This means we'll be able to* reach a far wider customer base – something we couldn't do before. (what / allow)
_____

10 *As far as I'm aware,* the work force is going be cut by 20%. (as / understand)
_____

11 *It'd be a good idea* to get your staff involved from the beginning. (encourage / all / you)
_____

12 *What concerns me is* whether we should include new staff. (reservations) _____

13 *Is there any guarantee* that there won't be any job losses? (us / assurance) _____

14 *What you say makes sense,* but I don't actually believe it'll cause any problems. (that / valid)
_____

15 *You've all got* a key role to play in this project. (each one)
_____

Re-write the phrases in *italics* using a passive form.

16 *We / just / inform* by senior management that no one can leave on Fridays before 5.00 p.m.
_____

17 Have you heard? John *finally / persuade* to join the team as IT assistant! _____

18 *a decision / take /* last week to do a print run of 5,000 brochures. _____

19 *It / going to / suggest* to the Marketing Department that we don't advertise in tabloid newspapers in the future.
_____

20 *It / proposed* at the meeting that Luc should cover for Fabian while he's on holiday.
_____

21 Now that Marianna has resigned, the project *coordinate / by* Suzy. _____

22 *It / decide* on Tuesday that everyone should give five euros towards flowers for Sally.
_____

Correct the two mistakes in each sentence. (2 points per sentence)

23 When Emma's away, I'll be expect to cover her work. I have to tell that I'm really not happy about that. _____

24 It was announced that a new project was been indicated – personal speaking, I'd love to be involved. _____

25 It's been told that your report was sub-standard – to tell you truth, I think you need to focus more on your writing skills. _____

26 I've been suggested that we allow for two part-time contracts, but to be honest to you, I think we'd be better off creating a job-share position. _____

Result _____ **/ 30 marks**

Role cards

Copy this page and cut out the role cards for the students. Students should do both role-plays. Then use the *Speaking test results* forms to evaluate each student's performance. You can then cut out the results and give them to the students.

Cut along this line

Student A

1 You are the Training Manager at an international company. Due to rising travel costs, Head Office have decided to replace face-to-face courses with distance training courses. Brief your staff on the following management decisions.
   - all training courses will now be distance courses (except interviewing skills)
   - training will be conducted online and via email

   During the briefing, remember to
   - maintain a personal distance
   - focus on the benefits (assignments and feedback can be uploaded easily; group forums for each course)
   - make people feel involved
   - respond to any concerns (extra study time will be allocated to participants).

2 Your colleague will tell you about plans for a festival. Listen carefully, then express your concerns, and ask for assurances on the following:
   - Some staff here aren't graduates; are any of our jobs in jeopardy?

Student B

1 Your Training Manager will tell you about a new training system. Listen carefully, then express your concerns, and ask for assurances on the following:
   - Will courses be run in our own time or in work time?

2 You work for a civil rights organization. In the summer you will have a stand at a youth festival to publicize what you do. Management have suggested recruiting university graduates to help. Brief your staff on the following management decisions.
   - interviews will take place early June
   - students will work in staff teams

   During the briefing, remember to
   - maintain a personal distance
   - focus on the benefits (students, not staff, will put together and distribute information packs; it will help us find potential future employees)
   - make people feel involved
   - respond to any concerns (students are being recruited on one-off short-term contracts).

Cut along this line

Speaking test results

Use these forms to evaluate the students.

Cut along this line

Student A

Can the student ...	Didn't do this (0 points)	Yes, but with some mistakes (1 point)	Yes, did this very well (2 points)
brief staff on decisions?			
focus on positive benefits?			
make people feel involved?			
respond to concerns?			
ask for assurances?			

Result _____ / 10 marks

Student B

Can the student ...	Didn't do this (0 points)	Yes, but with some mistakes (1 point)	Yes, did this very well (2 points)
brief staff on decisions?			
focus on positive benefits?			
make people feel involved?			
respond to concerns?			
ask for assurances?			

Result _____ / 10 marks

Cut along this line

Choose the correct answer from the words in *italics*.

1 It's out of the question to stop production in South Korea – it would be *significantly / irretrievably / potentially* disastrous.

2 Now that the price of oil has settled, transport costs are *relatively / unexpectedly / decreasingly* stable.

3 I have no idea why I keep getting all these unsolicited emails. It's *significantly / potentially / profoundly* worrying.

4 After last month's PR scandal, it looks like we have serious problems. The whole situation has been *profoundly / irretrievably / unexpectedly* damaging to the company.

Complete this extract from an appraisal document with the correct form of the words in the list.

> commit   conduct   pride   strive

Eamonn has had a good year, and has ⁵_____ business with our clients extremely professionally. He always ⁶_____ to achieve the best possible results, and takes ⁷_____ in his achievements. He remains ⁸_____ to our customers, and yet continues to exceed sales targets.

Use the words in *italics* to complete these sentences.

9 I'm sorry, but there's nothing I can do – *beyond / control*.
_____

10 I was thinking about another alternative – getting in a consultant: *that / something / you / consider*?
_____

11 Sam's going to be off for six months on a secondment – *you / make / do / part-time employee* as a replacement for the time being? _____

12 Your point about speeding up deliveries is an interesting one, and it's certainly *not / question*.
_____

13 The answer's no. That's all there is to it. *I / firm / this*.
_____

14 Mmm, *sound / feasible*. In fact, it seems a better idea, and I really think we might be able to make it work.
_____

15 I know it's not ideal, but there is nothing we can do about it. We *stuck / situation*.
_____

16 Look, we've already established that there are too many problems. Let's face it, *it / not / work*.
_____

Rewrite these sentences using an inversion and the words in brackets.

17 You should not enter the building through the rear door in any situation. (under no circumstances)
_____

18 The order was delayed and the goods were damaged! (not only) _____

19 You can only activate the virus scan program when you have restarted your computer. (not until)
_____

20 If you decided to take the job in Austria, you would have the chance to improve your German. (were)
_____

21 If I had known you were going to be in town today, I'd have changed my plans. (had)
_____

22 We shouldn't turn it down – it's not often we get an offer like this! (rarely) _____

Correct the two mistakes in each sentence. (2 points per sentence)

23 John, can I have a word? This is a bit dedicate. I don't mean sound rude, but that jacket just isn't appropriate for this event.

24 Please don't put this the wrong way, but this meeting is actually only for senior management, so you're not allowed to attend. Please don't give offence.

25 With respectful, your idea is unfeasible. I'm not quite sure where to put this, but from what I've heard your ideas are often poorly thought through.

26 I think it's quite as simple as that. You need understanding that there are far more people involved in this.

Result _____ / 30 marks

Role cards

Copy this page and cut out the role cards for the students. Students should do both role-plays.
Then use the *Speaking test results* forms to evaluate each student's performance. You can then cut out
the results and give them to the students.

Cut along this line

Student A

1 You are an office manager. An intruder recently entered offices at your company, threatened a member of staff, and stole some money. As a result, you want to introduce tighter security measures. Your preferences are:
   • Everyone should have their bags checked (including staff) when they enter the building.
   • Introduce a signing-in system for staff for six months.

   Meet a senior manager to discuss the situation.
   • state the situation and initiate negotiation
   • be prepared to negotiate on some aspects, but not all
   • reach an agreement

2 You are a senior manager. There are to be a series of one-week transport strikes in your city. Your preferences are:
   • Staff should try to get to work (car-share system).
   • Conference calls everyday for all senior staff.

   Meet the HR manager to discuss the situation.
   • listen and then present your own preferences
   • be prepared to negotiate on some aspects, but not all
   • reach an agreement

Student B

1 You are a senior manager. An intruder recently entered offices at your company, threatened a member of staff, and stole some money. Tighter security measures are to be introduced. Your preferences are:
   • Visitors should have their bags checked.
   • Introduce a signing-in system for two weeks.

   Meet an office manager to discuss the situation.
   • listen and then present your own preferences
   • be prepared to negotiate on some aspects, but not all
   • reach an agreement

2 You are the HR manager. There are to be a series of one-week transport strikes in your city. This will make it difficult for staff to get to work. Your preferences are:
   • Let staff work from home.
   • Ask staff to email a review of their work regularly.

   Meet a senior manager to discuss the situation.
   • state the situation and initiate negotiation
   • be prepared to negotiate on some aspects, but not all
   • reach an agreement

Cut along this line

Speaking test results

Use these forms to evaluate the students.

Cut along this line

Student A

Can the student …	Didn't do this (0 points)	Yes, but with some mistakes (1 point)	Yes, did this very well (2 points)
state the position?			
initiate negotiation?			
show he / she is happy to negotiate?			
show he / she is unhappy to negotiate?			
reach an agreement?			

Result _____ / 10 marks

Student B

Can the student …	Didn't do this (0 points)	Yes, but with some mistakes (1 point)	Yes, did this very well (2 points)
state the position?			
initiate negotiation?			
show he / she is happy to negotiate?			
show he / she is unhappy to negotiate?			
reach an agreement?			

Result _____ / 10 marks

Cut along this line

Each sentence contains one mistake. <u>Underline</u> it and write the correct word.

1 She was completely taken up by her boss when he told her the offices were moving to Australia – she didn't realize it was a joke. _____

2 I just don't buy the idea into of opening a new department. It simply doesn't seem viable at this stage. _____

3 Sally didn't accept the other job, but held out of the one she wanted – and eventually got it! _____

4 What you're asking for is difficult. I'm not sure we'll be able to live on to your expectations. _____

5 When Emma was going through the contracts, she picked on up a number of typing errors. _____

6 We can play to the fact that although we're a new company, we have employees with a lot of expertise. _____

7 The talk was just dreadful. The speaker didn't know how to put through what he was trying to say. _____

8 We need to tap up the expertise that Alec has – he's highly qualified and really knows what he's doing. _____

Choose the correct answer from the words in *italics*.

9 I'd like you to give serious *concern / consideration / ideas* to this expansion plan, even though it's fairly ambitious.

10 Frankly, we can't *accept / achieve / afford* to miss this opportunity.

11 Looking at the sales figures, it's become *recognized / apparent / achievable* that we need to rethink some of our products.

12 And *in addition / in consideration / in kind* to that, this will create opportunities for developing new skills.

13 I understand your reservations about diversification, but we have to *appear / know / acknowledge* that our competitors are doing much better than us.

14 I'm certain that this is *achievable / apparent / in addition*.

15 As you know, with figures like this, we are in an extremely strong *benefit / consideration / position*.

16 What comes *apparent / across / along* from talking to you is that you're all committed to the company.

Complete these extracts from an internal presentation to a sales department with a phrase from the list. Use the information in brackets to help you.

obviously	as I was saying	of course
anyway	admittedly	to tell you the truth
after all	so to speak	

'Our department has faced a lot of criticism recently. 17_____(I'm giving you some very frank information) it's the worst we've had for a long time. 18_____(I know this point weakens my position) – we should have recognized our sales had been consistently low, but we didn't and we've got to face the consequences. 19_____(this point is expected), management want to know what we're going to do about things. 20_____(this is clear), I'm not going to blame anyone, 21_____(I'm adding some additional, true information), it's no one's fault. ... So, moving on, we're suggesting that we regroup. This will refresh the team and, 22_____ (I've already mentioned this), the low sales are no one's fault, so there's no one person who should feel unhappy about moving teams. 23_____(I'm changing subject), on Monday it's going to be a clean slate 24_____(not literally, but figuratively) and I can't wait to begin!'

Correct the phrases in *italics* in these dialogues.

A 25 *That was a very worth meeting.* _____ Thanks for your contributions.

B You're welcome. They seem happy with our plan!

A I liked the email you wrote, Mike. It was very succinct.

B 26 *Glad you thought it so.* _____

A Congratulations on the presentation – it was great!

B Oh, thanks! 27 *I think it went quite good after all!* _____

A By the way, well done on your talk.

B Thanks – 28 *I was hope it'd be well received.* _____

A 29 *You looking well* – really tanned!

B It must be all the cycling to work in the sunshine.

A Fabulous photos. 30 *You did a great work!* _____

B Thanks. It was fun using the new camera!

Result _____ / 30 marks

Speaking test

Role cards

Copy this page and cut out the role cards for the students. Students should do both role-plays. Then use the *Speaking test results* forms to evaluate each student's performance. You can then cut out the results and give them to the students.

Cut along this line

Student A

1 You are the IT manager of a large property agency. You work with a number of key corporate clients on a regular basis and need an improved system of keeping records. You have recently found new software to do this. Meet a staff member (Student B) and tell them about your idea.

Rationale
- The software tracks all communications between staff and clients.
- The software is not difficult to use, and training is short.

During the meeting
- give reasons for the change
- build your argument / reinforce the message
- ask for their commitment
- conclude and deal with any concerns.

2 Your company has been taken over by a company based in Munich. Your manager will tell you about a new idea.
- Listen to the idea and rationale.
- Discuss the idea, give your opinion, and raise any concerns that you have.

Student B

1 Your company needs to improve the way they store client records. Your manager will tell you about a new idea.
- Listen to the idea and rationale.
- Discuss the idea, give your opinion, and raise any concerns that you have.

2 You are a senior manager. Your company has recently been taken over by a company based in Munich. You would like communication with Head Office to be in German from January onwards. Meet a staff member (Student A) and tell them about your idea.

Rationale
- Using German will improve communication with the parent company.
- Staff without good German will be given training.

During the meeting
- give reasons for the change
- build your argument / reinforce the message
- ask for their commitment
- conclude and deal with any concerns.

Cut along this line

Speaking test results

Use these forms to evaluate the students.

Cut along this line

Student A

Can the student ...	Didn't do this (0 points)	Yes, but with some mistakes (1 point)	Yes, did this very well (2 points)
establish the need for change?			
build the argument?			
ask for commitment?			
conclude?			
deal with concerns?			

Result _____ / 10 marks

Student B

Can the student ...	Didn't do this (0 points)	Yes, but with some mistakes (1 point)	Yes, did this very well (2 points)
establish the need for change?			
build the argument?			
ask for commitment?			
conclude?			
deal with concerns?			

Result _____ / 10 marks

Cut along this line

Unit 1

1 up-and-coming
2 outspoken
3 self-assured
4 easy-going
5 time-consuming
6 out-of-the-way
7 form an opinion
8 keep your eyes open
9 manage unknowns
10 build relationships
11 gives you an insight
12 weigh up the pros and cons
13 c
14 a
15 d
16 b
17 f
18 h
19 g
20 i
21 j
22 e
23 had planned
24 'll have finished
25 was talking
26 could have been
27 shouldn't have ordered
28 've bought
29 've been trying
30 is happening

Unit 2

1 stand
2 cling
3 move
4 stay
5 come
6 keep
7 stick
8 conventional
9 horizontally
10 grow
11 stage
12 broaden
13 backward / backwards
14 started
15 run
16 keen
17 come
18 Would(n't)
19 come
20 ahead
21 wondering
22 move

23 had ('d) been
24 would have (would've) happened
25 had
26 had ('d) thought
27 might have (might've) been
28 shouldn't have reacted
29 didn't cancel
30 had ('d) gone

Unit 3

1 entering
2 Carrying out
3 procedure
4 putting in place
5 transformation
6 means
7 option
8 implement
9 targets
10 enthusiasm
11 problems
12 information
13 progress
14 I'd like to start by
15 Just to fill you in on some of the background
16 Now, I don't know if you're familiar with
17 Perhaps here I should explain what I mean by
18 Just to digress for a second
19 I know what you **mean**, they **are going to make / will make** people …
20 a **tricky** time, expected **to work** overtime …
21 you might **well** / might **want**, little more **diplomatic**
22 **you'll be** flying, worth **trying**
23 **coming** from, we **will have been** working …
24 will **be**, for **certain**

Unit 4

1 anticipate
2 weigh up
3 expose
4 run
5 determine
6 minimize
7 over-cautious
8 sensible
9 reckless
10 rash
11 risk-averse
12 … interested **to hear / in hearing**

what you …
13 … to have **second** thoughts / serious **doubts / reservations**
14 … could just **bring** the conversation …
15 Could you **let** Jason …
16 I'd like to **draw** things …
17 to **sum** up their …
18 right
19 reservations
20 respect
21 getting
22 consensus
23 it's
24 that's
25 that was / it was
26 this
27 b
28 a
29 d
30 c

Unit 5

1 treats, unfairly
2 expressing, clearly
3 done, thoroughly
4 tread, carefully
5 work, closely
6 viewed, positively
7 with
8 of
9 to
10 of
11 to
12 understood
13 focused
14 deal
15 aware
16 would
17 honest
18 consider
19 prepared
20 What I'd really like to know is why they got rid of Tom.
21 Not only has the new finance manager stopped all new recruitment, but there's also talk of redundancies.
22 The reason (why) we're a successful team is because we get on so well together.
23 We have to finish this project by Friday which is why we're all working overtime at the moment.
24 What really worries me is the financial data for this quarter. / What's a real worry is the financial data for this quarter.

Unit 6

1. into
2. beyond
3. by
4. ahead of
5. around
6. off
7. back on
8. outside
9. out
10. clear
11. lines
12. wondering
13. concerned
14. supposing
15. stopping
16. worth
17. cause a stir
18. demand precision
19. outperform the competition
20. control costs
21. undergo change
22. Actually
23. just
24. totally
25. surprisingly
26. obviously
27. you're on the right track
28. I'm trying to think how
29. It's difficult for me to explain really
30. It just needs a bit more

Unit 7

1. personal development plan
2. shared vision
3. skills deficit
4. self-directed
5. bottom-up
6. b
7. e
8. f
9. c
10. h
11. g
12. d
13. a
14. Having seen how …
15. Given the shortage …
16. Faced with similar …
17. Knowing how hard you've worked, I think …
18. I was supposed to meet the visitors from Germany at the airport, but Harry went in my place.

19. I thought Elke would be a great addition to the team, but she's very lazy and hasn't fitted into the team.
20. I was going to finish the report before I left the office, but I couldn't because I had a long phone call.
21. The company intended to / had intended to review the pay scale in June, but there wasn't a review due to bad financial results.
22. use
23. head
24. expectations
25. limit
26. scratch

Unit 8

1. to
2. on
3. up
4. for
5. **put** my skills to the test, **take** pride in
6. **feel / be / become** part of, see a **future** for
7. was **coming** to that, **at** the moment
8. touch **on**, **would** be a good idea
9. sketch **out**, **unfortunately** I can't
10. the **exact** figures, **I'll** get back to you
11. **Off** the top, **double check** if you like
12. Why should I invest in your company?
13. Would you like me to show you the product? Can I / Should I / May I / Could I show you …?
14. You think this is a unique product, do you?
15. You're sure about that, are you?
16. I assume that you've already spoken to retailers about stocking your product?
17. Would you mind if I looked / Can I look / Could I look … at your business plan?
18. How much money are you looking for?
19. d
20. a
21. e
22. b
23. c

Unit 9

1. track record
2. quantifiable data
3. drain on resources
4. return on investment
5. knowledge base
6. mismanaged
7. allocated

8. squandering
9. utilize
10. consensus
11. perspective
12. picture
13. points
14. viability
15. position
16. strategy
17. wouldn't be experiencing
18. set up
19. 'd be / would be
20. Provided we do / did
21. wouldn't have invested
22. has become
23. hadn't already spent
24. would / might be able to
25. Sorry if I didn't make that clear
26. I was thinking more along the lines of
27. What I meant was
28. that's not exactly what I'm saying
29. That's not really what I meant
30. What I actually wanted to say was

Unit 10

1. committed
2. decisive
3. collaborative
4. self-aware
5. of
6. over
7. to
8. in
9. What this will allow us to do is …
10. As I understand it, …
11. I would / I'd encourage all of you …
12. I have some / serious reservations about …
13. Can you give us an assurance that …
14. That's a valid point, …
15. Each one of you has (got) …
16. We've just been informed
17. has finally been persuaded
18. A decision was taken
19. It's going to be suggested
20. It was proposed
21. will be / is going to be coordinated
22. It was decided
23. I'll be **expected** to, have to **say**
24. new project **has** been, **personally** speaking
25. **I've** been told / It's been **said**, tell you **the** truth
26. **It's** been suggested, to be honest **with** you

Progress test answer key

Unit 11

1 potentially
2 relatively
3 profoundly
4 irretrievably
5 conducted
6 strives
7 pride
8 committed
9 it's beyond my / our control
10 is that something you would / could / might consider?
11 could you make do with a part-time employee
12 not out of the question
13 I have to stay / stand firm on this
14 that / it sounds feasible
15 are stuck with the situation
16 it (just) won't work / it's not working
17 Under no circumstances should you enter the building through the rear door.
18 Not only was the order delayed, but the goods were also damaged.
19 Not until you have restarted your computer can you activate the virus scan program.
20 Were you to take the job in Austria, you would have the chance to improve your German.
21 Had I known you were going to be in town today, I would have changed my plans.
22 Rarely do we get an offer like this. We shouldn't turn it down.
23 a bit **delicate**, mean **to** sound rude
24 don't **take** this, don't **take** offence
25 With **respect**, not quite sure **how** to
26 I **don't** think, You need **to understand**

Unit 12

1 taken **in** by
2 buy **into the idea of**
3 held out **for** the one
4 live **up** to your
5 picked **up on** a number
6 play **on** the fact
7 how to put **across** what
8 to tap **into** the expertise
9 consideration
10 afford
11 apparent
12 in addition
13 acknowledge
14 achievable

15 position
16 across
17 To tell you the truth
18 Admittedly
19 Obviously,
20 Of course
21 after all
22 as I was saying
23 Anyway
24 so to speak
25 That was a very **worthwhile** meeting.
26 Glad you **thought so**.
27 I think it went quite **well** after all!
28 I was **hoping** it would be well received.
29 **You're** looking well. / You **look** well.
30 You did a great **job**.

Practice file answer key

Unit 1

Working with words

Exercise 1

1	read	2	build
3	weighed up	4	processed
5	keep	6	take
7	form	8	gave
9	build	10	work
11	managing	12	kept

Exercise 2

1 down to earth
2 out-of-the-way
3 outspoken
4 low-key
5 run-of-the-mill
6 unexpected
7 an easy-going
8 time-consuming
9 open-minded
10 self-assured
11 up-and-coming
12 tedious

Business communication skills

Exercise 1

1	convinced	2	anticipated
3	wouldn't	4	I'm not saying
5	wary	6	anything
7	've got to	8	confident
9	a reason	10	can't

Exercise 2

1 I'm **just not** 100% convinced
2 I'm **absolutely / quite** sure that
3 To be **fair / honest**, the whole matter
4 I **gathered** from your report
5 I wouldn't go **so far / as far** as to say
6 From **what** I could see

Exercise 3 *(suggested answers only)*

1 From what I could see, the meeting went much better than we expected.
2 I'm not saying the trip didn't go well – it's just that there were some problems.
3 I've got to say that / I'm fully confident the proposed site would be perfect for the company.
4 According to Fred / I gathered from Fred that the project is going fairly well.

Language at work

Exercise 1

1 are growing, has made
2 have expanded, have been
3 reflects, have continued
4 takes, is stepping

Exercise 2

1 We will have completed …
2 We had originally hoped …

3 … who have been working on it …
4 I'll be taking … / I'll take …
5 … there seems to be …
6 We're going to send … / We'll be sending … / We're sending … / We'll send …
7 I'm now handing over …, She has been working …
8 Our sales had been levelling off …
9 … I was thinking about this …

Unit 2

Working with words

Exercise 1

1 d	2 i	3 g	4 b	5 e	6 f
7 l	8 a	9 j	10 k	11 c	12 h

Exercise 2

1	stay ahead of	2	hold on to
3	get on with	4	look out for
5	stand up for	6	stand out from
7	cling on to	8	move on to
9	keep in with	10	come up with
11	stick up for	12	stand up to

Exercise 3

1	take	2	move
3	follow	4	Broadening
5	grow	6	goes
7	put	8	reach

Business communication skills

Exercise 1

1	get	2	talk
3	like	4	mention
5	understand	6	come back
7	suppose, think	8	keen on
9	come in	10	get on to

Exercise 2

a	2	b	7	c	1, 6, 10
d	3, 8	e	5	f	4, 9

Exercise 3

1 **Do** you want to … Would you **like** to
2 The obvious solution to this problem **must / would** be …
3 The **purpose** of today's meeting …
4 It's interesting you **said / say** that …
5 Could I **just** say something?
6 I'm not sure **what** your feelings are about …
7 But what makes you so **sure** …
8 Given that Arturo **doesn't** have …

Exercise 4

a	1	b	4, 7, 8	c	3
d	6	e	2	f	5

Language at work

Exercise 1

1 c	2 h	3 e	4 b	5 g
6 j	7 a	8 d	9 i	10 f

Exercise 2

1 Even if I had asked for a pay rise, I wouldn't have got one.
2 If the company had renewed our season ticket, I could have gone to the football game.
3 If only they hadn't got rid of the air-conditioning, the office wouldn't be so unbearably hot.
4 If the airport staff hadn't called off their strike yesterday, I wouldn't be in Spain now.

Exercise 3

1	should	2	might
3	would	4	have, had
5	should	6	have
7	had	8	might
9	would	10	should

Unit 3

Working with words

Exercise 1

1 efficient
2 entering, access
3 option
4 transformed
5 carried out
6 process, procedures
7 means
8 purpose
9 energetic, dynamic
10 installed

Exercise 2

1 targets
2 objections
3 ideas
4 performance
5 productivity
6 objections
7 development
8 potential difficulties

Exercise 3

1 measure the performance
2 exchange ideas
3 anticipate objections
4 facilitate productivity
5 assess the situation
6 accommodate the needs
7 generate enthusiasm
8 achieve good results

Business communication skills

Exercise 1

1 Just to fill you
2 something to think about
3 I'd like to start
4 put it another way

Practice file answer key

5 I mean
6 moving on
7 for example
8 turning to
9 I said earlier
10 This is where
11 Just to digress
12 And this brings me

Exercise 2
1 I've divided my talk up into …
2 First of all I'll … After that I'll …
3 I'll say more about that in a moment.
4 Just to fill you in on some of the background …
5 Now I don't know if you're familiar with …
6 And this is my key point.
7 I'll now be happy to take any questions. / I'll be happy to take any questions now.

Language at work

Exercise 1 (other forms are possible, but these are the best)
1 'll call
2 'll be rolling
3 'll give
4 'll have been listening … 'll take
5 'll learn
6 will have spoken
7 will yield / should yield
8 might / could / would be worth

Exercise 2
1 The consultants will probably suggest merging the departments.
2 They'll almost certainly deliver the stock in time.
3 The management are bound to ask our opinion before making the changes.
4 It's probable that the tax changes will turn investors away.
5 I've got to go now, but there's a good chance I'll see you at the launch party later.
6 The training course is unlikely to be useful. / It's unlikely that the training course will be useful.
7 The CEO is expected to make an announcement at the dinner. / It's expected that the CEO will make an announcement at the dinner.
8 They'll perhaps need more identification than a credit card. / Perhaps they'll need more identification than a credit card.

Unit 4

Working with words

Exercise 1
1 l	2 g	3 j	4 a	5 e	6 f
7 c	8 k	9 i	10 b	11 h	12 d

Exercise 2
1 reckless	2 over-cautious
3 prudent	4 rash
5 cautious	6 bold
7 foolhardy	8 risk-averse

Hidden word = sensible

Business communication skills

Exercise 1
1 could you talk us through this
2 Can I just check – we are now talking about
3 You're saying that
4 I'm not fully convinced as yet
5 Could you let Torsten finish, please
6 Maybe we're digressing a little
7 bring the conversation back to the agenda
8 I'd be really interested to hear what you think about the printer issue
9 we seem to have some sort of consensus …

Exercise 2
1 let	2 left
3 thoughts	4 respect
5 is getting	6 to sum up
7 reservations	8 in
9 draw	

Language at work

Exercise 1 (Other answers are possible, but these are the best.)
1 Yes, that was one of the most useful conferences I've been to.
2 Aleph's submitting his evaluation by email. It / That should be very helpful, I think.
3 We need to minimize the chances of a downturn. That would be disastrous.
4 We need to minimize the chances of a downturn. It's / That's just good business practice.
5 The auditors are arriving tomorrow. This is what's worrying me: firstly …
6 That's my problem too.

Exercise 2
1 That / It	2 That / This
3 It / This	4 This / That
5 This / That	

Exercise 3
1 b	2 a	3 a	4 b	5 a

Unit 5

Working with words

Exercise 1
1 c	2 b	3 a	4 c	5 b
6 a	7 c	8 b		

Exercise 2
1 pay, to	2 keeps, to
3 steer, of	4 fallen, of
5 focus, on	6 cope, with

Exercise 3
1 Admittedly, there are certain tasks that I tend to **neglect** …
2 Part of my job is making sure that the team **meets** the budget.
3 I like to **avoid** arguments at work …
4 I'm afraid your work **hasn't achieved** the standards …
5 Technical people are often able to **pinpoint** solutions …
6 I don't know how to **handle** this situation …

Business communication skills

Exercise 1
1 I just don't understand how …
2 Look, can we try and avoid any …?
3 How do you propose we deal with this issue?
4 Can we try and stay focused on the facts?
5 The real issue here is …
6 Do you understand what I'm trying to say?
7 I see what you mean, but …
8 Let's try not to get personal here.
9 Can I just make sure I've understood this correctly?
10 I don't know if you are aware …?

Exercise 2
1 if you are aware
2 I be right in thinking
3 just don't understand
4 prepared to
5 you be happy
6 a bit worried
7 what you mean
8 be more than happy
9 we try and avoid
10 not happy with

Language at work

Exercise 1
1 Only at the end did he contribute to the meeting.
2 My main question she didn't even answer / wasn't even answered.

3   It's her lack of professionalism I can't stand.
4   What's impressive is his boundless enthusiasm.
5   The person who's the best listener in our meetings is Zoe.
6   It's absolutely vital that you inform me of matters like that.
7   Creativity (is what) I value above anything else.
8   It's his constant need to make stupid jokes (that) I don't like.

Exercise 2
1   We were **very impressed indeed** with …
2   are **absolutely / really essential** …
3   She's **just so** close …
4   **Not only is the report** a month late …
5   Mo is **very / really** good …
6   **What was** annoying was …
7   What **I like** best about …
8   **Never have I / I have never** seen …
9   **Which is why** I decided …
10 The person **who** is chairing / The **person chairing**
11 **The** reason why I'm saying this
12 … **who** is on the phone / **Someone** from HR **is** on the phone.

Unit 6

Working with words
Exercise 1
1	figure	2	bounce
3	think	4	Look
5	hit	6	fall
7	get	8	try
9	run	10	get

Exercise 2
1 c	2 h	3 b	4 f	5 j
6 d	7 g	8 a	9 i	10 e

Business communication skills
Exercise 1
1   I'm not sure how this would work in practice, but how about …?
2   I would have thought it would be possible to …
3   What makes you think that would work?
4   Thinking about it, we could even …
5   Would you like to expand on that?
6   Well I just thought that in that way …
7   It's certainly worth thinking about.
8   Shouldn't we be thinking more about …?
9   I was thinking along the lines of …

Exercise 2 (*Other answers are possible in some gaps.*)
1   Couldn't we consider
2   Supposing we were to
3   Sorry, are you saying
4   so you're thinking
5   that's not such a bad idea
6   I'm concerned about
7   We should at least consider it

Language at work
Exercise 1
1	rather / quite	2	quite / rather
3	little	4	only
5	absolutely / quite	6	Even
7	quite / absolutely	8	all
9	just	10	actually

Exercise 2 (*Other answers are possible in some gaps.*)
1   quite / rather
2   absolutely / really / completely
3   honest
4   very / rather / quite / really
5   in fact / actually
6   even / quite
7   only / just
8   course
9   just
10 really
11 actually / definitely / easily

Unit 7

Working with words
Exercise 1
1   shared vision
2   structural change
3   collective aspiration
4   employee participation
5   performance management, personal development plans
6   paradigm shift
7   skills deficit

Exercise 2
across the board
get in the **real** world
in the long run
the **bigger** picture

Exercise 3
1	one-size-fits-all	2	centrally-driven
3	decentralized	4	job-specific
5	top-down	6	bottom-up
7	generic	8	self-directed

Business communication skills
Exercise 1
1   Could you clarify exactly what the problems were?
2   Do you mean that
3   What I'm saying is
4   What was the name of the other logistics company again?
5   That reminds me. Have you heard that Hans has handed in his notice?
6   By the way, talking about
7   Anyway, sorry. That's a bit of a digression.
8   Let's get back to the main issue.

Exercise 2
1	say	2	about	3	by
4	out	5	not	6	thought
7	doesn't				

Language at work
Exercise 1 (*suggested answers only*)
1   I was going to finish working on the Kelner case, but too many other things came up.
2   I was meeting Sue at 10.00 a.m., but she's off sick at the moment.
3   I was supposed to meet the Hungarian rep at 12.30 p.m. and take him for lunch, but his plane was delayed.
4   I was going to file my corporate credit card expenses, but I couldn't find my receipts.
5   I had intended to book flights for the Atlanta conference, but the airline's website kept crashing.
6   I was going to meet Sarah at Café Carlucci, but it was closed so we went to Spangio's instead.
7   I was going to check my bank account, but there's no point because we don't get paid until tomorrow.

Exercise 2 (*suggested answers only*)
1   Faced with a financial crisis, we cut 50 jobs.
2   Given the new interest rates, I think now is a good time to borrow some money.
3   Having retired, I decided to rethink my life.
4   Not understanding what to do, I asked for help.
5   Knowing what to do in situations like this, Paddy stayed calm throughout the meeting.

Unit 8

Working with words

Exercise 1
1 make, to
2 gained, for
3 have, in
4 feel, of
5 take, in
6 see, for

Exercise 2
1 live, up to
2 put, to
3 thinking, on
4 believe, in
5 seek, out
6 building, up
7 benefit, from
8 striving, for

Exercise 3
1 recognition
2 willingness
3 ability
4 desire

Business communication skills

Exercise 1
1 we are at the moment
2 just like to outline
3 it would be a good idea if I
4 the first thing is
5 a good point
6 remember exactly
7 I think you should be aware
8 have to admit that
9 I'll get back to you

Exercise 2
1 **I'd** like to …
2 … **we need to** address …
3 I don't have the **exact** figures …
4 I think this **is a really** / this **really is an** important point / I **really think** …
5 I can **double check** if you like?
6 I think that's **covered** everything.
7 … I **still need to** / **still have to** run that by ..

Language at work

Exercise 1
1 Would you say you have many weaknesses?
2 I'd like to know what attracted you to this position?
3 You're not unhappy in your present job, are you?
4 What salary are you looking for?
5 You must have some questions to ask us?

Exercise 2
1 a   2 b   3 a   4 b   5 a
6 b   7 b   8 b   9 a

Exercise 3
a 1, 8
b 2, 6
c 7
d 9
e 5

Unit 9

Working with words

Exercise 1
1 g   2 e   3 a   4 f
5 h   6 c   7 d   8 b

Exercise 2
1 corporate accountability
2 track record
3 knowledge base
4 assets
5 bottom line

Exercise 3
1 cost-benefit analysis
2 drain on resources
3 short-term profit
4 return on investment
5 quantifiable data
6 market value
7 long-term viability
8 competitive advantage

Business communication skills

Exercise 1
1 b   2 a   3 b   4 a
5 b   6 b   7 a   8 b

Exercise 2
1 provided we all work together
2 assuming we decided to hold
3 have to bear in mind the long-term viability
4 there's no point going ahead with this meeting if we don't

Language at work

Exercise 1
1 e   2 a   3 g   4 c   5 b
6 j   7 d   8 h   9 f   10 i

Exercise 2
1 If I **knew**
2 we **said** / **would say** so
3 **I'll** be amazed
4 wouldn't **have** so many
5 **had** had a pay rise
6 If they **offered** you

Unit 10

Working with words

Exercise 1
1   commitment
2   decisive
3   conviction
4   self-aware
5   people-focused
6   humble
7   collaborative
8   hands-off
9   adaptable
10 integrity
11 empathy
12 passionate
Hidden word = micromanages

Exercise 2
1   establish
2   instil
3   avoid
4   credibility
5   influence
6   generate
7   work together
8   culture of trust
9   sense of cohesion
10 be consistent in
11 recognize
12 reinforces

Business communication skills

Exercise 1
1   it has been agreed that
2   Apparently, the decision was taken
3   As I understand
4   what this will allow us to do is
5   Another great thing about this change is
6   my understanding
7   it will be well worth the inconvenience
8   the benefits are clear
9   you and your teams are crucial to
10 has a key role to play in
11 I would encourage all of you to

Exercise 2 *(suggested answers only)*
SH: This is something I wanted to bring up. **I like the idea of making** departments more accountable for their training budgets. We could all try to be more cost-effective, I'm sure. **But I'm not very happy about** having to make choices between competing training needs that are equally valid. How do we ensure that essential training will still take place? **Can you give us an assurance that** this will be taken into consideration?

CJ: Well, of course, **that's a valid point, but** the difference is that at the moment the HR Department decides how much of the budget is spent on job-specific training, IT skills, language training, etc. In future, individual departments will be free to choose their own priorities. **My understanding is** that it should make everyone's lives easier, so **let's give this a chance to work.**

Language at work

Exercise 1
1 Five of our products were being sold every minute in 2008.
2 Having been asked to email us details, he didn't get back in touch with us.
3 You will be interviewed before you are allowed to register for work here.
4 The flowers might have been sent yesterday.

5 To have been selected was a great honour.
6 Your order was being processed, but then the whole system crashed.
7 A formal reply is going to be written to address your complaints.
8 15,000 orders have been received – a staggering number.

Exercise 2
1 had been more than made up for
2 put
3 were published
4 showed
5 were divided
6 was reinvested
7 paid out
8 went
9 was raised
10 Looking
11 to have been invited
12 to put in
13 to build
14 Having been voted
15 we anticipate

Unit 11

Working with words

Exercise 1
1 In this day and age, it's really important for us to **conduct our business with** openness and integrity.
2 We **pride ourselves on** the fact that our engineers personally oversee the construction of each vehicle, from start to finish.
3 It's extremely important for us to **continue to be sensitive to** the needs of people in the communities where we conduct our business operations.
4 We want everyone to know that we **are committed to** our employees as well as our customers and stakeholders.
5 We **hold ourselves accountable to** all our stakeholders, no matter who they are or where they are.
6 We **have a passion for** technical innovation.
7 In everything we do, we always **strive to achieve** the highest possible standards.
8 We recognize the need to **work cohesively with** our colleagues in other industries.

Exercise 2
1 significantly	2 surprisingly
3 irretrievably	4 potentially
5 relatively	6 comparatively
7 irretrievably	8 potentially

Business communication skills

Exercise 1
1 beyond	2 stuck
3 possibly	4 firm
5 say to	6 out
7 way round	

Exercise 2
1 reached, where	2 employing
3 just not	4 budge
5 along	6 in
7 do	8 would
9 to say	

Exercise 3
We are in a **very difficult** situation …
… this idea about job-sharing **just won't** work.
… consider **re-allocating** jobs and **redefining** roles instead?
… I'd be willing **to hear** …
… I have to say no to **redefining** roles …
… that's **out** of the question …
I suppose that **is feasible / sounds feasible / would be feasible / could be feasible / might be feasible.**
Are we all agreed / Do we all agree that we need **to think** …

Language at work

Exercise 1
1 Eric didn't get your email, and neither did he get your voicemail message.
2 I don't know how often she's away from her desk. Nor do I care, really.
3 Seldom have so many strong applicants applied for a post with us.
4 Under no circumstances must / should visitors go beyond reception without a pass.
5 Never have / had I seen such a wonderful production.
6 Not until we're the market leader will I be satisfied.
7 Not only do they offer a very generous pension scheme, they also offer flexitime.
8 At no time have we failed to live up to our core values of decency, innovation, and trust.

Exercise 2
2 **Under no circumstances** will we accept food that hasn't been created with the sustainability of resources in mind.
3 **Nor** will we allow our food to travel thousands of miles unnecessarily.
4 **Only by** testing our produce regularly can we do this.
5 But **rarely** do we have to change suppliers …

Unit 12

Working with words

Exercise 1
1 generate a demand
2 reinforce an association
3 play on
4 tailor
5 promote the consumption of

Exercise 2
1 across	2 to	3 into
4 in	5 up	6 up
7 out	8 into	

Exercise 3
1 motivational
2 aspirational
3 market penetration
4 exploitative
5 status anxiety
6 USP
7 materialistic
8 consumer profiles

Business communication skills

Exercise 1
1 become apparent
2 comes across
3 first benefit
4 second point
5 having said
6 is achievable
7 strong position
8 Because we
9 very much
10 serious consideration

Exercise 2
1 c   2 f   3 a   4 e   5 b   6 d

Language at work

Exercise 1
1 Basically
2 obviously
3 Anyway
4 After all
5 Quite honestly
6 As a matter of fact
7 Admittedly
8 so to speak
9 Mind you
10 Of course
11 To tell you the truth

Exercise 2
1 b   2 a   3 b   4 b   5 a
6 a   7 b   8 a   9 a   10 b

Material used in the DVD

Business Result Advanced Student's Book, Unit 11, pages 86–87

Part 1 | Why do pre-work students need business English?

1 Read the typical characteristics of in-work business English students. Complete the second table with characteristics of pre-work students. See the example.

In-work students
Range of expertise and experience: These learners may be experts in certain areas of business or have a wide understanding of the world of work – they will often teach you a lot about business while you teach the language.
Goals and objectives: Some learners will have very specific goals relating to their job and they may have immediate needs. Others who don't currently use English in their work will usually recognize that it may be beneficial for their future career.
Time for learning: These people are working and may also have responsibilities at home. Time is often short, so the language training must be focused and time-efficient.
Motivation: As with any class, you will have highly-motivated students and less motivated students. However, there are often motivational reasons for taking the course, such as getting promotion, a pay rise, or fear of losing a job.
Language needs: In-work students might request reading and writing, but the majority will want to focus on improving speaking and listening. Because time is short they might also prioritize fluency over accuracy.

Pre-work students
Range of expertise and experience: These learners may have studied business in their own language, but in general they will have much less knowledge.
Goals and objectives:
Time for learning:
Motivation:
Language needs:

2 ▶ Watch this section and answer questions 1–2.

1 What was the topic of the lesson? Was it a difficult topic for the students to discuss?

_____

2 Make notes about the three students that were interviewed in this table.

	Why is the student studying English?	What area(s) of business would the student like to work in after their course?
Satoko		
Sonnie		
Kitiya		

3 Imagine you are teaching these three students on a course. Answer questions 1–2.

1 Are there any business topics that might be useful to include?

_____

2 Do you think these students would have any particular language needs for their future careers?

_____

Part 2 | How is teaching pre-work students different from teaching in-work students?

4 Match comments 1–5 from teachers of pre-work students to issues connected with teaching pre-work students a–e.

1 'If students don't understand why they are doing something, you may have to explain how the target vocabulary will help them in the future. And don't forget all those other tricks like making a language task competitive, varying the tasks, and giving regular praise.'

2 'Courses can be very broad, but it's a nice change after teaching in companies to be able to deal with language more generally and in a less specialized way.'

3 'Because the classes and courses are often longer you can do things like project work or set online research tasks.'

4 'It's true that they have less direct knowledge of business, but they are still consumers and have life experience that they can draw on.'

5 'One really rewarding aspect of teaching pre-work students is that some of them come on to a course with absolutely no idea of what they want to do in life, but after studying lots of different topics in their English lessons, they discover what areas of business really interest them.'

a Lack of experience _____   c Motivation _____   e Language needs _____
b Goals and objectives _____   d Time for learning _____

5 ▶ Watch this section and answer questions 1–3.

1 Which aspect of teaching pre-work students in **4** does Rebecca (the co-author) talk about? What does she think are the implications of this for the teacher?

_____

2 Does Jenny (the teacher) see students' lack of experience as a major problem for the teacher? What benefits of teaching pre-work students does she mention?

_____

3 What advice does Jenny give for teachers of advanced learners (both pre-work and in-work)?

_____

Material used in the DVD

Business Result Advanced Student's Book, Unit 11, pages 88–89

Part 1 | When do students negotiate?

1 **Which negotiations (a–e) would you expect to be formal and planned?**

   a negotiating for a cheaper price (e.g. for a mobile phone)
   b negotiating who's going to do a household chore
   c negotiating terms and conditions with a client or as a client
   d negotiating a time schedule or deadline (at work)
   e negotiating rates of pay with your boss

2 **Have you recently experienced any of the negotiations in 1? If so, what was the final outcome? Was it similar to one of these three negotiating outcomes?**

Outcome 1: Win-Win
In this case both sides come away from the negotiation pleased with what they achieved. They found an outcome that was suitable for both sides. This kind of result is good when you plan to have a long-term business relationship with the other side.
Outcome 2: Win-Lose
With this outcome, only one side leaves satisfied with the result. This is fine if you are the winner and don't need the other person to do business with you again in the future. However, it isn't good for a long-term business relationship.
Outcome 3: Lose-Lose
This describes what happens when a negotiation collapses and neither side can get what they want.

3 ▶ **Watch this section and answer questions 1–3.**

   1 Which negotiation from 1 did Tam (the student) have to do?

   _____

   2 Which two categories of negotiating does Rebecca (the co-author) describe?

   _____

   3 Conal (the teacher) begins by asking students to consider how negotiations might differ between nationalities. Eiko (Japanese student) describes how Japanese negotiators say 'no'. Which summary (a–c) reflects what she says?

   a Their answers are direct and they let the other side know if something is wrong.
   b They will say 'no' until they have achieved a win-lose outcome in their favour.
   c They want to be polite and indirect so will use other expressions to avoid saying 'no'.

4 **Based on Eiko's description, what cross-cultural problems could occur between a Japanese negotiator and negotiators from other cultures?**

   _____

5 **Think about a national culture you know well. How do you think the characteristics of this culture might affect the negotiating style?**

   _____

Part 2 | How do we teach negotiating?

6 Read the list of areas we might teach in a lesson on negotiating. Would you deal with everything on this list with your students? Would it depend on the students' level and experience?

1 **Different approaches to negotiating:** The theory of how to negotiate. This may be affected by national culture or company culture.

2 **Planning strategy:** Before meeting the other side, students will benefit from planning how they intend to approach the negotiation. For example, they may plan to ask for a much higher figure than they actually intend to get at the end. Similarly, they may try to guess what the other side will ask for. For non-native speakers the planning stage can also include thinking about what they will say during the negotiation.

3 **Stages of a negotiation:** Students can be taught about stages such as opening, stating your position, bargaining, closing, etc.

4 **Useful expressions for each stage:** For example, *could you make do with …? I'd be willing to ….*

5 **Different register:** Students need to know how to be more or less formal, more direct or tentative. They also need to recognize this in the other speaker.

6 **Active listening:** You need to show you are listening and you should check that you understand exactly what the other side wants so there are no unnecessary breakdowns in communication. To do this we use body language as well as expressions such as *Yes, I see …, So, what you're saying is ….*

7 **Note taking:** Students need to take notes on what the other side wants as well as making notes on what they want. This involves working on listening skills.

7 ▶ **Watch this section and answer questions 1–5.**

1 Which areas in **6** would Rebecca teach to students with less experience?

_____

2 In the clip of the Japanese student negotiating in a group with a Swiss student, how would you assess the Swiss student's level of directness and politeness? How does her approach to saying 'no' compare with the Japanese approach described earlier?

_____

3 Which areas in **6** would Rebecca work on with more experienced students?

_____

4 When Conal describes his lesson, what areas in **6** has he dealt with? What does he think makes a successful lesson on negotiating?

_____

5 In the final role-play between Irina (Swiss student) and Tam (Thai student), Irina wants to extend the deadline on a project and negotiates this with the client (Tam).
   • Do you think Irina had a strategy?
   • Was Irina's and Tam's language appropriate? What feedback would you give them?
   • What kind of outcome did the two students appear to reach (win-win, win-lose, lose-lose)?

Material used in the DVD

Business Result Writing bank lesson from the website, www.oup.com/elt/teacher/result

Part 1 | What business texts do students write?

1 What proportion of your students need help dealing with business writing?

2 ▶ Watch this section. What are the stages of the lesson we see? One involves students working together and the second is the teacher talking to the whole class.

Stage 1: _____

Stage 2: _____

3 After watching, answer questions 1–2.

  1 As well as the business texts that Rebecca (the co-author) mentions, what other written texts do you think people in business might have to read or write?

    _____

  2 What are the aims of the two stages that Jenny (the teacher) starts the lesson with?

    _____

Part 2 | What do we need to teach students in a business writing lesson?

4 Read Jenny's lesson plan. You have already watched the first two stages. Before watching the rest of the lesson, complete the lesson plan with the missing aims (a–e).

  a To develop students ability to plan a written text.
  b To encourage students to evaluate texts and note features of effective writing.
  c To focus on and introduce the use of fixed expressions in the text.
  d To practise drafting the business text.
  e To draw attention to the format and conventions of the text.

Aim of this stage	Procedure
1 To introduce a formal letter and provide students with a model.	Students re-order parts of a letter which is cut into separate pieces.
2	Students analyse the purpose of each part of the letter and note the typical conventions
3	Students read again and underline phrases that are often found in business letters.
4	The whole class brainstorms the information that would be required in a letter from a company to a new distributor.
5	Working in small groups, students decide where each piece of information will go and then write the letter. The teacher monitors and helps with content and form.
6	The groups swap their finished letters. They then give feedback to each other.

5 ▶ Watch this section.

1 As well as providing students with a model version of a business text, what else does Rebecca suggest you ask students to do? Why? _____

2 Teachers often think of writing as a solitary activity and set it as homework. What are three ways Jenny suggests to make it more interactive for the classroom?

Suggestion 1: _____

Suggestion 2: _____

Suggestion 3: _____

6 Plan a writing lesson based on the text below. Write the aim and procedure for each stage. The text can be adapted if necessary (e.g. cut it up or use as a gap fill).

To: All staff
From: Grace Helston
Date: 27th November
Subject: New roles after departmental restructuring

Further to the recent restructuring in the Sales Department, I wanted to clarify the roles of the following members of staff.

Patrick Chapman – Team leader
Patrick is now team leader and oversees the Sales Team, which includes Vaughan, Sarah, and Lisa. He reports directly to me. This means he is no longer part of Tony's team.

Hazel Cook – After-sales Assistant
We welcome Hazel to the department. She is now responsible for our current client list. She handles complaints and queries and is part of Tony's team.

Vaughan Sore – Sales Rep
Vaughan has moved from After-sales to the Sales Team. He now deals with potential new clients and is part of Patrick's team.

If anyone has further questions about the above, my door is always open.

GH

Aim of this stage	Procedure
1	
2	
3	
4	
5	

Pre-work students

1 Goals and objectives: Some pre-work students may not have clear goals for studying English and may not know how they will use the language in their future career. However, other students may have clear ideas on what they want to do in the future and so we can help with certain areas of English.

Time for learning: Many pre-work students will be taking extended courses and therefore will have time to study all aspects of English including all four skills plus grammar, vocabulary, pronunciation, and functions. They usually have more time for self-study.

Motivation: Pre-work students can also be highly motivated, but sometimes, if students aren't sure what career they want to follow, it can be harder for the teacher to motivate them. You may have to use extrinsic forms of motivation such as testing or exams.

Language needs: Pre-work courses usually include all four skills (speaking, listening, reading, and writing) and cover many areas of grammar and vocabulary so that accuracy is given a similar emphasis to fluency.

2 1 The topic is 'values' and students seemed to have plenty to say. The teacher started by asking them to define values in general and then the students applied their knowledge as consumers rather than as business people.

2 Satoko is studying English because she likes it and also because she thinks it will help her in her future career. After the course she wants to do global economic research. She'll need to interview people and discuss economic matters.

Sonnie is studying English because he's an MBA student and uses English in business contexts. After the course he wants to work for international companies. He doesn't say exactly what he wants to do, but as an MBA student he will probably need to learn about (and be interested in) many areas of business.

Kitiya is studying English because she thinks it will help her to communicate. Also her family's business exports furniture to America and Europe. She doesn't say exactly what she wants to do after the course, but assuming she will work in the family business, she will need to look at the topics of import / export and buying / selling.

3 They will need to cover a wide number of business topics, but they specifically mention areas such as economics, export, and trade. In terms of communication skills, areas such as presenting, discussion, and negotiating might all be useful areas to focus on.

4 1 c 2 e 3 d 4 a 5 b

5 1 Rebecca talks about lack of business experience. Because of this she believes the teacher may have to provide the content (information about business topics) as well as the language.

2 Jenny doesn't appear to see the students' lack of experience as a major problem. She mentions how resourceful and inventive they can be.

3 She suggests that teachers can work on pronunciation problems caused by L1 (first language) interference, collocation, idiomatic expressions, and register.

Negotiating

1 c, e, and possibly d would be formal and planned.

2 Answers will vary.

3 1 a Tam negotiated a cheaper price for a mobile phone.

2 The first type she mentions is 'formal and external' (e.g. negotiating terms and conditions) and the second is 'less formal' (e.g. times, deadlines) and might be the type of negotiations that happen in a company (perhaps with a colleague).

3 c

4 There could be misunderstandings. Negotiators from some cultures may only understand that someone does not want to agree to something if they hear a clear 'no', so they may assume that the Japanese negotiator is still undecided, and therefore they may persist in seeking their desired outcome. This could cause tension.

5 Answers will vary.

6 Answers will vary, although it's likely that if the students have little experience of negotiating (either in their own language or in English) a teacher may wish to focus on planning and the stages of a negotiation. For students with lower levels of English it would also make sense to focus on the language – the expressions that could be used in a negotiation.

7 1 Rebecca mentions point 3, but we can assume that 4 would also be dealt with.

2 The Swiss student says 'no', but she is still polite. It's interesting that she says this to the Japanese student who commented earlier on how anyone from her country would avoid saying 'no' directly like this.

3 Rebecca mentions 6 and 7.

4 Conal says he has dealt with the structure (3), the language (4), and planning (2). However, we also know he has dealt with 1 because we saw it earlier. He also mentions working on intonation, so to some extent he has addressed the issue of register (5). He thinks planning and strategy make a successful lesson on

negotiating – students need to plan what they want to say, what they think their opponents will say, and plan for reaching an outcome.

5 Irina appears to have a strategy because she makes an offer which is turned down, but she quickly makes a second offer. Although the two students negotiate an outcome, there are some points for feedback:

Irina communicates well in general and she applies a lot of techniques and language from the lesson. However, there are some errors which might cause confusion. She begins by saying 'we are in a delay' and uses incorrect word order with 'I want you to ask for longer schedules', when she means 'I want to ask you for …'. Her use of 'Can you make do with …?' on two occasions is slightly odd because she asks it as a question rather than offering something. She also ends by saying 'Are we all agreed?' when there are only two of them.
Tam is more advanced and performs well in the negotiation. She makes fewer obvious errors, but in feedback you might need to point out to her how strong the expression 'I refuse to budge on this' sounds and that it seems a little inappropriate for the situation. The negotiation is run in a friendly manner and both students seem happy with the final outcome, so it appears to be win-win.

Business writing

1 Answers will vary.

2 **Stage 1:** The students put parts of a letter in the correct order.

Stage 2: The teacher talks through each part and checks students understand its purpose.

3 1 People in business might also have to read or write texts such as manuals, notes, business cards, SMS messages, and notices.

2 The aim of stage 1 is to introduce a business text and provide students with a model version. The aim of stage 2 is to draw attention to the format and conventions of the text.

4 2 e 3 c 4 a 5 d 6 b

5 1 Rebecca suggests you ask students to bring in their business texts / documents from work and the teacher can use them in class. This will be more relevant for the students.

2 **Suggestion 1:** Brainstorm (a plan) in pairs.
Suggestion 2: Write the texts together in pairs or teams.
Suggestion 3: Encourage peer correction so that students give feedback to each other.

6 Possible answers for lesson plan.

1 **Aim:** To introduce memos / global emails as a business text and to check basic comprehension.
Procedure: Ask students to read and answer:
• What type of correspondence is it?
• What's the aim of the writer?
• Who is the reader?
Check answers and discuss with students if they write or receive similar memos.

2 **Aim:** To focus on and introduce conventions, headings, and use of fixed expressions in a memo / global email.
Procedure: Students read the text again and underline headings and fixed expressions that you normally find in memos / global emails.

3 **Aim:** To plan the content of a memo.
Procedure: Explain that their company is going to introduce a better system of security to enter and leave the company premises. Brainstorm with the class what could be introduced. For example: CCTV, identity swipe cards for doors, identity badges, and all visitors to sign in.

4 **Aim:** To draft a memo / global email.
Procedure: Students work in groups of three and write a memo / global email to all staff.

5 **Aim:** To encourage students to evaluate and note features of an effective memo / global email.
Procedure: The groups swap their finished texts and read them. They then give feedback to each other.